MW00791442

Preserving the History
of the Latter-day Saints

BRIGHAM YOUNG UNIVERSITY
Church History Symposium

PRESERVING THE HISTORY OF THE LATTER-DAY SAINTS

Edited by
RICHARD E. TURLEY JR. AND STEVEN C. HARPER

RELIGIOUS STUDIES CENTER
BRIGHAM YOUNG UNIVERSITY

PROPERTY OF
L   STITUTE
    d Street
T   AZ 85719

Published by the Religious Studies Center, Brigham Young University, Provo, Utah, in cooperation with Deseret Book Company, Salt Lake City
http://rsc.byu.edu

© 2010 by Brigham Young University
All rights reserved

Printed in the United States of America by Sheridan Books

Any uses of this material beyond those allowed by the exemptions in U.S. copyright law, such as section 107, "Fair Use," and section 108, "Library Copying," require the written permission of the publisher, Religious Studies Center, 167 HGB, Brigham Young University, Provo, Utah 84602. The views expressed herein are the responsibility of the authors and do not necessarily represent the position of Brigham Young University or the Religious Studies Center.

DESERET BOOK is a registered trademark of Deseret Book Company.

ISBN 978-0-8425-2777-4
Retail U.S. $21.99
Cover painting by Alvin Gittins © 1997 Intellectual Reserve, Inc. All rights reserved.
Cover design by Carmen Cole

Library of Congress Cataloging-in-Publication Data

Brigham Young University Church History Symposium (2009)
  Preserving the history of the Latter-day Saints / edited by Richard E. Turley, Jr., and Steven C. Harper.
    p. cm.
  "Brigham Young University Church History Symposium."
  Includes index.
  ISBN 978-0-8425-2777-4 (hard cover : alk. paper)
  1. Church of Jesus Christ of Latter-day Saints—Historiography—Congresses. 2. Mormon Church—Historiography—Congresses. I. Turley, Richard E. II. Harper, Steven Craig, 1970– III. Title.
BX8611.B725 2009
289.3072'2—dc22

                                                                                    2010034374

Contents

CONTENTS

Richard E. Turley Jr. and Steven C. Harper

PREFACE

UNLIKE most religious movements such as Judaism, Islam, Hinduism, and Buddhism, whose origins are somewhat veiled in antiquity, The Church of Jesus Christ of Latter-day Saints developed in a time of modern record keeping. Rather than being obscured by the passage of centuries or millennia, the origins of the church are situated in recent historical time. A written record has been kept at nearly every major step of the church's organization and growth.

The pattern of keeping records dates back to the earliest days of the church, when Joseph Smith, the church's founding prophet, announced the divine decree, "Behold, there shall be a record kept among you" (D&C 21:1). Leaders of the church have strived to obey that command. Contemporaneous records were kept of revelations received by the prophet, the calling and interaction of early leaders, missionary assignments, the building of temples, and much more.

The Latter-day Saints continue to be a record-keeping people. In fact, there may be no other people on earth of comparable size who have a richer record-keeping tradition than the people nicknamed Mormons. It is a part of the church's administrative system, reaching from small committees to the church's general conferences and from new members to the most senior leaders. Because of this tradition, scholars can readily evaluate Latter-day Saint history from a wealth of primary documents.

On February 27, 2009, professional historians and students of church history gathered for the fourth annual Brigham Young University Church History Symposium. It featured presentations on preserving the history of the Latter-day Saints and was a cooperative effort between the Religious Studies Center at BYU and the Church History Department at the church's headquarters in Salt Lake City.

Marlin K. Jensen, church historian and recorder of The Church of Jesus Christ of Latter-day Saints, delivered the symposium's keynote address. Assistant church historian and recorder Richard E. Turley Jr. spoke on the significance of his predecessors in that office. One of those former assistant church historians, James B. Allen, spoke on William Clayton's influential role in the preservation of the Latter-day Saint past. Other scholars addressed a variety of relevant topics that ranged from the church's earliest efforts at record keeping to the challenging task of preserving its increasingly global and complex history.

Many of the symposium's presentations are published in this volume. Readers will find these papers filled not only with research about the church's past but also the experiences and adventures of many who have taken seriously the commission to preserve the history of the Latter-day Saints.

Marlin K. Jensen

1

MAKING A CASE FOR
CHURCH HISTORY

CURRENTLY there is avid interest in Latter-day Saint history and the related discipline of Mormon studies. This is a welcome development, as it has resulted in a noticeable increase in public discourse and in the publishing of content dealing with both academic fields. I believe it is a development stimulated not only by the compelling nature of the subject matter but also by the stature of the participating scholars. Good scholars are always an important measure of the quality of the culture from which they spring. If Latter-day Saint scholars—particularly historians—will keep their faith and the sense of direction provided by the Lord's plan of salvation and His living prophets, they will be blessed to do their work aided by the Spirit of the Lord. If this occurs, the Spirit will give life to their productive efforts, and both the

---

Marlin K. Jensen is church historian and recorder and a member of the First Quorum of the Seventy of The Church of Jesus Christ of Latter-day Saints. Address given at the BYU Church History Symposium on February 27, 2009.

Elder Marlin K. Jensen is church historian and recorder of The Church of Jesus Christ of Latter-day Saints. (Courtesy of Brent R. Nordgren.)

scholarly and nonscholarly communities will continue to be fascinated with Latter-day Saint history, culture, and doctrine. And those who seek the truth will eventually know where to find it.

On a personal note, I feel compelled to acknowledge that more than forty-two years ago I enrolled in several history courses while attending Brigham Young University. Despite my rather modest attainments as a history student, my love of history—especially the history of the Latter-day Saints—has grown stronger and stronger through the intervening years. The once-small collection of church history volumes I purchased following my mission to Germany in the early 1960s has since grown to fill many bookshelves, and I happily spend much of my spare time reading and studying church history. My patient wife frequently pleads with me not to go so close to a bookstore that my irresistible bibliophilic impulses will get the best of me!

Small wonder, then, that when President Gordon B. Hinckley called me in April 2005 to be the church historian and recorder, I felt both delighted and daunted. To find the particulars of one's church calling and duties set forth in revelations given by the Lord to the Prophet Joseph Smith, and to contemplate the contributions of the men who preceded me in this office, is humbling to say the least. The first administrative directive of this dispensation may have been the Lord's command on the very day the church was organized that "there shall be a record kept among you" (D&C 21:1). These words set something wonderful in motion. They are worth pondering when considering the foundational role church history should play in the institutional church, as well as in the individual lives of Latter-day Saints.

As church historian and recorder, I feel no obligation more keenly than to help infuse church members with a sense of the practical spiritual benefit and the eternal importance—not to mention the joy—of acquiring a knowledge of church history. For this reason, I have titled this paper "Making a Case for Church History." Part of the appeal of such a title surely comes from my legal training. But more important, it seems in keeping with the Lord's way of encouraging His children to do the things they ought to do. With our moral agency always in mind, the Lord speaks of influencing our choices by inviting, enticing, and persuading us to do good (see Moroni 7:13–16; D&C 121:41–42). My hope is to offer some convincing reasons why the study and enjoyment of church history is an important part of a full life in the gospel of Jesus Christ.

THE LORD VALUES CHURCH HISTORY

It seems to me that the strongest case I can make for church history is to point out that the Lord Himself regards it as something of great value. From the earliest days of the church, He has directed church leaders to create and preserve a rich historical record. I have always found appealing the simple thought that what the Lord and His inspired leaders regard as important, we ought to regard as important—else what's a prophet for?

Several latter-day revelations speak to the subject of church history. In them the Lord clearly says He wants "a record kept" (D&C 21:1), and the record is to be kept "continually" (D&C 47:3). The record is to include "all things that transpire in Zion" (D&C 85:1) and is to chronicle the "manner of life" and the faith and works of the Latter-day Saints (D&C 85:2). It is to be written "for the good of the church, and for the rising generations that shall grow up on the land of Zion" (D&C 69:8). Those who keep the record—provided they are faithful—are promised "it shall be given [them] . . . by the Comforter, to write these things" (D&C 47:4).

These carefully revealed details of the Lord's program for church history seem to reflect the importance He places on this history. So does the timing of the command to keep a record: it was given even before the Lord began to reveal the essential details of church organization, procedure, and doctrine.

The Prophet Joseph Smith took these directions from the Lord very seriously. He went right to work to keep the church's history. This was typical of him. He was always resolute in his obedience to God's commands. In the midst of many pressures in Kirtland in 1834, his history recorded, "No month ever found me more busily engaged than November; but as my life consisted of activity and unyielding exertions, I made this my rule: *When the Lord commands, do it.*"[1]

Joseph wasn't without help in beginning the work of church history. His efforts in translating the Book of Mormon educated him in many ways. Because record keeping is an unmistakable theme of that unique book, the prophet's sensitivities to the value of history must have been awakened. He learned of Nephi's heroic efforts to obtain the brass plates, which contained "the record of the Jews" (1 Nephi 3:3); Joseph would have perceived that their contents had a marked effect on the entire course of Nephite civilization. Joseph must have also taken note of the careful way other prophet-historians in the Book of Mormon attended to record keeping. In addition, he would have pondered the plight of the people of Zarahemla. Without an adequate historical record, their language had become corrupted, and they had lost faith in their Creator (see Omni 1:17).

Even though he was instructed and motivated, the actual work of record keeping wouldn't have been easy for Joseph Smith. By training and inclination, he was neither a writer nor a historian. The mental and spiritual exertions required to create an acceptable historical record would have been taxing. A further complication was his demanding role as the prophet and leader of the fledgling church. His days were filled with official duties of all kinds, constant visitors, weighty decisions, vexatious lawsuits, and other distractions. Joseph's frustrated exclamation concerning record keeping contained in an 1832 letter to William W. Phelps speaks volumes: "Oh Lord God," he wrote, "deliver us in thy due time from the little narrow prison almost as it were totel darkness of paper pen and ink and a crooked broken scattered and imperfect language."[2]

Yet in spite of his limitations, over the all-too-short span of the prophet's adult life a steady stream of revelations, translations, letters, journals, discourses, and histories emerged under his hand or at his direction. He truly was the father of Latter-day Saint history. It is fitting that Joseph Smith himself was a major subject of the record he was commanded to keep: "And in it," said the Lord, "thou [Joseph] shalt be called a seer, a translator, a prophet, an apostle of Jesus Christ, an elder of the church through the will of God the Father, and the grace of your Lord Jesus Christ" (D&C 21:1). An important theme in church history will always be Joseph Smith's role in drawing us to Heavenly Father through His Son Jesus Christ.

In this connection, it is appropriate to note that currently about twenty-five historians and editors in the Church History Department are toiling full-time five days a week as participants in the Joseph Smith Papers Project. Their stated objective—to be accomplished over an approximately twenty-year period—is "to publish every extant document written by [Joseph] Smith or by his scribes in his behalf, as well as other records that were created under his direction or that reflect his personal instruction or involvement."[3] Think of it: it will take twenty-five scholars working five days a week over twenty years to get their arms around the documentary output of a busy and often distracted church president who was neither trained for nor inclined to record keeping and whose productive years totaled at most about sixteen! Can there be any doubt but that the power of the Lord rested upon Joseph Smith throughout his earthly ministry?

The historical enterprise Joseph Smith launched was faithfully carried on by the prophets who succeeded him. Three of them—Wilford Woodruff, Joseph Fielding Smith, and Howard W. Hunter—even served for periods of their lives as the church historian and recorder. As a result, an unmatched record of the church's history has been kept, is being kept, and will be kept in the future.

On June 20, 2009, President Thomas S. Monson dedicated the new Church History Library. This beautiful and spacious edifice was constructed during the previous three years at a prime location east of the Conference Center in downtown Salt Lake City. It is a superior facility containing both a library and archives. It provides an optimum preservation environment and needed security for the church's priceless historical collections. It will become the Mecca of church history to which interested people from all corners of the world will come. It will also stand as a symbol of the undeviating commitment of the First Presidency and Quorum of the Twelve to the Lord's command that "there shall be a record kept among you" (D&C 21:1). Because of the value the Lord and His inspired servants place on the keeping of that record, I invite every Latter-day Saint to make learning church history a lifelong pursuit.

A KNOWLEDGE OF CHURCH HISTORY PROVIDES A GODLY PERSPECTIVE

A continuing involvement with church history will affect our perspective on life. Although in the book of Isaiah the Lord tells us His thoughts are not our thoughts, neither are His ways our ways (see Isaiah 55:8), He nevertheless wants them to be. Like every loving and right-thinking parent, He wants us to mature and grow in all ways and thereby become like Him. An important step in that process is for Him to help us acquire His unmatched perspective and to begin to see life as He sees it. Acting out of such a perspective, we can make wiser choices and hasten the development of the attributes we must acquire to become like God and live again with Him.

At least two passages of scripture say that "all things are present before [the Lord's] eyes" (D&C 38:2; Moses 1:6; see also D&C 130:7). Thus, the Lord is simultaneously aware of all things—past, present, and future. This insight helps us understand why He has defined truth as a "knowledge of things as they are, and as they were, and as they are to come" (D&C 93:24). In our quest to become like God, knowing of "things as they are, and as they were, and as they are to come" provides us with a view of life that is Godlike. This is of critical importance.

The prophet Alma recognized the value of such a perspective. His incomparable sermon in Alma 5 (punctuated by a series of soul-stirring questions) begins with the query, "Have you sufficiently retained in remembrance the captivity of your fathers?" (Alma 5:6). Here, the starting point for Alma's efforts to motivate church members to greater faithfulness was to direct their minds back to the past. This approach is in keeping with the frequent use of the word *remember* in the holy scriptures, particularly the Book of Mormon. Prophetic admonitions to remember are usually calls to action: to listen, to see, to do, to obey, to repent.

Alma then proceeds in his sermon to ask questions of the members that deal with "things as they are," with "Have ye spiritually been born of God?" (Alma 5:14) being one of the key inquiries. And then, rounding out the desired godly perspective of life that includes a view of the past, present, and future, Alma asks, "Do you look forward with an eye of faith, and view this mortal body raised in immortality, and this corruption raised in incorruption, to stand before God to be judged according to the deeds which have been done in the mortal body?" (Alma 5:15).

The importance of the eternal perspective taught by Alma is reflected in the ceremonies of the church's temples as well. In the temple we have repeatedly rehearsed for us important details of our past, the critical nature of our present existence, and the glorious destiny that awaits us if we love God and our neighbor and are true to our covenants.

Most important, the temple experience—like our personal engagement with church history—impresses us with the significant place and role of the Savior in the history of mankind. His is the ruling hand in the affairs of humankind and of His church. He is literally the Beginning and the End of history, and He gives purpose and meaning to everything in between. He is the Author and the Finisher of our faith, the Creator, Redeemer, and final Judge of all. The highest purpose of church history—or any history—is to help us receive a witness of these truths and live accordingly.

CHURCH HISTORY AND THE POWER OF STORIES

A thoughtful reader of God's word will quickly discern that much scripture is expressed in narrative or story form. This is because most scripture is history, and the way to make history come alive, as historian Barbara Tuchman said in two words, is to "tell stories."[4] Being the master teacher, our Father in Heaven knows well the teaching and staying power of stories. So do composers of songs for Primary children. That is why we all still remember the words to "Tell Me the Stories of Jesus" and "Book of Mormon Stories"![5] The case I am making for the value of church history in our lives would not be complete without saying something about the benefit and power of historical narratives or stories.

The church began with Joseph Smith's simple story. I feel its canonized form in the Pearl of Great Price is the single most powerful and wonderful historical composition we have.

I remember some years ago reading an account of the conversion of a former professor at Brigham Young University, the late Arthur Henry King. He was a brilliant British scholar and rhetorician who joined the church at midlife in the 1960s. Speaking of his conversion and the missionaries who taught him, he said:

> I am glad that the first thing they did was to give me the pamphlet on Joseph Smith's vision. The style of the Joseph Smith story immediately struck me. He spoke to me, as soon as I read his testimony, as a great writer, transparently sincere and matter-of-fact. . . . When Joseph Smith describes his visions, he describes them not as a man who feels that he has to make the effort to persuade. He simply states what happened to him, and does it in a way that gives it credence. I am in this church because of the Joseph Smith story; my fundamental act of faith was to accept this as a remarkable document.[6]

For some years, when the gospel is introduced to a virgin nation and language, it has been church policy that one of the first items of church literature to be translated and provided for the use of missionaries and members is the Joseph Smith story. Like no other church, ours rises or falls on the strength of its history, especially its founding stories.

When President Gordon B. Hinckley was interviewed several years ago for a public television documentary on the church, he said of the Joseph Smith story, "It's either true or false. If it's false, we're engaged in a great fraud. If it's true, it's the most important thing in the world."[7] President Hinckley's simple logic was actually profound. The truth of our doctrine and our claim to priesthood authority as Latter-day Saints are rooted inescapably in our history. If the stories of angelic visitations by Moroni; John the Baptist; Peter, James, and John; Elijah; Elias; and others are not true, our claim to be the one true church is unsustainable. History—in story form—is truly the foundation of The Church of Jesus Christ of Latter-day Saints.

Not all the stories that make up our history are of the epic proportion of Joseph Smith's First Vision. Some remarkable stories come from the lives of ordinary Latter-day Saints. History is life, and from ordinary lives come stories that reinforce what we more ordinary people believe, what we stand for, and what we should do in the face of adversity.

Consider, for example, this excerpt from the personal history of Thomas Briggs, a British convert who suffered throughout his life with chronically poor health. Thomas joined the church at age sixteen, came to Utah in 1864, and in 1865 was living with his family in Bountiful, Utah:

> We had a very severe winter and the spring of 1865 was very late. I rented some land on shares from Thomas Fisher, and planted it to potatoes, and I also rented a piece of land from Brother Anson Call, on which I planted onions, beets, and carrots, also a little cane to make molasses. The main thing we had to eat was bread, and occasionally I would go to the mountains for wood, then haul it to Salt Lake City and sell it for what I could get. I had two running sores on my leg, and Ephraim, who was now eleven years of age, was the only help I had. The weather was very good, all our crops grew very fast, everything looked prosperous, and when Fall came we rejoiced to think that we had been blessed so much. We had two fat pigs in the pen, and I was able to haul considerable wood to the city. I was getting pretty well acquainted and a man in the

city told me if I would haul him five loads of good maple wood he would give me $100.

One day Ephraim and I started out for a load of wood, and when we were about a mile from home Brother Prescott stopped us, and said, "Brother Briggs, I am very sorry to tell you, but all of your stuff is burned up, your stable, and all that you had in the corral is gone." I asked him if everyone at home was all right and he said they were. I told him that last fall I came to Utah with nothing, and I had nothing now, and that I always dedicated everything to the Lord and if he thought fit to make a burnt offering of it, well and good. When I arrived home everything looked pretty bad. I comforted my wife the best I could. I then went to work with a stronger will than ever. I asked my Heavenly Father to give me strength of body, and prayed that He would help me through as He had many times before.[8]

A story like this can provide inspiration and balm for the soul.

The accounts of those who have gone before us can often teach us how to behave. Consider this statement from the journal of George Q. Cannon, who had associated intimately with the prophet Brigham Young, including serving as his counselor from 1873 until Brother Brigham's death in 1877:

To describe my feelings upon the death of this man of God, whom I loved so much and who had always treated me with such kindness and affection, is impossible. His family, because of his partiality and affection for me and the desire which he always manifested to have my company when I was at home, to eat with him, to spend my evenings with him, and when we visited the settlements on preaching excursions, to have me stop where he stopped, called me his last wife. I have endeavored to appreciate these manifestations of affection and love, and now that he has gone I feel exceedingly thankful that I had these up to the last—that nothing occurred to alienate his feelings from me. On my part, he was in my eyes as perfect a man as I ever knew. I never desired to see his faults; I closed my eyes to them. To me he was a prophet of God, the head of the dispensation on the earth, holding the keys under the prophet Joseph, and in my mind there clustered about him, holding this position, everything holy and sacred and to be revered. Some, I am satisfied, now as I write this in Washington, Jan. 17, 1878, have thought that I carried this feeling too far; but I know this, that in revering him as the prophet of the Lord, in obeying him, in being governed by his counsel, in bearing testimony to his teachings and his character I have been blessed of the Lord, peace has been in my heart, light has rested upon me, and the Lord has borne witness to me that my course was pleasing to Him. Now that Brother Brigham has gone I rejoice in this. I never criticised or found fault with his conduct, his counsel or his teachings at any time in my heart, much less in my words or actions. This is a pleasure to me now. The thought that ever was with me was: If I criticise or find fault with, or judge Brother Brigham, how far shall I go; if I commence, where shall I stop? I dared not to trust myself in such a course. I knew that apostasy frequently resulted from the indulgence of the spirit of criticising and fault-finding. Others, of greater strength, wisdom and experience than myself, might do many things and escape evil consequences which I dare not do.[9]

For those who tend to murmur and nitpick at the prophet and other church leaders, this wonderful expression of loyalty and devotion speaks for itself.

Stories can provide context that enriches and helps us better understand the revelations received in our day. Consider, for example, the story behind the fourth section of the Doctrine and Covenants. Most full-time missionaries commit this section to memory and frequently recite it at missionary gatherings, but few may have considered the historical setting in which it was received. The revelation was given through Joseph Smith to his father, Joseph Smith Sr., at Harmony, Pennsylvania, in February 1829. What was Father Smith doing more than one hundred miles from Palmyra in the dead of winter? What were Joseph and Emma's circumstances at that time?

Joseph and Emma had married in January of 1827 and had received the gold plates in September of that same year. Seeking peace to be able to translate, they went to Harmony in late fall of 1827 and settled near the home of Emma's father, Isaac Hale. Isaac had not been pleased with Emma's marriage to Joseph and was skeptical of Joseph's character.

Joseph was learning how to translate the plates when Martin Harris arrived in Harmony in February 1828 and began to serve as scribe. By mid-June of 1828, Joseph and Martin had completed 116 pages of text. Martin's uncertainty about Joseph's authenticity led to the well-known incident of the lost 116 pages. What is not as well known is that at the time Martin left to take the 116 pages to Palmyra, Emma gave birth to her first child, a son, after an exhausting labor. The son died the day he was born, and Emma nearly died herself.

After a brief time, Joseph went to Palmyra to check up on Martin Harris. When he learned that the 116 pages had been lost, he was distraught. "O, my God!" he exclaimed, "All is lost! all is lost! What shall I do?" His mother, Lucy Smith, later described what she termed "that day of darkness." "To us, at least," she said, "the heavens seemed clothed with blackness, and the earth shrouded with gloom." When Joseph went back to Harmony in July of 1828, his parents' concern for his welfare must have been acute.[10]

Once in Harmony, Joseph and Emma translated a little, but the practical need to prepare for winter occupied their time and effort. The Hales refused to assist with Joseph and Emma's obvious physical needs, so in early winter Joseph and Emma called on their good friend Joseph Knight Sr. in Colesville and revealed their predicament. They secured a little food and other necessities, but it must have been a humbling moment. Joseph seemed at this point to be struggling against considerable odds, without clear direction.[11]

Because Joseph's parents had heard nothing from him in nearly two months, and because they were mindful of the great distress he had been under in July over the loss of the 116 pages, they visited him in Harmony in February of 1829.[12] It was there and in the context of these discouraging and seemingly hopeless circumstances that Joseph received what is now section 4 of the Doctrine and Covenants. The revelation was directed to his beloved father but may well have been given as much for Joseph's benefit. "Now behold," said the Lord, "a marvelous work is about to come forth among the children of men" (v. 1). That bold declaration must have been as welcome and needed a message as ever reached Joseph's ears. He appears to have been rejuvenated after his parents' visit, and the work of translation began again in earnest. Can you see what a knowledge of the history that surrounds section 4, or any of God's directives, can do for our ability to appreciate and heed His counsel?

One does not have to go far back in time or search only on the American continent to find moving stories from church history.

Our religion is now a worldwide movement, and church history is being made every day in almost every land.

Between 2001 and 2004 my wife and I were able to associate with Helmi Luschin, the widow of Immo Luschin, through our church service in Europe. Immo was the church's lead German translator for more than forty years. He was a brilliant linguist and a strong-willed and wonderful man. He and his beloved Helmi met after the Second World War. Since both were interested in learning English, they courted by writing each other a letter in English each day and coming together after work in the evenings to read Shakespeare.

Helmi told us that shortly after she and Immo were married in the Catholic Church, he said to her one day, "We'll be together in heaven."

"Well," she replied, "I've never heard of that."

He then said, "If they don't have it when we get there, they'll invent it for us!" A few years later the full-time missionaries knocked on the Luschins' door in Gratz, Austria. Brother Luschin's first question was "What does your church teach about marriage and family?" The rest, as they say, is history.

A PERSONAL EXPERIENCE

As I conclude the case I have been making for studying church history, I realize I might have stressed many other benefits. For me personally, however, the most significant blessing of my engagement with church history is the spirit I feel when I read a pioneer journal, visit a church history site, or view a page from the original Book of Mormon manuscript. It is during these times that the peaceful whisperings of the Spirit assure me that Joseph Smith really saw what he said he saw and that the church he helped found is true and of God.

This feeling has never been more poignant than it was in November 2007 as my wife and I fulfilled an assignment to attend the Palmyra New York Stake conference. Since we had presided over the New York Rochester Mission from 1993 to 1995, we were thrilled to be sent back to a people and place we love. We arrived in Rochester on Friday evening and arose early Saturday morning so that we could visit the Smith farm and Sacred Grove before my official conference duties began.

It was a cool but clear November morning with the trees in brilliant fall colors as we arrived. We walked into the Sacred Grove as we had done dozens of times with new and departing missionaries during our mission. There were no other visitors that day, so Kathy and I walked deep into the grove and sat on a bench in blissful silence, watching an occasional leaf fall and listening to the morning songs of the birds.

As we sat together on that little bench in that sacred setting, my heart filled with love and appreciation for my wife and for the Restoration of the gospel that gives such purpose and meaning to our relationship and to our efforts to preside over a wonderful and ever-growing family. In the spirit of that moment, I turned to Kathy and did something I have not done often enough during our marriage: I bore my testimony just to her. I told her I knew that somewhere near where we were sitting, Joseph Smith had seen God and Christ and had been called as a prophet to restore the only true church. I told her I appreciated her faith in those truths and her willingness with me to stake the entire course of our adult lives on the veracity of Joseph Smith's story. When I finished, Kathy bore her testimony to me. It was one of the finest moments of our married life and the most persuasive and personal experience I might share about the Spirit emanating from the stories, people, and places of church history.

May we all be blessed to continue our love affair with the past so that we can take full advantage of the present and be prepared for our heavenly future. This is my hope and my prayer.

© 2010 by Intellectual Reserve, Inc. All rights reserved.

NOTES

1. *History of The Church of Jesus Christ of Latter-day Saints*, ed. B. H. Roberts, 2nd ed. rev. (Salt Lake City: Deseret Book, 1978), 2:170; emphasis in original.

2. Joseph Smith to William W. Phelps, November 27, 1832, in Joseph Smith Letterbook 1, p. 4, Joseph Smith Collection, Church History Library, The Church of Jesus Christ of Latter-day Saints, Salt Lake City.

3. Dean C. Jessee, Mark Ashurst-McGee, and Richard L. Jensen, eds., *Journals, Volume 1: 1832–1839*, vol. 1 of the Journals series, *The Joseph Smith Papers*, ed. Dean C. Jessee, Ronald K. Esplin, and Richard Lyman Bushman (Salt Lake City: Church Historian's Press, 2008), xv.

4. David McCullough, citing Barbara Tuchman, acceptance speech, November 15, 1995, National Book Awards.

5. *Children's Songbook* (Salt Lake City: The Church of Jesus Christ of Latter-day Saints, 1989), 57, 118–19.

6. Arthur Henry King, *The Abundance of the Heart* (Salt Lake City: Bookcraft, 1986), 25.

7. Gordon B. Hinckley, interview, January 2007, *The Mormons*, PBS, April 2007, www.pbs.org/mormons/interviews/hinckley.html.

8. Kate B. Carter, comp., *Our Pioneer Heritage* (Salt Lake City: Daughters of Utah Pioneers, 1960), 3:284–85.

9. George Q. Cannon, Journal, August 29–30, 1877, Church History Library. Although this passage is recorded under the dates of August 29 and 30, 1877, Cannon actually wrote it on January 17, 1878.

10. Lucy Smith, *Biographical Sketches of Joseph Smith, the Prophet, and His Progenitors for Many Generations* (Liverpool: S. W. Richards, 1853), 121, 124; Richard Lyman Bushman, *Joseph Smith: Rough Stone Rolling* (New York: Vintage Books, 2005), 53, 58–68.

11. Bushman, *Joseph Smith*, 70.

12. Smith, *Biographical Sketches of Joseph Smith*, 124.

2

ASSISTANT CHURCH HISTORIANS AND THE PUBLISHING OF CHURCH HISTORY

I was named assistant church historian and recorder for The Church of Jesus Christ of Latter-day Saints on March 12, 2008—a quarter century after anyone had borne that title. Most Latter-day Saints today may be unaware of the role played by assistant church historians since the early days of the church. I would like to describe the people who have served in this role and to survey some of the contributions they made to church history.

WILFORD WOODRUFF

Wilford Woodruff was an eyewitness to church history from an early date, having been baptized at the end of 1833. He marched with Zion's Camp in 1834, went on a series of missions in the United States, and became a member of the Quorum of the

---

Richard E. Turley Jr. is assistant church historian and recorder of The Church of Jesus Christ of Latter-day Saints.

Twelve Apostles in 1839. From 1839 to 1841 he served a mission with the quorum in Great Britain, where he worked closely with future church historian George A. Smith.[1]

When Elder Smith began his service as church historian in the 1850s, he turned to his friend Wilford Woodruff for help, not just because of Elder Woodruff's involvement in the events of the early church but also because of his personal journals. The journals proved invaluable during the process of compiling the histories of Joseph Smith and Brigham Young.[2]

On April 20, 1854, just a few days after George A. Smith was called as the church historian, Wilford Woodruff recorded in his journal that he spent the better part of the day in the Historian's Office and lent Elder Smith four volumes of his journal covering the years 1840 to 1846.[3] But Elder Woodruff did not just lend George A. Smith his journal. From time to time he also helped compile history. For example, his journal notes that he spent the week of June 20–24 "in the Historian's office with G. A. Smith & T Bullock In drawing off all the sermons & teachings of the Presidency & Twelve & of our Journey so they can be filled [filed] in the Historians office for the Church History."[4]

In March 1856 George A. Smith and John Taylor were chosen to go to Washington, D.C., to pursue Utah's admission to the union as a state. The timing of George A.'s trip would have conflicted with his assignment as church historian, for the "History of Joseph Smith" was almost complete, as was the construction of a new Historian's Office. Church leaders felt that someone needed to supervise matters in the Historian's Office while George A. Smith was away, and so they appointed Wilford Woodruff as assistant church historian. The appointment would last twenty-seven years.[5]

From April 1856 to May 1857, Elder Woodruff had direct charge of the Historian's Office. Over these months he supervised the move of the Historian's Office to the new building and dedicated the facilities.[6]

Wilford Woodruff was sustained as church historian in 1883 and served until 1889, when he became president of the church. Assistant church historian B. H. Roberts later offered this assessment of President Woodruff's journals: "Other men may found hospitals or temples or schools for the church, or endow special divisions or chairs of learning in them; or they may make consecrations of lands and other property to the church, but in point of important service, and in placing the church under permanent obligations, no one will surpass in excellence and permanence or largeness the service which Wilford Woodruff has given to the Church of Jesus Christ in the New Dispensation, by writing and preserving the beautiful and splendid *Journals* he kept through sixty-three eventful years—so far do the things of mind surpass material things."[7]

FRANKLIN D. RICHARDS

Franklin D. Richards, who served as assistant church historian from 1884 to 1889 and as church historian from 1889 to 1899, was the nephew of former church historian Willard Richards. In Nauvoo, Franklin D. worked for his uncle as a scribe. In 1849 he became a member of the Quorum of the Twelve Apostles at the young age of twenty-seven.[8]

Elder Richards served four missions to Europe before being called in 1869 as president of the Weber Stake in northern Utah. His second mission to Europe, where he served as British Mission president from January 1851 to May 1852, encompassed one of the most remarkable publication periods in the history of the

church. During this time he published the first edition of the
Pearl of Great Price, a new edition of the church hymnal, and a
new edition of the Book of Mormon. He also contracted to publish a new edition of the Doctrine and Covenants.[9]

His *Compendium of the Faith and Doctrines of The Church of
Jesus Christ of Latter-day Saints*, first published in 1857, reflected
his impressive gospel scholarship and was used by missionaries for
several decades.[10] The *Compendium* was reprinted twice during
Elder Richards's tenure as assistant church historian, which began on April 6, 1884. The volume was considered one of the key
Latter-day Saint doctrinal works of the nineteenth century.[11]
Elder Richards also provided a chapter for George Hagar's 1888
publication *What the World Believes*.[12]

Franklin D. Richards became church historian in 1889.[13] He
also served as president of the Genealogical Society of Utah and
as president of the Utah State Historical Society.[14]

JOHN JAQUES

John Jaques was a British convert to the church, baptized
in Derbyshire in 1845.[15] In 1854, while serving in the British
Mission, he published his *Catechism for Children, Exhibiting the
Prominent Doctrines of The Church of Jesus Christ of Latter-day
Saints*. The *Catechism* was reprinted the following year in Liver-
pool, with subsequent printings in the 1870s and 1880s in both
England and Salt Lake City. It was also translated and published
in Danish, Swedish, Dutch, German, and Hawaiian.[16]

Jaques immigrated in 1856, traveling to Utah with the
Martin handcart company. He eventually found a position as a
clerk in the Church Historian's Office, where he was employed
from 1859 to 1863. He left that position to work on a series of

newspapers and then returned to the Historian's Office staff. He was appointed assistant church historian in 1889.[17]

His duties in the office were varied. A major church historical project of the 1890s was Orson F. Whitney's four-volume *History of Utah*. Both the Historian's Office Journal and a diary Jaques kept for 1891 mention that he and church historian Franklin D. Richards spent many days in the office reading drafts of Whitney's history.[18] When the Genealogical Society of Utah was organized in 1894, John Jaques became its first librarian.[19] He died June 1, 1900, in Salt Lake City.

CHARLES W. PENROSE

Charles W. Penrose joined the church in London, England, in 1850 and immigrated to the United States in 1861. He returned to the British Isles on a mission in 1865. During the last two years of this mission, he helped mission president Franklin D. Richards edit the *Millennial Star*.[20]

After returning to Utah, Penrose was active in a number of business and community affairs and edited two newspapers, the *Ogden Junction* and the *Deseret News*. As a prominent member of the community and a newspaperman, he wrote and spoke on many topics important to the church and its history.[21]

After serving another mission to Great Britain in the 1880s, he returned to Utah and became the editor of the *Salt Lake Herald*. He was appointed assistant church historian in 1896 and was first assigned to begin compiling a scrapbook of church history that would become the Journal History of the Church.[22] He also worked with President Joseph F. Smith in comparing two published versions of Joseph Smith's letter from Liberty Jail.[23]

On July 8, 1896, Charles Penrose received an assignment to prepare biographies of the church presidents for an *Encyclopedia of American Biography*.[24] Previously, in 1882, he had published a small pamphlet on the teachings of the church titled *"Mormon" Doctrine, Plain and Simple, or, Leaves from the Tree of Life*; the second edition was printed in 1897.[25] That same year, the presidency of the British Mission requested from the First Presidency a series of missionary tracts along the lines of this pamphlet. The First Presidency asked Charles Penrose to write the material.[26] In just two months he penned a series of twelve tracts titled *Rays of Living Light*.[27] First published in 1898 in both Chicago and Liverpool, the *Rays of Living Light* pamphlets were translated into many languages and served as the church's basic missionary tracts for several decades.[28]

Charles W. Penrose was released as assistant church historian near the beginning of 1899 and was appointed by President Lorenzo Snow as the editor once again of the *Deseret News*.[29] He became a member of the Quorum of the Twelve Apostles in 1904 and later served as a counselor to Presidents Joseph F. Smith and Heber J. Grant.

ANDREW JENSON

Andrew Jenson was not quite four years old when his family joined the church in 1854.[30] In 1866 the family immigrated to the United States, and seven years later Jenson returned to his native Denmark to serve a mission.[31]

When his mission ended, he resumed his life in Utah as a manual laborer, but he also began working on his first historical project: a translation of the history of Joseph Smith into the Danish language. After publishing the book, Jenson was called to serve a second mission to Denmark, where he put his literary skills to work as an editor, writer, and translator. He continued to pursue these roles after returning to Utah.[32]

In 1886 he wrote to church president John Taylor requesting a position on the church historian's staff. President Taylor replied that a position was not available at the time, but he complimented Jenson for his historical work. Sometime later an arrangement was made for the aspiring historian to receive a monthly stipend for continuing his labors, although he still was not made a member of the Historian's Office staff.[33]

In 1888 the First Presidency assigned Jenson to tour the church's historic sites in New York, Ohio, Missouri, Illinois, Iowa, and Nebraska. Along the way Jenson conducted interviews and collected documents.[34] In 1889 he began an effort to record the history of each stake, mission, ward, and branch by gathering historical documents and interviewing long-time members throughout the church. His travels lasted many years and included a trip from 1895 to 1897 that took him around the world.[35] A summary of his local history work was published in 1941 as the *Encyclopedic History of The Church of Jesus Christ of Latter-day Saints.*[36]

Upon his return from his world tour, Andrew Jenson was appointed assistant church historian and worked on compiling the Journal History of the Church, begun by Charles W. Penrose.[37]

In 1888 Jenson published a collection of some two hundred sketches of Salt Lake City church leaders as a supplement to his periodical *The Historical Record.* He expanded this effort with the *Latter-day Saint Biographical Encyclopedia*, volumes of which were published in 1901, 1914, 1920, and 1936. The *Biographical Encyclopedia* was published on a subscription basis, and families whose members were featured in the encyclopedia were a prime audience for the books.[38]

Andrew Jenson passed away in 1941, leaving behind an amazing collection of organized, cataloged, and indexed research materials. His legacy of narrative history has benefited many who have studied the history of the church.

ORSON F. WHITNEY

Orson F. Whitney, the first assistant church historian originally from Utah, was the grandson of Heber C. Kimball, first counselor in the First Presidency. He was born in 1855 and was drawn to cultural and literary pursuits at an early age. After returning from a mission in the eastern United States, he embarked on a newspaper career with the *Deseret News*. In October 1881 he was called on another church mission, this time to Great Britain, where he worked in the editorial department of the *Millennial Star* and helped edit the *Journal of Discourses*.[39]

In 1887 Orson Whitney "prepared . . . a sketch of his grandfather's life," which he delivered at a reunion of the Heber C. Kimball family. The sketch was well received, and Whitney expanded it into a book-length biography that he published in 1888 with the title *Life of Heber C. Kimball, an Apostle; the Father and Founder of the British Mission*.[40]

Eventually he agreed to write a history of Utah for a project sponsored by entrepreneur John O. Williams of Colorado. Williams dropped out before the first volume was published, but Whitney continued with the work after George Q. Cannon & Sons picked up the project. While working on the history, Whitney was allowed to use a desk in the west wing of the Church President's Office and was told that the Historian's Office would be available to assist him. It is unclear exactly how much the Historian's Office contributed to the project, but the history was reviewed by a committee chaired by church historian Franklin D. Richards.[41]

In 1899 Whitney began working in the Historian's Office,[42] and in April 1902 he was sustained as assistant church historian at the church's general conference. "I had held this position for over three years, without bearing the title," he wrote. "Andrew Jenson, A. Milton Musser, and Brigham H. Roberts were likewise sustained as Assistant Church Historians. Busy as ever, I wrote for various publications in and out of the Church, often preparing articles for others to sign, whose names were more widely known, more influential, and consequently more potent for good. Occasionally, articles to be signed by myself were solicited for histories, magazines and other publications."[43]

Orson F. Whitney was released as an assistant church historian when he became a member of the Quorum of the Twelve Apostles in 1906.

AMOS MILTON MUSSER

Amos Milton Musser was born in 1830 in Pennsylvania. In about 1837 his mother remarried, and the family settled near Quincy, Illinois. In a few years they returned to Pennsylvania, where A. Milton's mother joined the church. After being driven from Illinois with the rest of the Saints in Nauvoo, Milton found a job as a clerk in Iowa and stayed there until 1851, when he left for Utah.[44]

There he found employment as a clerk in the Salt Lake City tithing office for a year before being called on a mission to India. He also served in England and Wales, returning to Utah in 1857. From 1858 to 1876 Musser served as a "traveling bishop," visiting the wards in Utah as an agent for the Presiding Bishopric and the First Presidency. In 1876 he left on a mission to the eastern states. After returning from his mission, he received a special commission from the First Presidency to work in the Historian's Office and keep track of all the persecutions of the church.[45]

At the founding of the Genealogical Society of Utah in 1894, A. Milton Musser was elected as its first treasurer.[46] In the latter half of 1896 he accepted a position on the staff of the Church Historian's Office, and in 1902 he was sustained as an assistant church historian. He passed away in 1909.[47]

BRIGHAM H. ROBERTS

B. H. Roberts's early life was not easy. He was born in 1857 in Lancashire, England. Both his parents joined the church while Roberts was an infant, but his father became an alcoholic and eventually deserted the family. His mother decided to move to Utah but could not afford to take her young son, then known as Harry. He spent four years in a difficult foster family arrangement until enough money could be obtained to bring him to the United States.[48]

Roberts served four missions, the fourth one to the British Isles, where he spent much of his time working as an assistant editor of the *Millennial Star*.[49] He returned from this mission in 1888 and was called to the First Council of the Seventy at age thirty-one. In 1902 Elder Roberts was called as an assistant church historian and immediately began a project to edit and publish Joseph Smith's history, which became known as the documentary *History of the Church*.[50] Begun in manuscript form under Joseph Smith's direction in 1838, the history was a compilation of documents put together in narrative format by the church historians and their staffs in a project spanning nearly two decades. Early portions of the history had been published in Nauvoo in the *Times and Seasons*, and the history was later published in the *Deseret News* in the 1850s and the *Millennial Star* in the 1850s and 1860s.[51] By the turn of the century, all of those earlier publications had long been out of print. B. H. Roberts edited the history and published it in six volumes, volume 1 appearing in 1902 and volume 6 in 1912.[52]

In 1909 Elder Roberts began publishing his own history of the church, which appeared in monthly installments in the *Americana Magazine* from 1909 to 1915. Later revised, the history was published in six volumes with the title *A Comprehensive History of the Church*. B. H. Roberts published many other books during his lifetime. He passed away in 1933.[53]

JOSEPH FIELDING SMITH

Joseph Fielding Smith was born in 1876. In October 1901, as a young returned missionary, he began a sixty-nine-year affiliation with the Church Historian's Office by working as a clerk under the direction of Anthon H. Lund.[54] Just days after the young clerk started his work, President Lorenzo Snow passed away, and Joseph Fielding's father, Joseph F. Smith, became president of the church. In addition to working in the Historian's Office, Joseph Fielding Smith served as his father's personal secretary and confidant.[55]

Ten months after beginning his work in the Historian's Office, Joseph Fielding Smith took a field trip to Massachusetts to gather genealogical information on the Smith family. His research on the trip led to his first publication, *Asahel Smith of Topsfield, Massachusetts, with Some Account of the Smith Family*. A second trip in 1904 took him to Missouri, where he visited church history sites and gathered information for the church archives.[56]

Two trips in 1905 added to Joseph Fielding Smith's understanding of the church's historic sites. In September he accompanied his father on a trip to the Mormon colonies in Mexico. That December he was part of a larger touring group that visited church sites in New York, Massachusetts, Vermont, and Ohio in conjunction with the dedication of a monument at the Prophet Joseph Smith's birthplace in Sharon, Vermont. The following year he published a small pamphlet describing the trip.[57]

Joseph Fielding Smith was an ardent defender of the church. One of his major assignments was to compile information useful to Reed Smoot during his confirmation hearings in Congress. The church at the time experienced criticism not just from politicians in Washington but also from Smith relatives in the Reorganized Church of Jesus Christ of Latter Day Saints. Joseph Fielding Smith had several spirited discussions with his cousin, future RLDS president Frederick M. Smith, in 1905 and also engaged in a written debate with Richard Evans, a counselor in the RLDS First Presidency. These activities led to two pamphlets published in 1905, *Blood Atonement and the Origin of Plural Marriage: A Discussion/Correspondence between Elder Joseph F. Smith, Jr. and Mr. Richard C. Evans* and *The "Reorganized" Church vs. Salvation for the Dead.*[58]

Joseph Fielding Smith was called as an assistant church historian in 1906. The following year he published another pamphlet, *Origin of the "Reorganized" Church: The Question of Succession.* Active in genealogy throughout his time in the Historian's Office, he served as secretary of the Genealogical Society of Utah starting in 1907, and within two years added the responsibilities of treasurer and librarian. He helped found and initially edited the *Utah Genealogical and Historical Magazine* and became the society's president in 1934.[59]

Joseph Fielding Smith was called to the Quorum of the Twelve Apostles in 1910. With his call to the apostleship, his church assignments also changed, although he continued to serve as assistant church historian until his call as historian in 1921. He served as church historian until 1970, when he was called as president of the church. His book *Essentials in Church History*, first issued in 1922, and many other writings published while he was church historian have been widely influential within the church.[60]

A. WILLIAM LUND

A. William Lund was born in 1886, the son of Anthon H. Lund. He served a mission to Great Britain from 1906 to 1908 and, after returning, found his dream job working with his father in the Church Historian's Office. When he began work on September 21, 1908, his father was second counselor in the First Presidency, as well as church historian and recorder.[61]

On April 9, 1911, twenty-four-year-old William was sustained in general conference as an assistant church historian. While he did participate in some limited publishing ventures, including the production of a map showing church trails in the United States and a reprinting of William Clayton's *Latter-day Saints' Emigrants' Guide*, A. William Lund's work mainly involved answering questions and helping people do research in the Historian's Office collections.[62] He had a sharp memory and could remember not only various facts about the history of the church but also where to find additional information. He became adept at reading manuscripts and suggesting avenues for further research.[63]

He interrupted his work in the Historian's Office to serve as president of the British Mission from 1928 to 1932. His familiarity with the records of the church led to assignments as a director of the Genealogical Society of Utah and as a member of the Deseret Sunday School Union general board.[64] Brother Lund believed first and foremost in furthering the interests of The Church of Jesus Christ of Latter-day Saints. He was generous in sharing his knowledge and expertise with anyone who he felt had the best interests of the church at heart, and he was less helpful if he felt the information would be used to the church's detriment.[65]

JUNIUS F. WELLS

Junius Free Wells was born in 1854 in Salt Lake City, the son of Daniel H. Wells, lieutenant-general of the Nauvoo Legion and future second counselor in the First Presidency. Junius served a mission to the British Isles from 1872 to 1874.[66] He was called by Brigham Young in June 1875 to organize the Young Men's Mutual Improvement Association (YMMIA). In December 1876 the YMMIA was organized on a general church level, and Junius, who had just returned from another mission, was called to be its president.[67] In 1879 he founded the *Contributor*, a monthly magazine issued on behalf of the YMMIA. He was editor of the magazine for thirteen years.[68]

A visit to Vermont in 1894 heightened Junius's interest in the Prophet Joseph Smith's birthplace. He wrote his impressions in a *Contributor* article published in February 1895. The idea of honoring Joseph Smith on the one hundredth anniversary of his birth took hold of him, and in 1905 he put his ideas into action. Over the course of the year he researched the site of Joseph Smith's birth, purchased the property on behalf of the church, and oversaw the construction of a granite monument that was dedicated by President Joseph F. Smith on December 23 of that year.[69]

In 1911 a monument to Oliver Cowdery was erected under Junius Wells's direction in Richmond, Missouri.[70] Seven years later he supervised the construction of a granite shaft to honor Hyrum Smith in the Salt Lake City Cemetery.[71]

In 1919 Wells was called on a mission to Great Britain, where he worked as the associate editor of the *Millennial Star*. While on his mission he was sustained at the April 1921 general conference of the church as an assistant church historian. Joseph Fielding Smith was sustained at that conference as church historian and general church recorder. From April to August 1921, Junius continued to edit the *Millennial Star.*[72]

After returning to Salt Lake City, he participated in a variety of activities in the Historian's Office. He was skilled in acquiring historical data, old photographs, and other materials useful for the church's historical collections.[73] He also authored articles on church history, including some that were published in church magazines. Especially noteworthy is the series of articles he wrote for the *Improvement Era* on the history of the YMMIA, as well as his *Instructor* article on portraits of Joseph Smith. He was active in planning the 1925 jubilee celebration of the YMMIA, and his articles on the history of that organization were a major contribution to the celebration.[74]

Before becoming associated with the Historian's Office, Wells had worked to have a monument placed at Martin Harris's gravesite. That work came to fruition in 1925 when President Heber J. Grant dedicated a granite shaft in honor of the Book of Mormon witness at the cemetery in Clarkston, Utah.[75]

Active as an assistant church historian for nine years, Junius F. Wells passed away in 1930.

PRESTON NIBLEY

Preston Nibley was born in 1884 in Logan, Utah. His father, Charles W. Nibley, was called to be Presiding Bishop in 1907 and second counselor in the First Presidency in 1925.

From 1903 to 1905, Preston served a mission to Germany and later attended the University of Chicago. He wrote for newspapers in Logan and Salt Lake City and was a prolific author of articles for the *Improvement Era*, beginning with the 1909 publication of "Lincoln and the Latter-day Saints" and ending with the 1963 publication of "Charles J. Thomas: Early Guide on Temple Square."[76] He also wrote a number of historical articles that appeared serially in the *Church News*.[77]

His church service was not limited to his writing. He served on the YMMIA General Board from 1919 to 1929 and as president of the Northwestern States Mission from 1937 to 1940. In February 1946 he became a member of the church historian's staff, and in 1957 he was sustained as an assistant church historian.[78]

Preston Nibley's most lasting contribution to the church may well be the many books he wrote. Most of his books were published before he was a member of the Historian's Office staff, with only one published after he became assistant church historian. For eight years, from 1940 to 1948, he produced at least one volume a year, a prolific publication output. The enduring value and popularity of many of these titles is reflected in the numerous reprints of several of his books. *The Presidents of the Church* was an important compilation of biographies of the church presidents; he updated and reprinted it every few years.[79]

Preston Nibley retired as assistant church historian in 1963 but continued to serve on the church's historic sites committee until his death in 1966.[80]

EARL E. OLSON

Earl E. Olson was born in Salt Lake City in 1916. He graduated from high school in 1933, when jobs were few because of the Great Depression. He found employment working as a typist for his grandfather Andrew Jenson in the Church Historian's Office, and he remained there until his retirement in 1986, with interruptions to serve a mission to Denmark from 1937 to 1939 and to serve in the United States military in World War II. Earl worked as a historical compiler, librarian, and archivist; was sustained as an assistant church historian in October 1965; was appointed church archivist in 1972; and became the assistant managing director of the Church Historical Department in 1974.[81]

Earl Olson was not trained as a writer or historian, although he did author a few articles on the Church Historian's Office and its collections.[82] From the beginning of his tenure he focused on the acquisition, organization, and preservation of historical documents. As his career advanced, he became involved with national and international archival organizations, keeping abreast of developments in the field.

He was particularly interested in compilations of information. Perhaps the most visible result of the work he directed is the compilation of early church statistical information published in the *Church Almanac*. Now in his nineties, Earl Olson lives in Bountiful, Utah.

JAMES B. ALLEN

James B. Allen was born in 1927 in Logan, Utah. He graduated from Utah State University in 1954 with a degree in history. During his senior year at Utah State University, he became acquainted with Leonard Arrington when they both took a graduate seminar from George Ellsworth. Jim Allen's paper from that seminar was published the next year in the *Utah Historical Quarterly*.[83]

After graduating from Utah State, he taught seminary and pursued a master's degree in history from BYU. He later was an Institute of Religion director while working on his PhD at the University of Southern California.[84]

After earning his doctorate, he joined the faculty of Brigham Young University. He coauthored a small volume, *Mormonism in the Twentieth Century*, with Richard O. Cowan in 1964. Long interested in the foundations of the church, James Allen published two thought-provoking articles on the First Vision. From 1970 to 1982, in collaboration with the Mormon History Association (MHA), he began editing a feature for *BYU Studies* titled "The Historians Corner," which focused on little-known, significant documents in church history. From 1972 to 1973 he served as MHA president.[85]

With Marvin S. Hill, he edited a compilation of scholarly essays titled *Mormonism and American Culture*, which included two essays by Leonard J. Arrington and was published in 1972.[86] That same year Leonard was appointed church historian and tapped Jim to work with him as an assistant church historian. Leonard Arrington, James Allen, and assistant church historian Davis Bitton together administered a program of church history that included significant contributions from a number of professional historians. Jim also worked personally on several historical projects. With Thomas G. Alexander, he edited the 1840–42 journals of William Clayton for publication.[87]

A major project of the Church Historical Department was the publication of a volume intended to replace Joseph Fielding Smith's *Essentials in Church History* as a basic survey of the history of the church. Jim coauthored the book with Glen M. Leonard, and it was published in 1976 under the title *The Story of the Latter-day Saints*.[88] A revised, enlarged, and updated second edition was published in 1992.[89] That year Jim also published *Men with a Mission: The Quorum of the Twelve Apostles in the British Isles, 1837–1841,* coauthored with Ronald K. Esplin and David J. Whittaker.[90]

After seven years as an assistant church historian, Jim left the Church Historical Department and returned to teaching full-time at BYU, where he served six years as chair of the Department of History. He then held the Lemuel Hardison Redd Jr. Chair in Western American History for five years.

James B. Allen's historical writing has won many awards. *Trials of Discipleship: The Story of William Clayton, a Mormon* won the prestigious David and Beatrice Evans Biography Award in 1986. The book was republished in 2002 with the title *No Toil nor Labor Fear: The Story of William Clayton*.[91] In 2000 Jim published *Studies in Mormon History, 1830–1997: An Indexed Bibliography*, with Ronald W. Walker and David J. Whittaker as coauthors. This invaluable bibliography, which received a special citation from the Mormon History Association in 2001, continues to be updated and is available online at mormonhistory.byu.edu.[92]

In 2008 Jim received the Leonard J. Arrington Award for his distinguished service to Mormon history.[93]

DAVIS BITTON

Davis Bitton was born in Blackfoot, Idaho, in 1930. While on a mission to France, he served as the editor of *L'Etoile*, the church's French-language magazine. Having taken first place in his home state of Idaho in a piano competition, he enrolled in piano during and after his mission. He gave concerts and many recitals in his lifetime. Following his mission Davis earned a bachelor's degree in history at BYU and received his master's and PhD degrees from Princeton University.[94]

After teaching at the University of Texas and the University of California at Santa Barbara, he joined the faculty of the University of Utah, where he taught for twenty-nine years until his retirement in 1995. Although his PhD was in modern European history, he remained active in Mormon studies, serving as president of the Mormon History Association from 1971 to 1972.[95]

In 1972 he was called as an assistant church historian to work with newly called church historian Leonard J. Arrington. Davis was a skilled reviewer and provided valuable critiques of articles and books that were proposed for publication.[96] He worked for some time with a number of students and research assistants to compile a bibliography of Mormon diaries and autobiographies, which was published in 1977.[97]

In the 1970s the Church Historical Department sought to produce a one-volume history that could be published by Alfred A. Knopf, a major trade publisher. The book would be a companion project to *The Story of the Latter-day Saints*, written by James B. Allen and Glen M. Leonard for a Latter-day Saint audience. Davis Bitton and Leonard Arrington collaborated on the volume for several years before it was finally published with the title *The Mormon Experience* in 1979.[98]

When the History Division of the Church Historical Department was transferred to Brigham Young University, Davis Bitton, who had remained a faculty member at the University of Utah, returned to full-time teaching. He continued working in church history for the rest of his life, writing numerous books and articles.[99] He coauthored the book *Mormons and Their Historians* with Leonard Arrington, and with Maureen Ursenbach Beecher he edited *New Views of Mormon History: A Collection of Essays in Honor of Leonard J. Arrington*.[100] His biography of George Q. Cannon, published in 1999, received the MHA Best Book Award and the David and Beatrice Evans Biography Award.[101]

Davis was a visiting professor at BYU–Hawaii from 2005 to 2006. In 2007 he passed away in Salt Lake City. Later that year he posthumously received the Leonard J. Arrington Award in recognition of his many contributions to Mormon history.[102]

CONCLUSION

The assistant church historians who preceded me performed invaluable service in laying the foundations for church history. We are indebted to these men for their diligence and dedication to the work. Collectively, they helped fulfill the charge given to the church historian in Doctrine and Covenants 69:3, 8 to "continue in writing and making a history of all the important things which he shall observe and know concerning my church, . . . preaching and expounding, writing, copying, selecting, and obtaining all things which shall be for the good of the church, and for the rising generations."

NOTES

1. A brief sketch of Wilford Woodruff's life can be found in Andrew Jenson, *Latter-day Saint Biographical Encyclopedia*, vol. 1 (Salt Lake City: Andrew Jenson History Company, 1901), 20–26.

2. The original Wilford Woodruff journals are housed in the Church History Library, The Church of Jesus Christ of Latter-day Saints, Salt Lake City. They are conveniently published in *Wilford Woodruff's Journal: 1833–1898, Typescript*, ed. Scott G. Kenney, 9 vols. (Midvale, UT: Signature Books, 1983–85).

3. Wilford Woodruff, Journal, April 20, 1854, Church History Library.

4. Woodruff, Journal, June 20–24, 1854.

5. Jenson, *Latter-day Saint Biographical Encyclopedia*, 1:41; Howard Clair Searle, "Early Mormon Historiography: Writing the History of the Mormons, 1830–1858" (PhD diss., University of California, Los Angeles, 1979), 133–353; Woodruff, Journal, April 7, 1856.

6. Searle, "Early Mormon Historiography," 133–35, 139, 142; Thomas G. Alexander, *Things in Heaven and Earth: The Life and Times of Wilford Woodruff, a Mormon Prophet* (Salt Lake City: Signature Books, 1991), 179–80.

7. B. H. Roberts, *A Comprehensive History of The Church of Jesus Christ of Latter-day Saints* (Salt Lake City: Deseret News, 1930), 6:355.

8. Jenson, *Latter-day Saint Biographical Encyclopedia*, 1:115–21.

9. Jenson, *Latter-day Saint Biographical Encyclopedia*, 1:116–20; Peter Crawley, *A Descriptive Bibliography of the Mormon Church, Volume Two, 1848–1852* (Provo, UT: Religious Studies Center, Brigham Young University, 2005), 234–38, 241–42, 311–13, 341–43; Rodney Turner, "Franklin D. Richards and the Pearl of Great Price," in *Regional Studies in Latter-day Saint Church History: British Isles*, ed. Donald Q. Cannon (Provo, UT: Brigham Young University Department of Church History and Doctrine, 1990), 177–91.

10. Franklin D. Richards, *A Compendium of the Faith and Doctrines of The Church of Jesus Christ of Latter-day Saints* (Liverpool: Orson Pratt, 1857).

11. The Church History Library collections include Salt Lake City printings in 1884 and 1886; see also Chad J. Flake and Larry W. Draper, eds., *A Mormon Bibliography, 1830–1930*, vol. 2 (Provo, UT: Religious Studies Center, Brigham Young University, 2004), 193–94.

12. George J. Hagar, ed., *What the World Believes* (New York: Gay Brothers, 1888), 586–613.

13. Franklin L. West, *Life of Franklin D. Richards, President of the Council of the Twelve Apostles, Church of Jesus Christ of Latter-day Saints* (Salt Lake City: Deseret News Press, 1924), 244.

14. James B. Allen, Jessie L. Embry, and Kahlile B. Mehr, *Hearts Turned to the Fathers: A History of the Genealogical Society of Utah, 1894–1994* (Provo, UT: BYU Studies, Brigham Young University, 1995), 267; West, *Life of Franklin D. Richards*, 245.

15. Jenson, *Latter-day Saint Biographical Encyclopedia*, 1:254–55.

16. Flake and Draper, *Mormon Bibliography*, 2:559–60.

17. Jenson, *Latter-day Saint Biographical Encyclopedia*, 1:254–55.

18. Historian's Office, Journal, 1844–1997, Church History Library; John Jaques, Diary, 1891, Church History Library.

19. Allen, Embry, and Mehr, *Hearts Turned to the Fathers*, 46.

20. Jenson, *Latter-day Saint Biographical Encyclopedia*, 1:256–58.

21. Jenson, *Latter-day Saint Biographical Encyclopedia*, 1:258–59; Kenneth W. Godfrey, "Charles W. Penrose: His Life and Thought," n.p. [2002], 189–91, copy located at the Church History Library; Charles W. Penrose, *Blood Atonement, As Taught by Leading Elders of The Church of Jesus Christ of Latter-day Saints* (Salt Lake City: Juvenile Instructor Office, 1884); Charles W. Penrose, *The Mountain Meadows Massacre: Who Were Guilty of the Crime?* (Salt Lake City: Juvenile Instructor Office, 1884).

22. Jenson, *Latter-day Saint Biographical Encyclopedia*, 1:256, 259–60; Godfrey, "Charles W. Penrose," 246; Davis Bitton and Leonard J. Arrington, *Mormons and Their Historians* (Salt Lake City: University of Utah Press, 1988), 49.

23. Charles W. Penrose, Journal, June 11, 1896, Church History Library.

24. Penrose Journal, July 8, 1896. The publication was more likely the *National Cyclopædia of American Biography*. See *The National Cyclopædia of American Biography* (New York: James T. White, 1897), 7:386–93.

25. Flake and Draper, *Mormon Bibliography*, 2:70.

26. Journal History of the Church, August 5, 1897, 2, Church History Library.

27. Journal History of the Church, October 1, 1897, 2.

28. Flake and Draper, *Mormon Bibliography*, 2:71–78.

29. West, *Life of Franklin D. Richards*, 245; Jenson, *Latter-day Saint Biographical Encyclopedia*, 1:261.

30. *Autobiography of Andrew Jenson* (Salt Lake City: Deseret News Press, 1938), 4.

31. Jenson, *Latter-day Saint Biographical Encyclopedia*, 1:261–62.

32. Bitton and Arrington, *Mormons and Their Historians,* 43–44; Jenson, *Latter-day Saint Biographical Encyclopedia*, 1:262.

33. Keith W. Perkins, "Andrew Jenson: Zealous Chronologist" (PhD diss., Brigham Young University, 1974), 77, 93.

34. Bitton and Arrington, *Mormons and Their Historians*, 46; Perkins, "Andrew Jenson," 79–92.

35. Bitton and Arrington, *Mormons and Their Historians*, 46–48; Jenson, *Latter-day Saint Biographical Encyclopedia*, 1:262–63.

36. Andrew Jenson, *Encyclopedic History of The Church of Jesus Christ of Latter-day Saints* (Salt Lake City: Deseret News, 1941).

37. Bitton and Arrington, *Mormons and Their Historians*, 48–49.

38. Bitton and Arrington, *Mormons and Their Historians*, 50–51.

39. Bitton and Arrington, *Mormons and Their Historians*, 56–57; Jenson, *Latter-day Saint Biographical Encyclopedia*, 1:658–62.

40. Bitton and Arrington, *Mormons and Their Historians*, 59; Orson F. Whitney, *Life of Heber C. Kimball, an Apostle; the Father and Founder of the British Mission* (Salt Lake City: Kimball Family, 1888).

41. Orson F. Whitney, *Through Memory's Halls* (Independence, MO.: Zion's Printing and Publishing, 1930), 201–3; *Some Facts Regarding the History of Utah* (Salt Lake City: George Q. Cannon & Sons, ca. 1894).

42. The Historian's Office Journal documents Orson F. Whitney's daily participation as a staff member beginning in 1899.

43. Whitney, *Through Memory's Halls*, 240.

44. Jenson, *Latter-day Saint Biographical Encyclopedia*, 1:381.

45. Jenson, *Latter-day Saint Biographical Encyclopedia*, 1:381–83.

46. Allen, Embry, and Mehr, *Hearts Turned to the Fathers*, 46.

47. Karl Brooks, "The Life of Amos Milton Musser" (master's thesis, Brigham Young University, 1961), 125n34. The Historian's Office Journal does not exist for the last half of 1896, but its first January entries for 1897 list A. Milton Musser as a member of the staff.

48. Bitton and Arrington, *Mormons and Their Historians*, 69–71.

49. Bitton and Arrington, *Mormons and Their Historians*, 72–73; Jenson, *Latter-day Saint Biographical Encyclopedia*, 1:205; *The Autobiography of B. H. Roberts*, ed. Gary James Bergera (Salt Lake City: Signature Books, 1990), 164–65.

50. Bitton and Arrington, *Mormons and Their Historians*, 73, 75.

51. Dean C. Jessee, "The Writing of Joseph Smith's History," *BYU Studies* 11, no. 4 (Summer 1971): 439–73; Searle, "Early Mormon Historiography," 220.

52. *History of The Church of Jesus Christ of Latter-day Saints*, ed. B. H. Roberts, 6 vols. (Salt Lake City: Deseret News, 1902–12).

53. Truman G. Madsen, *Defender of the Faith: The B. H. Roberts Story* (Salt Lake City: Bookcraft, 1980), 287; Roberts, *Comprehensive History of the Church*. Other titles include *The Gospel: An Exposition of Its First Principles*, 1888; *The Life of John Taylor*, 1892; *Outlines of Ecclesiastical History*, 1893; *Succession in the Presidency of The Church of Jesus Christ of Latter-day Saints*, 1894; *A New Witness for God*, 1895; *The Missouri Persecutions*, 1900; and *The Rise and Fall of Nauvoo*, 1900.

54. Historian's Office, Journal, October 4, 1901; Joseph Fielding Smith Jr. and John J. Stewart, *The Life of Joseph Fielding Smith* (Salt Lake City: Deseret Book, 1972), 126; Francis M. Gibbons, *Joseph Fielding Smith: Gospel Scholar, Prophet of God* (Salt Lake City: Deseret Book, 1992), 107.

55. Gibbons, *Joseph Fielding Smith*, 109, 113.

56. Gibbons, *Joseph Fielding Smith*, 114–17; Joseph F. Smith Jr., *Asahel Smith of Topsfield, Massachusetts, with Some Account of the Smith Family* (Topsfield, MA: Topsfield Historical Society, 1902).

57. Smith and Stewart, *Life of Joseph Fielding Smith*, 142–44; *Proceedings at the Dedication of the Joseph Smith Memorial Monument at Sharon, Windsor County, Vermont, December 23rd, 1905* (Salt Lake City: Deseret News, 1906).

58. Gibbons, *Joseph Fielding Smith*, 117, 121–23; Smith and Stewart, *Life of Joseph Fielding Smith*, 135–38.

59. Gibbons, *Joseph Fielding Smith*, 123–24; Smith and Stewart, *Life of Joseph Fielding Smith*, 139; Allen, Embry, and Mehr, *Hearts Turned to the Fathers*, 71–74, 267.

60. Joseph Fielding Smith, *Essentials in Church History* (Salt Lake City: Deseret News, 1922). Other titles include *Gospel Doctrine: Selections from the Sermons and Writings of Joseph F. Smith*, 1919; *The Way to Perfection*, 1931; *The Progress of Man*, 1936; *Teachings of the Prophet Joseph Smith*, 1938; *Life of Joseph F. Smith*, 1938; *The Signs of the Times*, 1942; *The Restoration of All Things*, 1945; *Church History and Modern Revelation* (Melchizedek Priesthood Course of Study), 1947–1950; *Man, His Origin and Destiny*, 1954; *Doctrines of Salvation*, 3 vols., 1954, 1955, 1956; *Answers to Gospel Questions*, 5 vols., 1957, 1958, 1960, 1963, 1966; *Take Heed to Yourselves!* 1966; *Seek Ye Earnestly*, 1970.

61. Albert L. Zobell Jr., "A. William Lund (1886–1971)," *Ensign*, March 1971, 75; Dorothy O. Rea, "A. William Lund . . . Keeper of History," *Church News*, August 6, 1966.

62. Zobell, "A. William Lund (1886–1971)," 75; Rea, "A. William Lund." See also *Map Showing the Movements of The Church of Jesus Christ of Latter-day Saints, Also the Routes of the Mormon Battalion, Zion's Camp and Important Data* (Salt Lake City: Deseret Book, 1929); W. Clayton, *The Latter-day Saints' Emigrants' Guide* (1848; repr., Salt Lake City, n.d., ca. 1950).

63. Zobell, "A. William Lund (1886–1971)," 75; Albert L. Zobell Jr., "A. William Lund: Assistant Church Historian for Fifty Years," *Improvement Era* 64 (April 1961): 240.

64. Zobell, "A. William Lund: Assistant Church Historian," 240; Zobell, "A. William Lund," 75; Rea, "A. William Lund."

65. See T. Edgar Lyon, "Church Historians I Have Known," *Dialogue* 11 (Winter 1978): 19–21.

66. Andrew Jenson, *Latter-day Saint Biographical Encyclopedia*, vol. 4 (Salt Lake City: Andrew Jenson Memorial Association, 1936), 249.

67. Junius F. Wells, "Historic[al] Sketch of the Y. M. M. I. A., First Period," *Improvement Era* 28 (June 1925): 713–29; Leon M. Strong, "A History of the

Young Men's Mutual Improvement Association, 1875–1938" (master's thesis, Brigham Young University, 1939), 11–16, 19.

68. Junius F. Wells, "The Contributor," *Improvement Era* 33 (November 1929): 55–57.

69. Junius F. Wells, "Birthplace of the Prophet Joseph Smith," *Contributor* 16, no. 4 (February 1895): 203–11; Keith A. Erekson, "American Prophet, New England Town: The Memory of Joseph Smith in Vermont" (master's thesis, Brigham Young University, 2002), 58–130; *Proceedings at the Dedication of the Joseph Smith Memorial Monument*; Keith A. Erekson, "'Out of the Mists of Memory': Remembering Joseph Smith in Vermont," *Journal of Mormon History* 32, no. 2 (Summer 2005): 30–69; Richard Neitzel Holzapfel and Paul H. Peterson, "New Photographs of Joseph F. Smith's Centennial Memorial Trip to Vermont, 1905," *BYU Studies* 39, no. 4 (2000): 107–14.

70. Richard Neitzel Holzapfel and Robert F. Schwartz, "The Dedication of the Oliver Cowdery Monument in Richmond, Missouri, 1911," *BYU Studies* 44, no. 3 (2005): 99–121.

71. "Original Y. M. M. I. A. Worker Called Home," *Improvement Era* 33 (June 1930): 549.

72. J. M. Sjodahl, "Farewell!" *Latter-day Saints' Millennial Star* 81 (April 17, 1919): 248; *Ninety-First Annual Conference of The Church of Jesus Christ of Latter-day Saints* (Salt Lake City: Deseret Book, 1921), 189; Missionary record index, 1830–1971, microfilm, Church History Library.

73. Junius F. Wells, Papers, 1867–1930, Church History Library. Wells's papers do not include much outgoing correspondence but do include many incoming letters responding to his historical inquiries.

74. Junius F. Wells, "Historic[al] Sketch of the Y. M. M. I. A., First Period," *Improvement Era* 28 (June, July, September, and October 1925): 713–29, 873–82, 1069–74, 1149–54; Junius F. Wells, "Portraits of Joseph Smith the Prophet," *Instructor* 65 (February 1930): 79–80; "Original Y. M. M. I. A. Worker Called Home," 549.

75. Junius F. Wells to Heber J. Grant and Counselors, August 26, 1924, Junius F. Wells Papers; "Statue Unveiled to Martin Harris; Thousand Attend," *Deseret News*, July 11, 1925, in Journal History of the Church, July 10, 1925, 3.

76. Albert L. Zobell Jr., "Preston Nibley, Noted Church Writer, Passes Away," *Improvement Era* 69 (March 1966): 166; Preston Nibley, "Lincoln and the Latter-day Saints," *Improvement Era* 12 (March 1909): 333–37; Preston

Nibley, "Charles J. Thomas: Early Guide on Temple Square," *Improvement Era* 66 (March 1963): 166–67, 202–6.

77. See, for example, "Joseph J. Daynes Was the First Salt Lake Tabernacle Organist," *Church News*, March 5, 1955; "Danquart A. Weggeland Was a Distinguished Pioneer Artist," *Church News*, March 19, 1955; "Albert King Thurber Served as President of Sevier Stake," *Church News*, March 26, 1955.

78. Zobell, "Preston Nibley," 166.

79. Preston Nibley, *The Presidents of the Church* (Salt Lake City: Deseret Book, 1974). Other important titles include: *Brigham Young: The Man and His Work*, 1936; *Pioneer Stories*, 1940; *Inspirational Talks for Youth*, 1941; *Missionary Experiences*, 1942; *Faith Promoting Stories*, 1943; *Joseph Smith the Prophet*, 1944; *Three Mormon Classics*, 1944; *History of Joseph Smith by His Mother, Lucy Mack Smith*, 1945; *The Witnesses of the Book of Mormon*, 1946; *Exodus to Greatness*, 1947; *Sharing the Gospel with Others: Excerpts from the Sermons of President [George Albert] Smith*, 1948; *L.D.S. Adventure Stories*, 1953; *Stalwarts of Mormonism*, 1954; *L.D.S. Stories of Faith and Courage*, 1957.

80. Zobell, "Preston Nibley," 166.

81. Gerry Avant, "For 50 Years, He Has Seen History up Close," *Church News*, April 8, 1984; "40 Years Bring Changes," *Church News*, May 16, 1981.

82. See Earl E. Olson, "The Chronology of the Ohio Revelations," *BYU Studies* 11 (Summer 1971): 329–49; Earl E. Olson, "When the Books Are Opened," *Library Journal* 86 (January 1, 1961): 33–36.

83. Leonard J. Arrington, *Adventures of a Church Historian* (Urbana: University of Illinois Press, 1998), 82; James B. Allen, "The Evolution of County Boundaries in Utah," *Utah Historical Quarterly* 23 (July 1955): 261–78.

84. Arrington, *Adventures of a Church Historian*, 82.

85. Arrington, *Adventures of a Church Historian,* 82; James B. Allen and Richard O. Cowan, *Mormonism in the Twentieth Century* (Provo, UT: Extension Publications Division of Continuing Education/Brigham Young University Press, 1964); James B. Allen, "The Significance of Joseph Smith's 'First Vision' in Mormon Thought," *Dialogue: A Journal of Mormon Thought* 1 (Autumn 1966): 29–45; James B. Allen, "Eight Contemporary Accounts of Joseph Smith's First Vision—What Do We Learn from Them?" *Improvement Era* 73 (April 1970): 4–13; James B. Allen, ed., "The Historians Corner," *BYU Studies* 10 (Summer 1970): 479–80; James B. Allen, "The Historians Corner," *BYU Studies* 22 (Summer 1982): 357; "Past MHA Presidents,"

Mormon History Association, www.mhahome.org/about/past_presidents.php.

86. Marvin S. Hill and James B. Allen, *Mormonism and American Culture* (New York: Harper & Row, 1972).

87. James B. Allen and Thomas G. Alexander, eds., *Manchester Mormons: The Journal of William Clayton, 1840 to 1842* (Santa Barbara: Peregrine Smith, 1974).

88. James B. Allen and Glen M. Leonard, *The Story of the Latter-day Saints* (Salt Lake City: Deseret Book, 1976).

89. James B. Allen and Glen M. Leonard, *The Story of the Latter-day Saints*, 2nd ed. (Salt Lake City: Deseret Book, 1992).

90. James B. Allen, Ronald K. Esplin, and David J. Whittaker, *Men with a Mission: The Quorum of the Twelve Apostles in the British Isles, 1837–1841* (Salt Lake City: Deseret Book, 1992).

91. *Trials of Discipleship: The Story of William Clayton, a Mormon* (Urbana: University of Illinois Press, 1987); *No Toil nor Labor Fear: The Story of William Clayton* (Provo, UT: Brigham Young University Press, 2002); "Previous Winners—Evans Biography Award," www.usu.edu/mountainwest/prevwinners.pdf. The book received the Evans award while still in manuscript form.

92. James B. Allen, Ronald W. Walker, and David J. Whittaker, *Studies in Mormon History, 1830–1997: An Indexed Bibliography* (Urbana: University of Illinois Press, 2000). Other major book titles include *Mormons & Gentiles: A History of Salt Lake City*, 1984, with Thomas G. Alexander; *Hearts Turned to the Fathers: A History of the Genealogical Society of Utah*, 1995, with Jessie L. Embry and Kahlile B. Mehr; *Mormon History*, 2001, with Ronald W. Walker and David J. Whittaker.

93. "MHA 2008 Award Winners," Mormon History Association, www.mhahome.org/awards/2007.php.

94. Arrington, *Adventures of a Church Historian*, 82–83.

95. Arrington, *Adventures of a Church Historian*, 82–83; "Past MHA Presidents," Mormon History Association, www.mhahome.org/about/past_presidents.php.

96. Arrington, *Adventures of a Church Historian*, 83.

97. Davis Bitton, *Guide to Mormon Diaries & Autobiographies* (Provo, UT: Brigham Young University Press, 1977).

98. Leonard J. Arrington and Davis Bitton, *The Mormon Experience: A History of the Latter-day Saints* (New York: Alfred A. Knopf, 1979); Arrington, *Adventures of a Church Historian*, 186–94.

99. Major book titles include *The Redoubtable John Pack: Pioneer, Proselyter, Patriarch*, 1982; *The Mormon Graphic Image, 1834–1914: Cartoons, Caricatures, and Illustrations*, 1983, with Gary L. Bunker; *The Martyrdom Remembered*, 1994; *Mormons, Scripture, and the Ancient World: Studies in Honor of John L. Sorenson*, edited by Davis Bitton, 1998; *The Ritualization of Mormon History and Other Essays*, 1994; *Historical Dictionary of Mormonism*, 1994; *Images of the Prophet Joseph Smith*, 1996.

100. Bitton and Arrington, *Mormons and Their Historians*; Davis Bitton and Maureen Ursenbach Beecher, *New Views of Mormon History: A Collection of Essays in Honor of Leonard J. Arrington* (Salt Lake City: University of Utah Press, 1987).

101. Davis Bitton, *George Q. Cannon: A Biography* (Salt Lake City: Deseret Book, 1999); "MHA Awards," Mormon History Association, www.mhahome.org/awards/07_Awards.pdf; "Previous Winners-Evans Biography Award," www.usu.edu/mountainwest/prevwinners.pdf.

102. "MHA 2007 Award Winners," Mormon History Association, www.mhahome.org/awards/2006.php?PHPSESSID=1d00476228792e120fa438d200bd3ed6 _Summary_2008.pdf.

In March 1831, John Whitmer "was appointed by the voice of the Elders" in Kirtland "to keep the Church Record." (Courtesy of Church History Library, Salt Lake City.)

3

"A History of All the Important Things" (D&C 69:3): John Whitmer's Record of Church History

JOHN Whitmer's tenure as church historian began inauspiciously and ended acrimoniously. Charged "by the voice of the Elders to keep the Church Record," Whitmer's reaction was, "I would rather not do it." But he would comply, he said, if the Lord manifested his will "through Joseph the Seer."[1] In March 1831, Joseph Smith received a revelation directing John to "write and keep a regular history . . . [and] to keep the church record and history continually" (D&C 47:1, 3). Eight months later, Whitmer was further counseled through revelation to "continue in writing and making a history" (D&C 69:3). These directives formed the basis for his record, "the Book of John Whitmer, kept by commandment."[2]

Though John Whitmer began his history with the goal of recording "all the important things which he shall observe and

---

Scott C. Esplin is an assistant professor of church history and doctrine at Brigham Young University.

know . . . for the good of the church, and for the rising generations that shall grow up on the land of Zion" (D&C 69:3, 8), his
official record keeping ended with his excommunication in 1838.
Afterward, Joseph Smith and Sidney Rigdon sought the history.
A letter they sent to Whitmer reflected not only their perceptions
of his record but also the divide evident between him and the
leaders of the church. Accusing him of "incompetency as a historian, . . . never . . . capable of writing a history," they wrote, "We
were desirous of honoring you by giving publicity to your notes on
the history of the Church of Latter-day Saints, after making such
corrections as we thought would be necessary, knowing . . . that
writings coming from your pen, could not be put to press without
our correcting them, or else the Church must suffer reproach."[3]

Cut off from the church and possibly hurt by the accusation
of incompetency, John Whitmer refused the request to surrender
the history, keeping it in his possession while the Prophet Joseph
Smith and his associates began a new record, now known as *History of the Church.*

Accurate or not, Joseph Smith and Sidney Rigdon's negative
assessment both of John Whitmer as a historian and of the useful-
ness of his account continues to plague his record. What happened
to "The Book of John Whitmer" after his parting from the church?
In addition to Joseph's initial efforts, what other attempts were
made by church leaders to acquire the history? How did it eventually come into the possession of the Reorganized Church of Jesus
Christ of Latter Day Saints (now Community of Christ) and subsequently get published? What misunderstandings have persisted
over the years regarding John Whitmer's contributions and record?
This paper analyzes these questions, seeking to chronicle the history of Whitmer's manuscript over more than 175 years.

CHURCH LEADER AND HISTORIAN

The third son of Peter and Mary Whitmer, John Whitmer was born August 27, 1802, near Harrisburg, Pennsylvania. As a young boy he moved with his family to New York in 1809, and they eventually settled with other German families near Fayette. There, through his younger brother David and future brother-in-law Oliver Cowdery, John was introduced to the Book of Mormon translation Joseph Smith was doing. His interest in the work increased when Joseph and Oliver moved to the Whitmer home in Fayette in June 1829 to complete the translation.[4]

John's association with Joseph led to his receiving a revelation outlining "the thing which [would] be of the most worth unto [him]" (D&C 15:6), his baptism in June 1829, and a call as one of the Eight Witnesses to the Book of Mormon. At the first confer-ence of the church, held on June 9, 1830, John was listed as one of seven elders in the fledgling organization.[5] Later that year he was called to serve a mission near Fayette, New York (see D&C 30:10).

His call to serve as church historian was connected with the missionary efforts of the early church leaders. At a church con-ference in September 1830, Oliver Cowdery, who had formerly fulfilled the command to keep a historical record (see D&C 21:1), was called to head a mission to the Lamanites more than a thousand miles away on the western frontier of Missouri (see D&C 28:8–9). While traveling to Missouri, Cowdery and his associates achieved great success in Kirtland, Ohio, causing the Prophet Joseph to send John Whitmer to preside over the new congregation there.

In March 1831, with Cowdery still in Missouri on his mis-sion, Whitmer "was appointed by the voice of the Elders" in Kirtland "to keep the Church Record."[6] In the divine directive Joseph Smith received for Whitmer, the latter was appointed "to keep the church record and history continually; for Oliver Cowdery I have appointed to another office" (D&C 47:3). John's own history states: "Oliver Cowdery has written the commencement of the church history, commencing at the time of the finding of the plates, up to June 12th, 1831. From this day I have written the things that I have written, and they are a mere sketch of the things that have transpired, they are however all that seemed to me wisdom to write."[7]

Eight months after John Whitmer's appointment, further revelation was given directing him to accompany Oliver Cowdery from Kirtland to Independence, Missouri, where publication of the Book of Commandments would occur (see D&C 69). Leaving Ohio on November 10, 1831, Cowdery and Whitmer arrived in Independence on January 5, 1832. This first visit by John to Missouri introduced him to the region where he would spend much of the remainder of his life. Assisting with the publication of the Book of Commandments, Whitmer lived in the Independence area from January 1832 until the expulsion of the Saints in November 1833.

A leader of the church and witness to the Missouri persecutions, Whitmer recorded, "The whole County turned out and surrounded us came to W W Phelps, and my house and took us upon the publick Square, as did Partridge, Corrill, Morly, and Gilbert and were determined to massacre us unless we agreed to leave the county immediately. Finally we agreed to leave."[8] Settling in nearby Clay County, Whitmer continued as a leader of the church in Missouri while chronicling the struggles of the Saints, including their negotiations with the governor and the arrival of Zion's Camp in 1834.

While in Missouri with Zion's Camp, the Prophet Joseph Smith organized the presidency of the church in Missouri, appointing David Whitmer as president, with William W. Phelps and John Whitmer as counselors. The new presidency was subsequently instructed to return to Kirtland and "receive [their] endowment . . . with power from on high."[9] Obedient to the directive, John went to Kirtland in May 1835, where he witnessed and wrote about the organization of the Quorums of the Twelve and the Seventy and the dedication of the Kirtland Temple.

Returning to Missouri, he resumed his duties in the presidency while continuing to write the history. Chief among these responsibilities was the assignment to direct land purchases in the Saints' new settlement of Far West. By 1837 and 1838, however, the apostasy that ruined the church in Kirtland began to infiltrate John Whitmer's heart as well. In February 1838 the entire Missouri presidency was rejected by the church membership, an action sustained by the high council a month later.[10] Specifically, John Whitmer was charged with "persisting in unchristian-like conduct" and misusing church funds.[11]

Whitmer's being "cut off from the Church" and "given over to the buffetings of Satan" led to the disagreement about his manuscript and the end of his record keeping.[12] During these 1838 conflicts Whitmer concluded, "The situation of the Church both here and in Kirtland is in an unpleasant situation in consequence of the reorganization of its authorities, which was not satisfactory to all concerned. And has terminated in the expulsion of some members, as also some temporal movements have not proved satisfactory to all parties [and] has also terminated in the expulsion of many members."[13]

Whitmer's account continues, adding (in words he or someone else later crossed out), "among whom is W. W. Phelps and myself. Therefore I close this history of the church of Latter Day Saints, Hoping that I may be for given of my faults, and my sins be bloted out and in the last day be saved in the kingdom of God notwithstanding my present situation, which I hope will soon be bettered and I find favor in the eyes of God and All men his Saints Farewell March. 1838."[14]

Whitmer fled Far West in the summer of 1838, a foreshadowing of the church's expulsion from Missouri entirely in 1838–39. As feelings cooled, however, he returned to the region, taking advantage of reduced rates on property to become a prosperous farmer in the deserted city of Far West.[15] For nearly four decades he resided in the area, where he was known as "a highly respected and law abiding citizen." At his death on July 11, 1878, he left behind an estate of 625 acres, livestock, farm machinery, and a beautiful two-story home.[16] He also left behind his history of the church, which at that point passed to other hands.

LATTER-DAY SAINT ATTEMPTS TO ACQUIRE JOHN WHITMER'S HISTORY

Though out of the church in 1838, John Whitmer and his history continued to attract interest. Joseph Smith and Sidney Rigdon tried to acquire the history as early as April of that year through their aforementioned letter. There is no record of a response from John Whitmer.

A second dialogue regarding the record exists from the Nauvoo era. This time the history was used as a bartering chip in a possible business transaction. On March 4, 1840, two years after their joint excommunication, William W. Phelps wrote John Whitmer about property in Far West. Writing from Ohio, Phelps reminisced, "I long for the days when we can do as we used to, enjoying ourselves in a happiness that does not exist only where 'brethren dwell together in unity.' Say what you will of the world, and think what you may of the Church of Christ, when new members walked in the path marked out by the finger of God, the world has no Joys as pure as hers." Phelps then continued:

> As to the debts we contracted, I have ever done and meant to do my part. My house and lot, and some small parcels around town, after paying Mr. Boyce the post office deficit, I want sold to apply on those concerns: The printing office and lot I will deed to you as soon as I can get to some place where I can tarry long enough to do the business. The whole matter shall be arranged as speedily as possible. It would have been arranged on my part last summer with Frye, but sickness prevented, and I barely escaped to a healthier climate by the threads of life, which held soul and body together for the time being. I am in great needs now and mean to realize some money besides cancelling the old debts in Mo from the avails of those lands there.[17]

As with the letter from Joseph Smith and Sidney Rigdon, no immediate response from Whitmer has survived.

Discussion of transferring land titles, however, did eventually lead Whitmer to reopen conversation about the church history. Four years later, in 1844, Whitmer wrote Phelps, wondering why the land transaction still wasn't resolved:

> I should like to know how you are a doing and how you are feeling in regard to what we talked in regard to the old Frye concern before you left this place. I hope you are willing to do the clean thing, and why is it that that matter is not settled agreeable to your letter written to me at Dayton, Ohio, in which you said that as soon as you became settled and found a resting place you would close our business. I feel anxious to have it closed.

Connecting the matter to the history, Whitmer continued:

[Lyman E. Johnson] stated a few things to me from you in regard to the old Fry concern and also respecting the Church history, which is at my control, but not in my possession, and can be had at a fair price. . . . You have land in this county which is going to distruction. The timber that is valuable is pretty much destroyed. Now, if you will come here in the spring, I will sell to you the history for property, etc, provided we can agree as to price, and I think there will be but little difficulty in that. You own a small quantity of land north of us, joining my field, which I should like to own.[18]

Word of John Whitmer's attempt to part with the history reached Joseph Smith in Nauvoo, probably through Phelps himself, who was now faithfully back in the church. Joseph Smith's journal for February 23, 1844, notes that "W. W. Phelps rec[eive]d letter from J. Whitmer on Church history on which Dr Richards replied to."[19] Like Joseph and Sidney's 1838 letter seeking the history, Willard Richards's 1844 letter forcefully attacks Whitmer's labors as a historian as well as the record itself:

Your Letter of the 8th of January to W. W. Phelps came in to our beloved Brother Joseph Smith's office this day. As you mention something about the church records it becomes necessary to reply. We have already compiled about 800 pages of church history. ([Large pages][20] closely written. One page, probably, contains about 4 times the amount of matter of 1 which you wrote.) Which covers all the ground of which you took notes, therefore any thing which you have in the shape of church history would be of little or no consequence to the church at large.

You enquire about Bro Phelps prospects. He owns <u>no</u> property in <u>Nauvoo</u>, but labors diligently for the Church, and like all other Righteous men hardly gets a comfortable living, as the time has scarcely arrived for the "<u>meek to possess the earth</u>."

Yours respectfully,
Willard Richards
Recorder and Historian for the whole Church of Jesus
Christ of Latter Day Saints[21]

Nothing further resulted from Willard Richards's tersely written missive to John Whitmer.

The physical separation between John Whitmer and the church created by the Latter-day Saints' move to Salt Lake City further divided the two parties. At his death in Far West, Missouri, on July 11, 1878, John Whitmer still had control of the manuscript, leaving church leaders to speculate about its contents.

Whitmer was survived by two children, Jacob D. Whitmer and Sarah Elizabeth Whitmer. While his home and farm in Far West passed into their hands, the record, together with other church materials John owned—including a portion of the Joseph Smith translation of the Bible—were passed to his brother David Whitmer in Richmond, Missouri. David added these materials to other significant church artifacts he had received from Oliver Cowdery before his death in 1850. Prominent among these relics was the printer's copy of the Book of Mormon translation. When David Whitmer assumed control of John Whitmer's record, the history became linked with the more famous Book of Mormon manuscript for the remainder of the nineteenth century.

Two months after John Whitmer's death, Orson Pratt and Joseph F. Smith visited David Whitmer in Richmond, Missouri. Traveling east to visit church history sites, the pair met with this last of the Three Witnesses to interview him and preserve his account of early church history. During their conversation, reported later that year in the church's *Millennial Star*, Elders Pratt and Smith inquired about the Book of Mormon manuscript and what would be done with it upon David's death. Whitmer reported his plan to pass the manuscript on to his nephew, David P. Whitmer, son of his brother Jacob. When pressed about "part[ing] with [the manuscript] to a purchaser," Whitmer refused, responding, "Oliver charged me to keep it, and Joseph said my Fathers house should 'keep the Records.' I consider these things sacred and would not part with, nor barter them for money."[22]

Joseph F. Smith stated, "We would not offer you money in the light of bartering for the [pages], but we would like to see them preserved in some manner where they would be safe from casualties and from the caprices of men, in some institution that will not die as man does." Countering this reasoning, David Whitmer responded by referring to the recent tornado that had devastated the Richmond area, severely damaging the Whitmer home except the room where the Book of Mormon manuscript was kept. David's nephew Philander Page, who was present during the conversation, added, "Do you think . . . that the Almighty cannot take care of his own?"[23] David and his family were determined to keep the documents.

The next day, Pratt "again felt closely after the subject of procuring the [pages]." Denied again, Pratt and Smith later summarized: "We found that nothing would move him on this point. The whole Whitmer family are deeply impressed with the sacredness of this relic. And so thoroughly imbued are they with the idea and faith that it is under the immediate protection of the Almighty, that, in their estimation, not only is the [manuscript] itself safe from all possible contingencies, but that it is a source of protection to the place or house in which it may be kept, and, it may be to those who have possession of them."[24]

Word of church efforts to acquire the Book of Mormon manuscript, and probably John Whitmer's history with it, was quickly spread and sensationalized. Two weeks after their visit, the *Kansas City Journal* reported: "Orson Pratt and J. F. Smith, two of the leaders of the Mormon Church, visited Ray County to secure this original copy of their sacred book for deposit in the archives of the Church. . . . The Mormon elders offered Mr. Whitmer almost any price for it, but in vain."[25] Seven years later, the *Chicago Tribune* further enhanced the story:

> The original manuscript from which the Book of Mormon was printed is still in Mr. Whitmer's possession, and most of it is in the handwriting of his brother Christian and his brother-in-law, Oliver Cowdery. Mr. Whitmer also has an exhaustive history of the Church, which was compiled by his brother, and an accurate copy of several plates from which the Book of Mormon was translated. These records he has preserved against all temptations and in the face of death. Several years ago a delegation of Mormons came to Richmond from Salt Lake and made every overture to Mr. Whitmer in a vain attempt to gain possession of the records, but he stood aloof and declined every offer. A prominent businessman of the place, at that time engaged in banking, informed your correspondent that he knows of his own knowledge that the Mormon Church would have willingly paid Mr. Whitmer $100,000 for the documents, and that the delegation returned home thoroughly convinced that Mr. Whitmer was proof against all financial temptation so far as concerned his records.[26]

The story, including the reported $100,000 offer to purchase the documents, continued to hound the church. Nearly two decades after Pratt and Smith's visit, Chicago's *Daily Inter Ocean* called the Book of Mormon document "the most valuable manuscript now owned within the limits of the United States, the Federal constitution and the declaration of Independence alone excepted." The conclusion was based, in part, on rumors that "the Salt Lake hierarchy offered $100,000 in gold for it, and it is believed that they would have made an offer of $500,000 had they thought there was a prospect of Mr. Whitmer parting with it."[27]

On September 21, 1899, the *New York Times* repeated the story, embellishing again the attempted acquisition by linking it with plural marriage. "Once," the paper observed, church leaders "offered $100,000 in cash for the old and yellow manuscript, but its keeper, David Whitmer, one of the founders of the Church, refused the offer because he believed the Utah branch of the Church wished to get hold of the manuscript to insert into it by forgery a clause that would authorize and sanction the practice of polygamy." The paper further reported that "last week two representatives of the Mormon Church of Utah were [in Richmond, Missouri,] making another attempt to buy the manuscript."[28]

These and other accounts of church efforts to acquire the historic documents so exasperated Joseph F. Smith that he refuted them in a letter written on March 19, 1901:

> The [Book of Mormon] manuscript . . . possesses no value whatever. It has been repeatedly offered to us, and numerous false reports have been put in circulation with regard to our desire to obtain possession of it, but we have at no time regarded it as of any value, neither have we ever offered any money to procure it, all the stories to the contrary notwithstanding, for we have always known it was not the original, as aforesaid, and as many editions of the Book of Mormon have been printed, and tens of thousands of copies of it circulated throughout the world you can readily perceive that this manuscript really

is of no value to anyone. There is no principle involved in its possession, there could be nothing lost if it were utterly destroyed; it can neither add to or diminish aught from the word of God as contained in the printed work which has already come to the world and been translated into many languages. Indeed, it is not worth the time and paper I am using to convey these thoughts to you.[29]

As evidenced by President Smith's response, the Book of Mormon was the focus of most stories then circulating about the church's attempts to acquire the Whitmer manuscripts. But the *Chicago Tribune* account of 1885 indicates that individuals also apparently knew that "Mr. Whitmer also has an exhaustive history of the Church, which was compiled by his brother."[30]

John Whitmer's history remained linked to the Book of Mormon manuscript following David Whitmer's death on January 25, 1888. But the Whitmer collection did not pass to David Whitmer's nephew David P., as originally intended. This nephew preceded his uncle in death in 1883, so David Whitmer instead conferred the artifacts on his own son, David J. Whitmer.

Near the end of the nineteenth century, the church's focus shifted from the Book of Mormon printer's manuscript back to John Whitmer's history. Attempts to access the document during the late 1880s and early 1890s were headed by Andrew Jenson, who later became assistant church historian. Following David Whitmer's death, Jenson, together with Edward Stevenson and Joseph S. Black, visited David J. Whitmer in Richmond, Missouri, and examined the Book of Mormon manuscript in his possession.[31] Five years later, Jenson returned to Richmond. There he found the history in the care of George W. Schweich, David J.'s nephew. Describing the experience later in his autobiography, Jenson recorded:

I went to work immediately copying John Whitmer's old record, in the store of Geo. Schweich, who assisted me some in reading proof. Mr. Schweich did not think that the little old book with faded writing was the very book that I had been hunting for, but as I perused it, I came to the conclusion, without telling him so, that it contained all that John Whitmer ever wrote on Church history; hence I was anxious to copy every word contained in it. Mr. Schweich reluctantly allowed me to take it to my hotel where I spent all night copying, and in the morning returned the original to him. I was very pleased indeed to obtain a copy of this old Whitmer record.[32]

This autobiographical account was published more than three decades after the discovery. Andrew Jenson's contemporary journal entries paint an even more complete picture of how he obtained the church's first copy of John Whitmer's history. On Tuesday, September 5, 1893, Jenson described his search for the record: "Took train to Richmond, Ray Co. . . . where I met David J. Whitmer and Geo Schweich, and succeeded in getting sight of the old John Whitmer Church history; was busy perusing it most of the day."[33]

Nearly three weeks later, Jenson returned to Richmond, where his journal continues, describing the multiday ordeal of copying the record: "Monday 25. . . . I went to work immediately copying John Whitmer's old record in the store of Geo Schweich, who assisted me some in reading proof after I had copied part. . . . Tuesday 26 Continued my labors copying at Mr. Schweich's store and finished the work at my lodging place about 12 midnight. Wed. 27. Mr. Schweich helped me again comparing what I had written with the original record after which I proceeded to the railway station at Richmond."[34]

Returning the transcription to Salt Lake City, Jenson made several copies, appending a note that explained the state of the original record. Jenson observed: "The original Whitmer record from which this is copied, is a book, containing nearly 300 pages of unruled paper, of which only the first 96 are written, the remaining pages remaining blank. The size of the book is 12½ × 8½ inches, bound very plain, with paper sides and cloth back. The writing is that of an ordinary hand, without any pretence of advanced penmanship; the spelling and punctuation are bad." Trying to be as accurate as possible, Jenson even traced the length and width of the book, drawing lines to represent its dimensions. Describing the cover, he added, the "book is plainly bound, of the old timers; cloth back, paper sides; size ordinary fools cap folio."[35]

In addition to including a physical description of the record, Jenson's appended introduction also explains his transcription method. "During my visit to Missouri in September last," Jenson recorded, "I obtained permission from said David J. Whitmer to make a copy of the old Whitmer record in his possession. I spent several days doing this labor and was very careful to copy verbatim everything which the record contained, except certain revelations, letters and documents, which are already contained in the history of Joseph Smith. These, as produced in the following pages are copied from said printed history as published in the Mill. Star vol. 14. Hence the following is a full, complete and accurate copy of the original record as written by John Whitmer."[36]

Jenson's copy reveals his knowledge of church scripture and history, as he simply refers to Doctrine and Covenants passages rather than copying them. The fact that this was an unplanned effort at transcription is also evident, as the document is largely written on what appears to be scrap paper. Ten of Jenson's pages are written on the back of George Schweich's business letterhead.

Numerous other pages are written on the backs of pages torn from Jenson's monthly periodical, *The Historical Record*.

Jenson also describes any alterations he made to the transcription: "I have corrected . . . errors and introduced some punctuation, but have not altered the construction of sentences in any degree whatever, except in a very few instances where I have introduced single words in brackets in order to make the sense more complete, and in a few other instances where I (also in brackets) have given correct dates after wrong ones given by Mr. Whitmer. The few words thus inserted by me are all underlined in this copy."[37]

Furthermore, Jenson's introductory reflections offer his assessment of John Whitmer's history. His evaluation includes a discussion of how Whitmer may have written the history and added material following Joseph's death. "Whoever reads this copy," Jenson noted, "should observe that Mr. Whitmer closes his record as historian in 1838, at the end of his Chapter 19; but that he subsequently adds three more chapters which are written in altogether a different spirit to that which dictated the first part of the history. It is evident that Mr. Whitmer, after his excommunication from the Church, became very bitter in his feelings toward Joseph the Prophet and the Church generally, and also that he changed his views on different points as he grew older, particularly in regard to the successorship in the Presidency of the Church. This is proven by the erasures which he made of that which he had formerly written, all of which is shown in this copy."[38]

Most important, Andrew Jenson added one additional piece of information regarding the physical state of the manuscript that aids the reader immensely in assessing the record. At the end of the transcription Jenson summarized: "Here the Whitmer record suddenly ends, on the bottom of page 96, the following four pages having been torn off. This is evident from the fact that there are small fragments of the leaves left in the book, and the number of the next page left intact is 101. No other writing however appears on this page, nor on any of the succeeding pages, about two hundred in number."[39] This information is critical because it helps the researcher know that by 1893, up to four pages were missing from the extant Whitmer record.

BRINGING JOHN WHITMER'S RECORD TO LIGHT—THE REORGANIZED CHURCH'S ACQUISITION AND PUBLICATION

With a copy of John Whitmer's long-missing record in hand, church leaders in Salt Lake City were finally able to satisfy themselves regarding its contents. But individuals and institutions with ties to Mormon history continued to be interested in the original. At the beginning of the twentieth century, this interest culminated in the Reorganized Church of Jesus Christ of Latter Day Saints successfully acquiring the document from Whitmer family members and leading efforts to see it published.

As noted in Andrew Jenson's 1893 account, while the record was owned by David J. Whitmer, George W. Schweich maintained some control over the document. A dry goods merchant in Richmond, Schweich was the grandson of David Whitmer, his mother being David's only daughter, Julia Ann Whitmer Schweich. When his uncle David J. Whitmer died tragically from a sandbar collapse in 1895, George Schweich gained exclusive control over the Whitmer family artifacts, including the Book of Mormon printer's manuscript and John Whitmer's history.

Unlike his grandfather, Schweich seemed willing to exhibit and possibly part with the sacred family artifacts. Aware of this possibility, interested parties within the Reorganized Church began inquiring about the documents as early as January 1886, long before Schweich actually received them. At that time RLDS Church president Joseph Smith III wrote Albert D. Hager, secretary of the Chicago Historical Society:

> It will be comparatively useless for me to approach Eld[er] David Whitmer on the subject of depositing the Mss of the Book of Mormon in his care, in the Archives of the Historical Society at Chicago. He believes himself divinely appointed as the custodian of that Mss, and as such he will not consent to part with it while he lives.
>
> There is in Chicago, or was, in the Customs Office, a Col. VanCleve. . . . He was the husband of a grand daughter of David Whitmer, and I think has great influence with the family. I suggest that you see Col. VanCleve and his wife, and talk the matter over with them. It is my opinion that when father Whitmer dies, he will put the Mss in the hand of his grandson George Schweich, of Richmond, brother of Col. VanCleve's wife. Hence, if you can succeed with the Colonel it may aid you further on.
>
> It will give me pleasure to forward your efforts to secure all that throws light on the history of Mormonism being myself a learner though a believer in it. I Expect to meet the exact truth hereafter, and I desire to be as honest and brave now as I will be compelled to be then. Personally, I have nothing to hide in reference to Mormonism.[40]

Ten years later, following the passing of all Whitmer materials into the possession of George Schweich, the RLDS Church made a specific attempt to contact him regarding the records. In 1896, as RLDS apostle and church historian Heman C. Smith was compiling the official church history of his denomination, he asked Schweich for material from the Whitmer history. In a letter Smith explained, "When I met you near a month ago you kindly agreed to find out the where-a-bouts of the manuscript history written by Mr. John Whitmer, and permit us the use of it in compilling the work in which we are now engaged. Have you yet learned any more regarding its where abouts?" Specifically, Smith asked for the "complete and verbatim account as it appears in the account kept by John Whitmer" of the "ordination of High Priests in 1831."[41]

Due to the increasing number of inquiries regarding the history, Schweich may have become aware of the financial value of the document as well as his other relics from early Mormon history. Apparently this led him to seek to profit financially from his family's connections to Mormonism. In 1891 he wrote Angus M. Cannon, Salt Lake Stake president and brother to First Presidency member George Q. Cannon, about an artifact in his collection: "I own now the table on which the book of Mormon was written by Oliver Cowdery & others while the prophet translated it. I send you a photo. Can't you find some of your wealthy men who would give me as much as $5000[00] for it. If you can I shall consider the sale of it. Would rather let some one of your upright men have it. . . . I hate to sell it to an unbeliever which I can now do. I have a good motive in this and am not so mercenary as it seems. Please know that this is a private letter to one who I think a friend."[42]

At the turn of the century, Schweich entrusted a portion of his collection with William E. Benjamin, a wealthy rare book collector in New York City. Writing the Reverend O. R. Beardsley about the arrangement, Schweich mentioned: "I am the owner of the Original M.S of the Book of Mor. It is now in New York City with W. E. Benjamin. . . . I consider the M.S. an important document for the American people[.] I also have M.S. History of the Church for some unpublished periods."[43]

News of Schweich's willingness to part with the Whitmer family collection eventually reached RLDS Church president Joseph Smith III. In April 1897 he wrote Schweich, inquiring specifically about the Book of Mormon manuscript:

Dear Sir and Bro:—

Elder William Vaughan, of Huntsville, Mo., in attendance here at Conference, stated to me . . . that on his way here he called on you and had a chat. He further stated that you expressed a willingness that we should have the custody of the Manuscript of the Book of Mormon, of which your Grandfather was so long the faithful guardian; provided that I would come for it, and engage to keep it safe from mutilation, soiling, or destruction. He stated that you so stated to him that if I would come for it I could get it.

While, I would quite willingly undertake to keep the manuscript with the same fidelity and jealous care that I would the mss of the Holy Scriptures, which my mother kept so long and faithfully, if they were confided to me; I would not have you to think that I would not ask you to surrender the charge delivered to you by your Grandfather for the sake of anything I might say to you; as I have full satisfaction that your Grandfather was made the custodian of them; and, felt contented that they were safe in your hands, believing you to be honorable in your fidelity to the ways of the Lord. . . .

If for any reason satisfactory to you, you are willing to confide the manuscript to my care; or if you are desirous of relieving yourself of the care and anxiety which such a constant custody of them involves; and you will trust them to me, I will come to Richmond for them at any time set by you. . . .

If Elder Vaughan has misunderstood you in this affair, please pardon the intrusion of this letter; for believe me, I do not seek to deprive you of that committed to your care; or desire in any ignoble or unworthy way to get possession of these manuscripts.[44]

President Smith's conciliatory manner seems to have opened a door between the RLDS Church and George Schweich, not merely for the transfer of the Book of Mormon manuscript but also for other artifacts, including the John Whitmer history. Deliberate negotiations apparently ensued, with the minutes of the First Presidency of the RLDS Church recording on April 24, 1902:

> Joseph Smith and Fred M. Smith, of the First Presidency, E. L. Kelley of the Bishopric, and W. H. Kelley, F. A. Smith, J. W. Wight, of the Twelve, met in the First Presidency's office at three o'clock in the afternoon, to consider the advisability of accepting an offer from George W. Schweich, of Richmond, Missouri, to turn over to the Reorganized Church, for a money consideration of twenty five hundred dollars the manuscript of the Book of Mormon. All seemed to be agreed that if some other papers which he possessed could be secured together with the Book of Mormon manuscript, they would be worth the price asked. Hence a motion prevailed that negotiations be opened with him for that purpose.[45]

A year later the transaction was finalized when, on April 18, 1903, Schweich delivered to Joseph Smith III and other RLDS leaders the Book of Mormon printer's manuscript, John Whitmer's manuscript history, parts of Joseph Smith's translation of the Bible, manuscript copies of several revelations, and a piece of paper containing copied Book of Mormon characters.[46] An announcement was made at the RLDS Church conference, with a subsequent Presiding Bishop's report summarizing: "The present year the Church has been at some considerable special expense, outside of keeping up proper repairs and protection of its property, for matters that will not come up in the future and yet essential to the interests of the work. Of this list the sum of $2,450 was expended for the original manuscripts of the Book of Mormon, and notes of church history in the hands of relatives of David and John Whitmer, deceased."[47] A far cry from the rumored six-figure amount offered twenty-five years earlier by Orson Pratt and Joseph F. Smith, the sale finally transferred John Whitmer's history from private to institutional hands.

MAKING JOHN WHITMER'S HISTORY ACCESSIBLE TO THE PUBLIC

Once it possessed the original manuscript of the history, the Reorganized Church quickly sought to make the document accessible to its members. But the manuscript was nearly destroyed by fire shortly after its acquisition. On January 5, 1907, flames ravaged the RLDS Herald Publishing House in Lamoni, Iowa, reducing to ashes nearly 2,800 volumes dealing with the early church and its reorganization that were housed in the historian's office and library. Because the fire occurred at 7:40 a.m., however—prior to the vault materials being opened for the day—the record of John Whitmer and other priceless historical treasures were providentially preserved.[48]

A year later, RLDS Church historian Heman C. Smith first published John Whitmer's record in the January, April, and July 1908 issues of the RLDS periodical *Journal of History* under the title "Church History." Smith concluded the published account with John Whitmer's benediction, written after his 1838 expulsion: "Therefore I close the history of the church of Latter

Day Saints, hoping that I may be forgiven of my faults and my sins be blotted out and in the last days be saved in the kingdom of God notwithstanding my present situation, which I hope will soon be bettered and I find favor in the eyes of God and all men his Saints. Farewell. March, 1838."[49] But this farewell was not the end of the record. At the time, RLDS leaders decided not to publish the final three chapters, representing eleven manuscript pages John Whitmer wrote sometime after his disaffection from The Church of Jesus Christ of Latter-day Saints.

Following official publication of the record, discussion ensued regarding the accuracy of Andrew Jenson's 1893 transcript copy. In 1918 Heman C. Smith wrote RLDS Church president Frederick M. Smith, describing both the record and the controversy: "[John Whitmer's record] is written in a blank book all in one hand presumably that of John Whitmer. . . . It has since developed that the Utah people claim to have made a copy prior to its coming into our hands. I am of the opinion that there is some truth in the statement. How faithfully they have been in copying is impossible to tell from the evidence now in our possession."[50]

The dispute over differing copies caused continued interest in John Whitmer's history, leading to additional publication efforts. In 1960 disaffected RLDS member Pauline Hancock produced a typescript copy of the entire manuscript. Explaining her labors, Hancock wrote: "The manuscript up to page 85 was published by the [RLDS Church in 1908]. . . . This includes entries made up to March 1838, but the last three chapters have never been published. . . . We have now obtained the microfilm of John Whitmer's complete history and have had it printed f[ro]m the microfilm and bound into a book so that others may also read these items of history that have been held back by the churches that have the original history."[51] Six years later, Jerald and Sandra Tanner similarly published a version in Salt Lake City.[52]

Aware of discrepancies between these different versions, the RLDS Church's Herald Publishing House issued a new version in 1980. The account, edited by historians F. Mark McKiernan and Roger D. Launius, included the disputed final three chapters omitted from the earlier *Journal of History* printing. To aid the reader, it also included extensive explanatory footnotes, an introductory essay on John Whitmer and his history, a detailed biographical essay, and an index. According to Community of Christ archivist Ron Romig, however, "the McKiernan and Launius edition was subject to some editorial oversights and differs in places from both John Whitmer's manuscript and Jenson's typescript."[53]

Latter-day Saint scholar Bruce N. Westergren produced the next edition of John Whitmer's history in 1995. This annotated version attempted to preserve the accuracy of the text, with "spelling, punctuation, and capitalization . . . retained as they appear in the original. . . . Characters and words stricken out in the original [were] retained." Effort was made to indicate missing or illegible characters and words, with all editorial insertions indicated.[54]

Care has also been taken regarding the manuscript itself. Following the near destruction of the document in the 1907 Herald House fire, efforts were made to ensure its protection. The construction of the RLDS auditorium in Independence, Missouri, in the early twentieth century provided a fireproof repository within the building for the manuscript. There it remained in the historian's office and later the RLDS library and archives until 1992, when it was moved to the nearby temple complex then under construction.[55] Most recently, John Whitmer's original manuscript has been displayed at the new Community of Christ visitors center adjacent to the temple in Kirtland, Ohio.

Moreover, while the original manuscript has been preserved, cooperative efforts have developed between the RLDS (now Community of Christ) and LDS Churches to increase access to the document. In 1974, LDS and RLDS officials exchanged microfilmed historical materials, including the John Whitmer manuscript. In an effort to preserve it for future use, RLDS Church historian Richard P. Howard arranged for the pages to be removed from their binding, laminated, and rebound in a modern cover during the early 1970s.[56]

More recently, as part of the Joseph Smith Papers Project, officials from the two churches have worked closely together to preserve the manuscript, employing advanced techniques, including reversing the process of lamination. According to Community of Christ archivist Ron Romig, during 2005 and 2006, officials from The Church of Jesus Christ of Latter-day Saints in Salt Lake City took John Whitmer's ninety-six handwritten pages and "carefully delaminated, cleaned, washed, deacidified, stabilized, repaired, and reassembled [them] back into their original ledger book covers." At the same time, additional study was made of the original manuscript pages, the transcription of which will be included in subsequent Joseph Smith Papers publications.[57]

ASSESSING JOHN WHITMER'S RECORD

From its inception, "the Book of John Whitmer, kept by commandment" has followed a long and twisted path. Reluctantly begun by commandment, it remained a point of contention during John Whitmer's lifetime and a subject of mystery following his death. This history, as well as the conflict and obscurity that surrounded it, influenced ways in which church members, leaders, and scholars viewed the record.

For decades, skepticism and even ridicule have haunted the document. This began with Joseph Smith and Sidney Rigdon's 1838 letter to John requesting he give up the manuscript and continued through Willard Richards's 1844 rebuff of Whitmer's attempt to sell it. But these decidedly negative statements should be considered within the emotionally charged contexts in which they were delivered. For example, the 1838 letter criticizing Whitmer's "incompetency as a historian" was written following the Kirtland apostasy and the prophet's loss of numerous leaders and close friends, including the entire Whitmer family. The heated 1844 dialogue came as the prophet was discovering the threats both from within and without that ultimately led to his death four months later. The pressures caused by these contexts may have colored any dialogue regarding the history.

Without access to the record itself, The Church of Jesus Christ of Latter-day Saints was unfortunately left to rely on these confrontational statements when assessing John Whitmer's history. Describing his own recording efforts, including filling in the gaps created by the absence of John's record, Wilford Woodruff observed: "I have recorded nearly all the sermons and teachings that I ever heard from the Prophet Joseph, I have in my journal many of the sermons of President Brigham Young, and such men as Orson Hyde, Parley P. Pratt and others." He explained that one "reason I was moved upon to write in the early days was that nearly all the historians appointed in those times apostatized and took the journals away with them."[58]

Others in the Utah church made specific reference to John Whitmer and his failings. In 1907, First Presidency member Anthon H. Lund applauded the efforts of Matthew, Mark, Luke, John, Nephi, and Alma in producing scriptural records. Then, calling John Whitmer's command to write a church history "a very important matter," President Lund continued,

> I wish that commandment had been more strictly obeyed and more elaborate records had been kept from the beginning of the Church. What history we have is correct, but John Whitmer's record and the records of the early recorders of the Church are not very extensive, and if it were not for the history of the Prophet Joseph, and the journals kept by some of our leading men in those early days, our knowledge of the interesting events of that remarkable period of our history would be very meager.[59]

Because his reluctance and subsequent command to keep the church record are described in the *History of the Church* as well as in the record itself, negative feelings about John Whitmer and his history are also common in Latter-day Saint scriptural commentaries. For example, one source critiques "the meager results of his labors" and mentions that John Whitmer's service as church historian was performed "not always with exemplary diligence."[60] Another source, emphasizing the brevity of Whitmer's account, highlights that "his writings, which included revelations given by Joseph Smith during that seven-year period, were only eighty-five pages in length."[61] A third calls his account "a sketchy history."[62] Even the church-produced *Doctrine and Covenants Student Manual* notes, "John Whitmer's history of the Church is a mere sketch of events that actually transpired between 1831 and 1838. His work consisted of eighty-five pages, which included many of the revelations given to the Prophet Joseph Smith."[63]

To be fair, these assessments reflect the emotional feelings of those who originally sought John Whitmer's record as well as the longing by modern scholars for more information, especially from its official historian, about the early church. But directing criti-cism at the record's shortcomings or evaluating it against modern standards may be improper. Rather, the history should be valued for the contributions it does make while assessing it against the expectation and charge delivered to Whitmer. Doing so empha-sizes the fact that, in some measure, content matters more than coverage.

As one of the earliest elders in the New York area in 1830 and the presiding elder in Kirtland prior to Joseph Smith's arrival in February 1831, Whitmer offers unique insights into early New York and Ohio church history throughout his record. Andrew Jenson himself noted about the transcription, "It contained only a little of historical value. Yet John Whitmer recorded events which are not recorded elsewhere."[64] Especially important are his details about the opposition the church faced in New York, the migration of members to Ohio, and the revelations manifested in Kirtland by Mrs. Hubble and others "led away with foolish and vain imaginations."[65] Later, as Whitmer was reassigned to Missouri, he recorded historical details regarding the expulsion from Zion, the subsequent attempts by the Saints to reclaim their promised land, and the settling of Far West. Finally, as one re-cent commentary observed, though John "becomes quite cyni-cal about the Church as [he] apostatized in 1838," the record "is an important but sketchy source of early Church history."[66] Even these cynical portions surrounding his disaffection help modern readers understand better the emotion of the time. For these and other reasons, as one author noted, "[John Whitmer's] ninety-six written pages are considered by some historians to be the most authoritative history of the Church before 1838."[67]

With increased availability, John Whitmer's manuscript might be moving to a new era in its history. Gone are the confrontations

over access to the account and the corresponding negative con-
notations that it spawned. In its place, we hopefully gain insight
from the contributions that his record, kept by commandment of
the Lord, offers.

Describing these labors, as well as his desire to be accepted by
the Lord and his servants, John Whitmer himself wrote to Oliver
Cowdery in 1833, "I want you to remember me to Joseph in a
special manner, and enquire of him respecting my clerkship[;]
you very well know what I mean & also my great desire of doing
all things according to the mind of the Lord."[68] As modern bene-
ficiaries of one historian's attempt to please the Lord, we too now
remember John Whitmer and his record in a "special manner,"
applying lessons from his life to our own historical endeavors.

NOTES

The author expresses special appreciation to Robin Jensen of the Church History
Library in Salt Lake City, Ron Romig of the Community of Christ Archives, and
David Whittaker at Brigham Young University for their willingness to share both
expertise and resources on this topic.

1.   F. Mark McKiernan and Roger D. Launius, eds., *An Early Latter Day Saint
     History: The Book of John Whitmer, Kept by Commandment* (Independence,
     MO: Herald Publishing House, 1980), 56.
2.   This title is taken from the first line on the first page of John Whitmer's
     manuscript record.
3.   *History of The Church of Jesus Christ of Latter-day Saints*, ed. B. H. Roberts,
     2nd ed. rev. (Salt Lake City: Deseret Book, 1978), 3:15–16.
4.   Larry C. Porter, "A Study of the Origins of The Church of Jesus Christ of
     Latter-day Saints in the States of New York and Pennsylvania, 1816–1831"
     (PhD diss., Brigham Young University, 1971, 2000), 91; Andrew Jenson,
     Latter-day Saint Biographical Encyclopedia, vol. 1 (Salt Lake City: Andrew
     Jenson History Company, 1901), 251.

5. Donald Q. Cannon and Lyndon W. Cook, eds., *Far West Record: Minutes of The Church of Jesus Christ of Latter-day Saints, 1830–1844* (Salt Lake City: Deseret Book, 1983), 1.

6. McKiernan and Launius, *Early Latter Day Saint History*, 56.

7. McKiernan and Launius, *Early Latter Day Saint History*, 56.

8. McKiernan and Launius, *Early Latter Day Saint History*, 93.

9. Cannon and Cook, *Far West Record*, 68.

10. See *History of the Church*, 3:5–8.

11. *History of the Church*, 3:6–7. *History of the Church* refers to a disagreement involving $2,000 in Church funds, appropriated for the building of the temple in Far West but retained by Whitmer and Phelps. The financial disagreement is a complicated one, however, and centers on earlier properties purchased by Whitmer and Phelps during the founding of Far West. The *Far West Record* records the allegations leveled against church leaders, as well as their counter-argument that the council was "contrary to the principles of the revelations of Jesus Christ." See Cannon and Cook, *Far West Record*, 146–49.

12. *History of the Church*, 3:8, 11.

13. Bruce N. Westergren, ed., *From Historian to Dissident: The Book of John Whitmer* (Salt Lake City: Signature Books, 1995), 180.

14. Westergren, *From Historian to Dissident*, 180.

15. Jenson, *Latter-day Saint Biographical Encyclopedia*, 1:252.

16. Richard Lloyd Anderson, *Investigating the Book of Mormon Witnesses* (Salt Lake City: Deseret Book, 1981), 131.

17. William W. Phelps to John Whitmer, March 4, 1840, L. Tom Perry Special Collections, Harold B. Lee Library, Brigham Young University, Provo, Utah. The Frye concern mentioned in this letter by Phelps (and in the follow-up letter four years later by Whitmer—see note 18) involves a loan contracted by Phelps and Whitmer with Mr. William Frye when they purchased property on behalf of the Church in Far West in 1836. Controversy over the repayment of this debt continued for years following the original transaction.

18. John Whitmer to Wm. W. Phelps, January 8, 1844, Journal History of the Church, Church History Library, The Church of Jesus Christ of Latter-day Saints, Salt Lake City, Utah.

19. Joseph Smith, Journal, February 23, 1844, Church History Library.

20. The original letter seems to read "Lage Demi." The corresponding typescript version of the same letter in the Journal History also reads "Lage Demi," but

someone has written over it, in pencil, the words "Large pages." The exact meaning of "Lage Demi" is uncertain.

21. Willard Richards to John Whitmer, February 23, 1844, Willard Richards Papers, 1821–54, Church History Library. The original to this document includes some words that were lined through and therefore deleted. These have been omitted, without ellipses, from the document as quoted.

22. Orson Pratt and Joseph F. Smith to John Taylor and Council of the Twelve, September 17, 1878, in *Selected Collections from the Archives of The Church of Jesus Christ of Latter-day Saints*, ed. Richard E. Turley Jr., 2 vols. (Provo, UT: Brigham Young University Press, 2002), DVD 27: Joseph F. Smith Incoming Correspondence; also in "Report of Elders Orson Pratt and Joseph F. Smith," *Millennial Star*, December 9, 1878, 773.

23. Pratt and Smith to Taylor and Council of the Twelve, September 17, 1878.

24. Pratt and Smith to Taylor and Council of the Twelve, September 17, 1878.

25. "The Book of Mormon," *Kansas City Journal*, September 22, 1878.

26. *Chicago Tribune*, December 15, 1885, cited in "David Whitmer," *Deseret News*, December 24, 1885.

27. "Book of Mormon Manuscript," *Chicago Daily Inter Ocean*, September 9, 1895. The authenticity of the $100,000 offering can be questioned. Jacob T. Child, a resident of Richmond referred to as Colonel Childs in Pratt and Smith's published account, later wrote: "I was present when Elders Orson Pratt and Smith, from Salt Lake City, called on your grandfather in regard to the manuscript of the 'Book of Mormon,' and upon it being shown to them Elder Pratt recognized the handwriting of Oliver Cowdery and Mrs. Smith. After some conversation Elder Pratt asked Mr. Whitmer if he would dispose of the manuscript, stating that he would give anything in reason for it, as the archives of the Church were incomplete without it. There was no fixed sum named but your grandfather was afraid that if he parted with it that they might interpolate." Jacob T. Child to George W. Schweich, August 28, 1896, cited in I. Woodbridge Riley, *The Founder of Mormonism: A Psychological Study of Joseph Smith, Jr.* (London: William Heinemann, 1903), 98n55.

28. "The Book of Mormon: The Original Manuscript Said to Be in a Missouri Town," *New York Times*, September 21, 1899.

29. Joseph F. Smith to Samuel Russell, March 19, 1901, Perry Special Collections.

30. *Chicago Tribune*, December 15, 1885, cited in "David Whitmer."

31. Andrew Jenson, Edward Stevenson, and Joseph S. Black, letter to the editor, September 13, 1888, in "Historical Landmarks," *Deseret Evening News*, September 17, 1888.

32. *Autobiography of Andrew Jenson* (Salt Lake City: Deseret News Press, 1938), 209.

33. Andrew Jenson, Journal, September 5, 1893, Autobiography and Journals, 1864–1941, Church History Library.

34. Jenson Journal, September 25–27, 1893.

35. Andrew Jenson, Manuscript and Typescript, Andrew Jenson Collection [ca. 1871–1942], Church History Library. At one point the original document is unclear. Before the words "of the old timers" is another word, perhaps "and" or "one." That word may be crossed out in the original.

36. Jenson, Manuscript and Typescript. The original to this document includes some words that were lined through and therefore deleted. These have been omitted, without ellipses, from the document as quoted.

37. Jenson, Manuscript and Typescript.

38. Jenson, Manuscript and Typescript.

39. Jenson, Manuscript and Typescript.

40. Joseph Smith III to Albert D. Hager, January 11, 1886, Community of Christ Archives, Independence, Missouri; original located in Collection of Manuscripts about Mormons, Chicago Historical Society, Chicago, Illinois.

41. Heman C. Smith to George W. Schweich, July 20, 1896, Community of Christ Archives.

42. George W. Schweich to Angus M. Cannon, August 19, 1891, Angus M. Cannon Collection, Church History Library. Schweich's fascination with Church relics did not apparently end with this table. A 1914 Kansas City newspaper account reports that he "is said to be the possessor of the sword of Laban as well as the golden plates from which the Mormon Bible was translated, and other Mormon relics." Schweich refused to confirm whether he had the plates, replying, "If I had I should not want to make any announcements about it." He fueled the rumors, however, by giving a description of the plates. See "Tells of Mormon Relics," *Kansas City Star*, December 27, 1914.

43. George W. Schweich to O. R. Beardsley, January 17, 1900, Perry Special Collections.

44. Joseph Smith III to George W. Schweich, April 5, 1897, Joseph Smith Letter Book, P6, LB 7, 479–81, Community of Christ Archives.

45. First Presidency Minutes, Reports, and Correspondence, April 24, 1902, microfilm, Community of Christ Archives.

46. Ronald E. Romig, "The New Translation Materials since 1844," in Scott H. Faulring, Kent P. Jackson, and Robert J. Matthews, eds., *Joseph Smith's New Translation of the Bible* (Provo, UT: Religious Studies Center, Brigham Young University, 2004), 37.

47. "General Conference Minutes: Presiding Bishop's Report," *Supplement to Saints' Herald* (Lamoni, IA: Reorganized Church of Jesus Christ of Latter Day Saints, 1904), 689. Some question as to the legality of the sale persisted following the transaction. During his 1907 visit to Church history sites, photographer George Edward Anderson described his visit with Whitmer relatives in Far West: "Question with Mr. [John David] Whitmer if George Schweich had a right to sell [?] the manuscript of the Book of Mormon. He thought they might belong to the original church and that could be settled by court." Importantly, Anderson's interview with John David Whitmer also speculates as to why Schweich sold the documents: "Said George Schweich mortgaged the manuscript for $1,800. Then had to raise the money." Richard Neitzel Holzapfel, T. Jeffery Cottle, and Ted D. Stoddard, eds., *Church History in Black and White* (Provo, UT: Religious Studies Center, Brigham Young University, 1995), 82.

48. Romig, "New Translation Materials since 1844," 37–38.

49. "Church History," *Journal of History* (July 1908): 305.

50. Heman C. Smith to Frederick M. Smith, March 11, 1918, P10, f 19, Community of Christ Archives.

51. Ronald E. Romig, "Provenance of 'The Book of John Whitmer,'" November 8, 2007, typescript, Community of Christ Archives.

52. Westergren, *From Historian to Dissident*, xii.

53. Romig, "Book of John Whitmer"; McKiernan and Launius, *An Early Latter Day Saint History.*

54. Westergren, *From Historian to Dissident*, xii–xiii.

55. Romig, "Provenance of 'The Book of John Whitmer.'"

56. Romig, "Provenance of 'The Book of John Whitmer.'"

57. Romig, "Provenance of 'The Book of John Whitmer.'"

58. Matthias F. Cowley, *Wilford Woodruff: History of His Life and Labors* (Salt Lake City: Bookcraft, 1964), 477.

59. Anthon H. Lund, in *Seventy-Seventh Annual Conference of The Church of Jesus Christ of Latter-day Saints* (Salt Lake City: Deseret News, 1907), 54.

60. Stephen E. Robinson and H. Dean Garrett, *A Commentary on the Doctrine and Covenants* (Salt Lake City: Deseret Book, 2001), 2:84.

61. Joseph Fielding McConkie and Craig J. Ostler, *Revelations of the Restoration* (Salt Lake City: Deseret Book, 2000), 370. By referring to eighty-five pages of text, the authors seem to be referring to Whitmer's record up to 1838. As previously discussed, Whitmer wrote eleven additional pages of manuscript sometime after his disaffection, bringing the remaining manuscript total to ninety-six pages. Also, as is evident in Andrew Jenson's account of transcribing the original, apparently four pages at the end of the text were missing by 1893.

62. Richard O. Cowan, *Doctrine & Covenants: Our Modern Scripture* (Provo, UT: Brigham Young University Press, 1978), 85.

63. Church Educational System, *Doctrine and Covenants Student Manual: Religion 324–325* (Salt Lake City: The Church of Jesus Christ of Latter-day Saints, 1981), 102.

64. *Autobiography of Andrew Jenson*, 209.

65. McKiernan and Launius, *Early Latter Day Saint History*, 61.

66. Steven C. Harper, *Making Sense of the Doctrine & Covenants* (Salt Lake City: Deseret Book, 2008), 163.

67. Susan Easton Black, *Who's Who in the Doctrine & Covenants* (Salt Lake City: Bookcraft, 1997), 332.

68. Whitmer to Cowdery, July 29, 1833, quoted in Lyndon W. Cook, *The Revelations of the Prophet Joseph Smith* (Salt Lake City: Deseret Book, 1985), 64–65.

James B. Allen

4

WILLIAM CLAYTON AND THE RECORDS OF CHURCH HISTORY

A MONTH before his martyrdom, the Prophet Joseph Smith remarked, "For the last three years . . . I have kept several good, faithful, and efficient clerks in constant employ; they have accompanied me everywhere, and carefully kept my history, and they have written down what I have done, where I have been, and what I have said."[1] One of those clerks was twenty-nine-year-old William Clayton.

William Clayton is an obscure figure to many Latter-day Saints, as are most of Joseph Smith's clerks and scribes. If his name is recognized at all, it is likely due to his authorship of one of Mormonism's most beloved hymns, "Come, Come, Ye Saints," or perhaps his remarkable pioneer journal. Yet if not for Clayton and many people like him, we would have practically no recorded

James B. Allen is a former assistant church historian of The Church of Jesus Christ of Latter-day Saints and professor emeritus of history, Brigham Young University.

history of the early church. This paper will attempt to shed light on this important but little-known record keeper from the past.

A SACRED TRUST

On January 29, 1845, seven months after the prophet's death, William Clayton spent nearly all day working at the Church Recorder's Office. He interrupted his activities, however, to attend and record the proceedings of a special meeting conducted by President Brigham Young of the Quorum of the Twelve Apostles. Also in attendance were two other members of the quorum, Heber C. Kimball and Orson Hyde; the two trustees-in-trust of the church, Newel K. Whitney and George Miller; and two members of the Nauvoo Temple committee, Alpheas Cutler and Reynolds Cahoon. The purpose of the meeting was to consider a special request by the members of the temple committee. Their assignment, Reynolds Cahoon explained, required considerable extra effort, including working on Sundays, going to bed late, and getting up at all hours of the night to serve those who brought in property for the temple. They wanted this extra work, for which they were not paid, to be entered on the books as full payment of their tithing. After all, the committee members explained, Joseph Smith intended for them to have this tithing arrangement when they were first asked to serve.

During the discussion, Brigham Young said that he and the other church leaders were determined to carry out Joseph's wishes in every respect. He also commented on the "unceasing and indefatigable labors of the Twelve and others" who were spending all their time working for the benefit of the church. He recommended that tithing should be entered as paid in full for the committee and the Twelve, and everyone agreed. William Clayton then made the same request. In the end, all the apostles, the trustees, members of the temple committee, and William Clayton, as well as the late Joseph and Hyrum Smith and city marshal John P. Green, had their tithing shown on the record as paid in full.

For William Clayton, perhaps the most spiritually satisfying part of the meeting happened after the decision about tithing was made. At that point Elders Young and Kimball gave him a special blessing in which he was told that "he should be a scribe for this church in the resurrection." He made note of the blessing not only in the minutes of the meeting but also in his personal journal.[2] Keeping the records of the church was a sacred trust to him, one in which he had reveled since he was appointed as a scribe to the Prophet Joseph Smith in 1842. To have his labors and abilities so recognized by church leaders, with the assurance that this recognition would continue in the eternities, must have given him exhilaration that little else could match.

DEDICATED AND INDUSTRIOUS SAINT

William Clayton grew up in Penwortham, England, where, at the time of his conversion, he worked as a clerk in a factory. Of a meticulous, methodical nature, he was a gifted musician (he played the violin, drum, and French horn), a lover of fine craftsmanship, and a devoted husband and father. On October 21, 1837, he was baptized by Heber C. Kimball, who was leading the first Latter-day Saint mission to England and remained Clayton's friend and confidant until Kimball's death in 1868.[3]

Clayton made rapid progress in his newfound faith, and church leaders quickly recognized his talents. Less than six months after his conversion he was ordained a high priest and made a member of the British Mission presidency. In October 1838 he quit his job to work full time in his ministry. Almost immediately he was assigned to serve in Manchester, where he spent

William Clayton and his wife Diantha. (Courtesy of Utah State Historical Society.)

the next two years and built up the second largest congregation in England. In January 1840 he began keeping a diary, which is now an important source for the early history of the church in that area.[4] In addition, members of the Quorum of the Twelve in England assigned him to be the official conference clerk at the April and July 1840 general conferences.

Clayton and his family left England early in September 1840, arriving at Nauvoo, Illinois, on November 24. The diary Clayton began in Manchester continues with a remarkably detailed account of the emigration process and life aboard an emigrant ship.

It also provides some interesting though brief details of life in Zarahemla, Iowa, the community across the river from Nauvoo, where Hyrum Smith encouraged Clayton to settle and which Joseph Smith once predicted would become as great as Nauvoo itself. When a stake was organized in Zarahemla, Clayton was at first a member of the high council and later, as might be expected, the stake clerk.

Clayton was miserable in Zarahemla, however, and failed in his effort to become a self-sufficient Iowa farmer—just as Joseph Smith's high hopes for the Iowa settlement also eventually failed. On December 14, 1841, he moved back across the river to Nauvoo, where he soon found himself engaged in work that was more in tune with his competence and natural skills: clerking and record keeping.

On February 10, 1842, Heber C. Kimball told Clayton to report to Joseph Smith's office. Willard Richards was acting as recorder for the Nauvoo Temple, but he was overworked and needed an assistant. Joseph Smith gave Clayton the assignment. On June 29, all the work of the prophet's office was turned over to Clayton, as Richards had to travel east. Then, on September 3, Joseph called him in and said, "Brother Clayton I want you to take care of the records and papers, and from this time I appoint you Temple Recorder, and when I have any revelations to write, you shall write them."[5] The assignment must have been deeply satisfying to the twenty-eight-year old Clayton, who had been an ardent, unquestioning disciple of the prophet since they first met and would continue to be so throughout his life. With this assignment, he would be in the almost constant company of Joseph Smith.

The closeness that existed between the two men was indicated by a note sent by the prophet about a month after Clayton was appointed temple recorder. Clayton had previously asked for permission to do something (the nature of which is unknown), and on October 7—the same day Joseph temporarily left Nauvoo to escape from Missourians on their way to capture him—Joseph hurriedly wrote a curious but heartwarming response:

Brother Clayton

Dear Sir

I received your Short note I reply in Short be shure you are right and then go ahead David Crocket like and now Johnathan what shall I write more only that I am well and am your best Friend

Joseph Smith to William Clayton

or David

or his mark

———X———[6]

Clayton undoubtedly felt honored to have their friendship compared to that of David and Jonathan. Like Jonathan of old, he would do anything for this modern David.

Clayton's life in America was exceptionally busy. In Nauvoo he was city treasurer, recorder and clerk of the Nauvoo City Council, secretary *pro tem* of the Nauvoo Masonic Lodge, an officer of the Nauvoo Music Association, a member of the committee responsible for erecting the Music Hall, and a member of the Nauvoo brass band. In 1844 he became a member of Joseph Smith's private prayer circle, where the temple ordinances were first introduced. That same year he was invited to become part of the somewhat secretive Council of Fifty, for which he kept the minutes. He also took time to build a brick home, where he lived for the last two years of his time in Nauvoo. After Joseph Smith introduced to him the principle of plural marriage, the married Clayton took on four additional wives. One soon left him, but when he was forced to leave Nauvoo in February 1846, he was accompanied by three wives, four children, a mother-in-law, and a few other in-laws, while another pregnant wife remained temporarily behind.

In Utah, Clayton became one of Salt Lake City's most prominent and well-respected citizens. He built an adobe home just two blocks west of Brigham Young's estate and was granted U.S. citizenship in 1853. He no longer worked full time for the church, though he was employed for a short while in the church's mint in Salt Lake City, making coins from California gold. He also continued to work part time with the financial records of the church, and at least into the 1860s it was he who read the financial report of the trustee-in-trust in general conference. Yet he increasingly directed much of his personal energy into private business and public service. He needed to, for after marrying five additional wives, he had many mouths to feed. In total, he was the husband of ten women and father of forty-two children, though four of his wives left him for various reasons. When he died at age sixty-five, he left four living widows, thirty-three living children ranging in age from ten to forty-three, and one child on the way.

Clayton's private and public business activities were highly varied. In 1850 he set up a bookshop in Salt Lake City's Council House. He also opened a boarding house for emigrants who were passing through. In 1849 he was appointed public auditor for the State of Deseret, and in 1852, after the Territory of Utah was organized, he was appointed territorial auditor as well as territorial recorder of marks and brands. He was reappointed to these positions after returning from his 1852–53 mission to England and continued in this service until his death in 1879.

Neither of these positions paid enough to sustain all his needs, and so he took on whatever additional work he could. In 1867 he was appointed treasurer of the newly incorporated Deseret Tele-graph Company. With encouragement from Brigham Young, he established a foreign collection agency intended to collect money in Europe for immigrants who had been unable to collect from those who owed them. When Zion's Cooperative Mercantile Institution (ZCMI) was established in 1868, Clayton became its first secretary. He threw himself into the new cooperative effort so intently that it consumed nearly all his time and forced him to give up nearly all his other businesses. He finally resigned in 1871 and went into the stock business to try to increase his earnings. He also ventured into such private business efforts as filing land claims, acting as an attorney, lending money, merchandising, working in the lumber business, farming, and speculating in mining. Some of these businesses, including some partnerships, did not serve him well, and he was never really comfortable financially.

At the same time, Clayton's talents were recognized by Brigham Young, who tried to help him reestablish some of his businesses after he left ZCMI. One way was by introducing him to the School of the Prophets on November 10, 1873, where he was unanimously admitted as a member. In introducing him, President Young described him "as the most capable man in the community to make out Wills in strict conformity to law and recommended the bretheren to avail themselves of his services."[7]

RECORD KEEPING

Clayton kept numerous kinds of records. Some were secular in nature, while others were directly involved with Joseph Smith and the church. He thought of these, including his journals, as sacred records that would help preserve for all time the workings and activities of the kingdom of God.

Nothing was intentionally whitewashed. Some of Clayton's records, especially his personal journals and letters, are filled with comments on various problems and controversies within the church, and even criticism of some leaders. Nevertheless, his devotion to Joseph Smith probably blinded him to any of the prophet's weaknesses. The prophet came off almost perfect in anything Clayton wrote about him. "If I were in England," he wrote to his friends in Manchester in December 1840, "I would raise my voice and testify that Joseph is a man of God, which will roll forth unto the ends of the earth and gather together all the good there is on the earth." He also wrote that the prophet was "no friend to iniquity but cuts at it wherever he sees it. . . . He has a great measure of the spirit of God. . . . He says 'I am a man of like passions with yourselves,' but truly I wish I was such a man."[8]

Clayton wrote to William Hardman in March 1842, "My faith in this doctrine, and in the prophet and officers is firm, unshaken, and unmoved; nay, rather, it is strengthened and settled firmer than ever. . . . For me to write any thing concerning the character of president Joseph Smith would be superfluous. All evil reports concerning him I treat with utter contempt. . . . I will add that, the more I am with him, the more I love him; the more I know of him, and the more confidence I have in him; and I am sorry that people should give heed to evil reports concerning him, when we all know the great service he *has rendered the church*."[9] Such was the Joseph Smith who appeared in anything Clayton wrote.

It may be that some of Clayton's records are lost, but here is a brief review of the extant records that directly reflect various aspects of the history of the church.

Personal journal from Manchester to Nauvoo. As mentioned, Clayton began keeping his personal journal in January 1840 while doing full-time missionary work in Manchester. It is a marvelously detailed volume that reveals the concerns and problems as well as the brotherhood and spirituality of the Manchester Saints, along with Clayton's own selflessness and sense of responsibility as a church leader. Through this journal we see different sides of human nature as expressed within that early Mormon community. We see working-class people with all their foibles and problems but also with faith and concern for each other. We see their love for and generosity to William Clayton, and we see his gratitude as he frequently recorded the food and even water they gave when he visited them. We see him weeping at times over the problems faced by some branch members. And we also see him struggling to overcome weaknesses of his own.

Beyond all that, the diary provides wonderful insight into the process of emigration, as Clayton describes in detail the preparations he and his family made as well as the voyage across the ocean. After that, the diary becomes more sketchy, but it still provides insight into the problems of Zarahemla and Clayton's decision to leave. It ends on February 18, 1842, with Clayton listening as "Joseph read a great portion of his history."[10]

Nauvoo journals. Clayton made the first entry in his three Nauvoo journals on November 27, 1842. For some reason there is a more than eight-month-long gap after the end of the Manchester journal, though it is possible, even probable, that Clayton kept some kind of record that has been lost. But the Nauvoo journals provide intimate details of both the secular and spiritual life of Nauvoo through the eyes of one of Joseph Smith's most devoted followers. The journals are a bit difficult to follow, for the entries are not always strictly chronological. Apparently Clayton began writing in one journal, moved to another for some reason, and then moved back to the original. As a result, the researcher must move back and forth between volumes. Sometimes there are two entries for the same day. It is not clear why.

Nevertheless, the journals are a tremendously important though still somewhat untapped source for insights into various aspects of Nauvoo life as well as the life of Joseph Smith. Clayton was candid about the problems as well as the positive things he saw in Nauvoo. Through his eyes we see the building of the temple and the activities of the Quorum of the Anointed and the Council of Fifty. We learn about Joseph Smith's public as well as private life, his problems and frequent need to flee Nauvoo to escape his enemies, his business activities, and the events leading to the Martyrdom. We also learn about plural marriage and what it meant to William Clayton.

Clayton spent considerable time assisting the Prophet Joseph in his real-estate business and other secular activities. The land office business probably consumed more of Clayton's time than any other business activity, as he was constantly looking at property, showing and selling lots, meeting land agents, making out-of-town business trips for the prophet, and keeping the records. He reported on much of this work, though often tersely, in his Nauvoo journals. On occasion he went to Carthage to pay taxes, he sometimes went on other trips to obtain supplies, and he frequently spent time examining the books of various business ventures. On September 21, 1843, for example, Joseph Smith instructed him to spend the next month on the *Maid of Iowa*, a little stern-wheeler the prophet partly owned, to set in order its books. Clayton stayed there only a few days, but the fact that Joseph trusted him with such errands was a source of great satisfaction.

Clayton's multifaceted temperament may be seen in the "Reflections" he recorded on New Year's Day, 1845. Still agonizing over the brutal murder of Joseph Smith, he described the problems of 1844 in language that oozed bitterness and disgust at the "un-godly generation" that allowed it all to happen. Nevertheless, he saw the martyrdom of the prophet as fulfilling at least some important purpose. It would permanently stain the wicked state of Illinois "with the innocent blood of two of the best men who ever lived on the earth," and it would indelibly write in the hearts of the Saints the memory of that horrible day. In this, at least, Clayton was prophetic, for the story of the martyrdom has taken its place alongside the First Vision and the coming forth of the Book of Mormon as one of the three most oft-repeated stories in Mormon piety.

Clayton's year-end reflections were not all negative. He was delighted that he had received two new "companions," by which he meant two new wives, Margaret Moon and Alice Hardman. He also had a "good prospect of adding another crown to my family which is a source of great consolation to me." Here he referred to sixteen-year-old Diantha Farr, whom he would marry on January 9. He was also thankful that the Saints were united in sustaining the Twelve as leaders and that, on the whole, the year ended "with the blessing of the Almighty God in the midst of his Saints and their never seemed to be a better feeling than at present." All this and more, including a long but tender prayer of thanksgiving for all his blessings, reveals much about Clayton himself as well as about life among the Saints in Nauvoo.

As one of Joseph Smith's scribes, Clayton was on the committee that originally began to prepare Joseph Smith's *History of the Church* for publication. It is well known that much of this history was not written or dictated by Joseph himself but rather was based on journal entries of his scribes and other people. When these entries were made part of the *History*, the third-person references to Joseph were simply changed to the first person, an accepted practice at the time. Other changes were made to the text, though they usually were minor. George A. Smith and Wilford Woodruff finished the work in 1856 and published it serially in the *Deseret News*. A half-century later, B. H. Roberts edited the text, and the church published it in six volumes. Clayton's Nauvoo journals were among the valuable resources for this history.[11]

For example, some of the revelations now included in the *History* and in the Doctrine and Covenants were originally recorded in Clayton's journals. On the evening of February 9, 1843, for instance, Clayton was at the home of Joseph Smith, along with several other people, when the prophet gave them historical as well as doctrinal instruction. Among other things, he told them of the two kinds of beings in heaven: angels, or resurrected beings, and the spirits of just men "made perfect." He then described three keys by which they could distinguish between angels, spirits of just men, or "the devil as an angel of light." The entry in Clayton's journal became, practically verbatim, the entry in the *History* and, later, section 129 of the Doctrine and Covenants. Something similar is true for much of section 130, recorded on April 2, 1843, as well as a few other sections.

Some of the entries in the *History*, based on Clayton's journal, reveal the potential problems with this kind of history. The story of the infamous Kinderhook plates is an example. On May 1, 1843, Clayton recorded the following:

> I have seen 6 brass plates which were found in Adams County by some persons who were digging in a mound They found a skeleton about 6 feet from the surface of the earth which was 9 foot high [tracing of plate] The plates were on the breast of the skeleton. This diagram shows the size of the plates being drawn on the edge of one of them. They are covered with ancient characters of language containing from 30 to 40 on

each side of the plates. Prest J. has translated a portion and says they contain the history of the person with whom they were found & he was a descendant of Ham through the loins of Pharaoh king of Egypt, and that he received his kingdom from the ruler of heaven & earth.[12]

That same entry, with some slight modifications, appeared in the *History* as follows:

I insert fac-similes of the six brass plates found near Kinderhook, in Pike county, Illinois, on April 23, by Mr. Robert Wiley and others, while excavating a large mound. They found a skeleton about six feet from the surface of the earth, which must have stood nine feet high. The plates were found on the breast of the skeleton and were covered on both sides with ancient characters.

I have translated a portion of them, and find they contain the history of the person with whom they were found. He was a descendant of Ham, through the loins of Pharaoh, king of Egypt, and that he received his kingdom from the Ruler of heaven and earth.[13]

The problem here is that the Kinderhook plates were a hoax, and because we know this, the entry seems to show that Joseph Smith was hopelessly duped. It must be noted, however, that in his diary Clayton did not quote Joseph directly—he only reported what he thought was happening. Whether Joseph actually told Clayton that he had translated the plates, or whether Clayton was simply reporting what he heard from a variety of sources, is not clear. The latter appears to be the case, especially when one realizes that Clayton's account contains several inaccuracies. The so-called "discovery" took place in Pike County, not Adams County, and there was no skeleton with the plates, only some bones.

Further, William Clayton's account is not consistent with a similar account by Parley P. Pratt, which was also probably obtained by hearsay rather than from the prophet himself. There is no evidence of any direct statement by Joseph Smith about the authenticity of the plates and no evidence that he ever attempted a translation. As historian Stanley B. Kimball has demonstrated, all kinds of stories about the plates were circulating, but Joseph Smith did not get involved with the plates at all.[14] What is clear is simply that the unfortunate entry got into the *History* before any of its editors knew the truth.

A different kind of problem arises from an account in the *History* that was reported to have come from Clayton's journal but that actually did not—at least not from the journals now extant. On May 18, 1843, Joseph Smith and William Clayton were in Carthage, where they dined with Judge Stephen A. Douglas at the home of Sheriff Jacob Backenstos. Some of that conversation is recorded in Clayton's journal, but not the way it later appeared in the *History*. However, in putting the conversation in the *History*, the editors did not follow their usual pattern of entering whatever they could gather without citing the source. Instead, they took pains to state that "the following brief account . . . is from the journal of William Clayton, who was present." That account, which is not actually in Clayton's Nauvoo journal, includes the now-famous statement: "Judge, you will aspire to the presidency of the United States; and if ever you turn your hand against me or the Latter-day Saints, you will feel the weight of the hand of [the] Almighty upon you; . . . for the conversation of this day will stick to you through life."[15]

The question is where this expanded version of Clayton's original entry came from. If, somehow, it really came from Clayton, there are only two possibilities. One is that Clayton wrote in more than one journal that day, perhaps in a source that is no longer extant. The other is simply that Clayton, who was still working with the church historians when they were putting all this together, was asked about the prophecy and, drawing on a vivid memory of the occasion, provided the expanded account. It is certainly possible that the account reflected the gist of that dramatic confrontation, even after many years.

Beyond what he wrote in his journals, Clayton also recorded many other important words of Joseph Smith. The famous King Follett sermon, for example, was eventually amalgamated and placed into the *History* from four different sources, including a transcription by Clayton. In addition, Clayton recorded the famous revelation on marriage, now known as section 132 of the Doctrine and Covenants.

Clayton's Nauvoo journals end on January 30, 1846, as Clayton was preparing to leave Nauvoo and head west.

Pioneer journal. Clayton's most well known and widely available contribution to church history is the journal he began on February 8, 1846, and ended on October 21, 1847. It was published by the Clayton Family Association in 1921 with the title *William Clayton's Journal* and has been republished several times since then. One of the finest firsthand accounts of the memorable crossing of the plains, it allows the reader to see the experience through the eyes of one who was not a leader but, rather, a faithful follower and veritable workhorse in his commitment to building the kingdom.[16]

Clayton seemed to know that his pioneer journal would be read by future Saints, and one can see a kind of historic sense in many of his entries. For one thing, possibly to satisfy what he thought would be the natural curiosity of his readers, he recorded the now-famous tally in the 1847 pioneer company of 143 men and boys, 3 women, 2 children, and "72 wagons, 93 horses, 52 mules, 66 oxen, 19 cows, and 17 dogs, and chickens."[17]

Included in the journal are such significant stories as the crossing of the Mississippi River in midwinter; the terrible conditions on the plains of Iowa; the events that led to Clayton's writing of "Come, Come, Ye Saints"; Clayton's difficulties in taking care of his family and personal needs while at the same time writing for Heber C. Kimball, making maps for Willard Richards, and acting as camp clerk while crossing Iowa; the settlement at Winter Quarters; the experiences of the vanguard company that scouted out the trail to the Great Basin; Clayton keeping an accurate record of the mileage they traveled each day from Winter Quarters to the Salt Lake Valley and eventually contributing to the construction of the pioneer "roadometer"; the events on the return trip he and several others made to Winter Quarters; and the story of his planning and writing the important *Latter-day Saints' Emigrants' Guide*.[18]

Southern exploring expedition. Clayton apparently wrote only two small journals after the conclusion of the pioneer journal—at least, only two exist today. One was a short journal he kept in 1852 when he was appointed camp historian for Brigham Young's second trip to southern Utah. The group had an ambitious mission: "visiting the southern settlements; exploring the country; ascertaining the situation of the Indians; making roads; building bridges; killing snakes; preaching the gospel; and doing and performing all other acts and things needed to be done, as they may be led by the Good Spirit."[19]

The expedition lasted only a month, and Clayton kept a daily journal, though today it is found in a rather unusual place. Beginning on April 21, 1852, and concluding on May 16, 1852, it is found in the back of Edward Hunter's account book, 1857–79.[20]

One must turn the account book upside down to read the journal. It provides interesting descriptions of the early Mormon settlements they passed through, meetings with American Indians, and some brief exploring.

British mission journal. Clayton's final journal covers his 1852–53 mission to England. He was part of a group of nearly one hundred missionaries called during a special conference on August 28 and 29, 1852, to go to the nations of the world. Their assignment was not only to preach the gospel but also, for the first time in church history, to preach publicly the doctrine of plural marriage. By that time Clayton was the husband of four living wives and the father of fifteen children, with two more on the way. His enthusiasm for the gospel, however, left no question in his mind—he would go wherever and whenever the living prophet sent him.

The mission turned out to be a bittersweet experience. He loved being back in England and reuniting with old friends. But he got into difficulty for two reasons: someone accused him of drunkenness, and someone else accused him of immorality. The drunkenness charge may have been true, for Clayton had an off-and-on problem with alcohol. Nevertheless, he convinced the mission president that it was not a problem then, and therefore he was not disciplined. But the charge of immorality was most likely connected to his enthusiastic advocacy of plural marriage, which clearly clashed with some English sensibilities. In any case, he became controversial enough that he was finally advised to return home after fewer than six months on his mission. His missionary diary, along with a poignant letter written to his friend Thomas Bullock, provides a telling story of one Latter-day Saint's faith, determination, exhilaration, and disappointment.[21]

Temple records. Other than his personal journals, perhaps no records were more important to William Clayton than those he kept of the Nauvoo Temple. From the time he went to work for Joseph Smith until he left Nauvoo four years later, he was bound to the temple as much as to the church itself. He kept its records, wrote its history, and participated in its sacred ceremonies.

By the time Clayton received these records, the construction of the temple was well on its way. As the edifice continued to rise, Clayton kept track of donations, purchases, and all other financial transactions. His authorized salary was two dollars per day. At first he worked in the counting room of Joseph Smith's red brick store, but because the work was so voluminous and he needed more room, the temple committee eventually erected a small brick office for him near the temple site.

Joseph Smith introduced the sacred temple endowment ceremony first to his private prayer circle, sometimes called the "Anointed Quorum" or the "Quorum of the Anointed." Clayton became a member of this select group in January 1844. He must have been tempted to write about what he was learning in his diary, but, believing as he did that sacred things must be kept sacred, he simply noted his attendance at the prayer circle meetings and left out the details of the ceremony itself. Once in a while he did provide a few comments that reveal the special nature of those meetings, which continued after the death of Joseph Smith.

One such occasion came on Sunday, November 30, 1845, when a select group of men, all members of the Anointed Quorum, met in the temple for the dedication of the attic, where the temple endowment would soon be given to the general membership of the church. William Clayton kept the minutes, which he recorded in his personal journal. During the meeting the group donned their temple robes and rehearsed parts of the temple ordinances "to get them more perfect."[22] Another such occasion came a week later, when several members of the Anointed Quorum again met in the temple, dressed in their ceremonial robes. It became a kind of testimony meeting, with prayer, the administering of the sacrament of the Lord's supper, expressions of gratitude from several people, and an address by Brigham Young that Clayton recorded, at least in part. Among other things, the new church leader said

> that a few of the quorum had met twice a week ever since Joseph and Hyrum were killed and during the last excitement, every day and in the hotest part of it twice a day to offer up the signs and pray to our heavenly father to deliver his people and this is the cord which has bound this people together. If this quorum and those who shall be admitted into it will be as dillegent in prayer as a few has been I promise you in the name of Israels God that we shall accomplish the will of God and go out in due time from the gentiles with power and plenty and no power shall stay us.[23]

Clayton's journal is the only place where we find some of these details, for much was left out of the published *History of the Church*.

On December 10 the full endowment ceremony was conducted for the first time in the temple, and of course it fell to Clayton to keep the records. From that day until they began to flee Nauvoo nearly two months later, the Saints flocked to the temple to receive their endowments and other temple blessings, thus ending the exclusive nature of the Anointed Quorum.

Temple history. As he kept the records of the Nauvoo Temple, Clayton also began to compile the notes from which he would write his history of the temple. He was so sure that future generations would want to know of the unique efforts and faith-promoting stories that went into the construction of this sacred building that he reported some of them in his history. Early in 1844, for example, Hyrum Smith asked the women of the church to pledge one cent per week for glass and nails, promising them their first choice of seats in the temple when it was finished.[24] When Clayton wrote his temple history in 1845, he noted that many women paid a year in advance and that already two thousand dollars had been received.

He also told of other subjects that did not find their way into the published *History of the Church*, such as an unusual contribution from the women of the La Harpe and Macedonia branches. Convinced that a new crane was needed to speed construction, in July 1844 they offered to provide the means to build it. The committee accepted the offer, and by the end of August the crane was complete and in operation.

A version of Clayton's temple history was first published in the *Juvenile Instructor* in 1886 under the title "An Interesting Journal." The editors of the magazine had mistitled the work, however, for it was not a "journal" as such; it was a manuscript history. They also made some grammatical changes and shortened or paraphrased some of the sections. The *Juvenile Instructor* version was published again in 1991 in a book of Clayton documents. A literal transcription from Clayton's original manuscript was published in full, for the first time, as an appendix in the second edition of this author's biography of William Clayton.[25]

Book of the Law of the Lord. When Willard Richards turned over to Clayton all the records pertaining to the temple, the collection included the "Book of the Law of the Lord." Clayton then became one of several scribes who contributed to this record. This large, leather-bound book primarily contains a list of tithing contributions for the building of the temple, and 370 of its pages are in Clayton's handwriting. The book also contains some manuscript sources used in compiling Joseph Smith's *History of the Church*, and Clayton wrote about sixty-one of these pages. The language was written mostly in the third person and was later changed to first person for the sake of the published history. The book also contains some direct dictation from Joseph, such as a letter to Emma that Clayton entered and then presumably copied and sent her.[26]

Among the more tender items Clayton recorded in the "Book of the Law of the Lord" were Joseph Smith's reflections on the loyalty of his friends, dated August 16 and 23, 1842. These reflections eventually found their way into the *History of the Church*. They were precipitated by the arrest of the prophet and Orrin Porter Rockwell on August 8 for their alleged role in the attempted murder of Lilburn W. Boggs, former governor of Missouri. The Nauvoo municipal court released the two on a writ of habeas corpus, whereupon the Adams County officers appealed to Illinois governor Thomas Carlin. When the officers left, Joseph went into hiding. The prophet remained in hiding for several weeks, being visited only clandestinely by a few trusted friends, including William Clayton.

On August 11 Joseph sent word that he wanted to meet with his scribe as well as a few others. After dark that night, Clayton, Emma Smith, Hyrum Smith, William Law, Newel K. Whitney, George Miller, and Dimick Huntington took a skiff to an island in the Mississippi. They were soon joined from the Iowa side by Joseph Smith and Erastus Derby. The group decided that Joseph should be taken to another location up river and continue to hide out until the danger passed. It was a deeply emotional time. Five days later the prophet began to dictate his feelings to his scribe; he continued that dictation on August 23. Together the two dictations formed a long, tender soliloquy that captured the love Joseph had for his friends as well as the meaning of genuine friendship. He said, in part:

> My heart was overjoyed as I took the faithful band by the hand, that stood upon the shore, one by one. . . .
>
> I do not think to mention the particulars of the history of that sacred night, which shall forever be remembered by me; but the names of the faithful are what I wish to record in this place. These I have met in prosperity, and they were my friends; and I now meet them in adversity, and they are still my warmer friends. These love the God that I serve; they love the truths that I promulgate; they love those virtuous, and those holy doctrines that I cherish in my bosom with the warmest feelings of my heart, and with that zeal which cannot be denied. I love friendship and truth; I love virtue and law; I love the God of Abraham, of Isaac, and of Jacob; and they are my brethren, and I shall live; and because I live they shall live also.[27]

The "Book of the Law of the Lord" also contains the original manuscripts of some of Joseph Smith's revelations in Clayton's handwriting. An example is section 127 of the Doctrine and Covenants, which is a letter about baptism for the dead.

Because Clayton believed his responsibility to keep church records was sacred, he must have felt devastated after an experience around the time of Joseph Smith's martyrdom. At 1 a.m. on Sunday, June 23, 1844, he was roused from his bed with the message that Joseph Smith wanted to see him. Joseph and his brother Hyrum, aware of plots to kill them, had determined to flee across the Mississippi. When Clayton met him at the river, Joseph whispered to him some alarming instructions about the records of the kingdom of God (that is, the Council of Fifty). He was either to give them to a faithful man who would take them to safety, or he was to burn or bury them. The devout scribe could hardly bear either to part with or destroy the sacred records he had worked so hard to compile. He hurried home, gathered up not only the private records but also all the public records he possessed, and buried them. Ten days later, after Joseph Smith was dead, Clayton dug up the records, only to find that in his haste he had not adequately waterproofed them, and moisture had seeped in and damaged them. One can only imagine his horror.

Other Nauvoo records. As indicated earlier, William Clayton also kept tithing records—not just those having to do with donations to the temple but other such records as well. In addition, he made numerous entries in the record book of the Nauvoo Masonic Lodge.[28]

Minutes of the Council of Fifty. The Council of Fifty was another highly confidential body established by Joseph Smith and consisting of men he felt he could trust, for their loyalty had already been tested. It was a quasi-secular body set up to plan and work for the eventual establishment of the political kingdom of God on earth. Among other things, the council planned and directed Joseph Smith's run for the presidency of the United States, directed Nauvoo's industrial development after his death, and exercised important political influence in the Territory of Utah. It was officially organized on March 11, 1844, and the next day William Clayton was appointed "Clerk of the Kingdom," a title he no doubt relished.

The meetings of the Council of Fifty were confidential, so Clayton made only brief notations in his personal journal, but he apparently kept careful notes and spent long hours recording them in the official minute books.[29] Anticipating a glorious future for the kingdom, he once wrote that in these meetings "the principles of eternal truths rolled forth to the hearers without reserve and the hearts of the servants of God [were] made to rejoice exceedingly."[30] On April 11 they even voted to make Joseph Smith their "Prophet, Priest, and King," confirming him with "loud Hosannas."[31] Although the Council of Fifty was ostensibly a secular body, it had great spiritual significance for its clerk.

Heber C. Kimball's journals. It is not surprising that others occasionally wanted to make use of Clayton's talents as a record keeper and scribe. Before Heber C. Kimball left England in 1840, he asked Clayton to write his history, which Clayton was happy to do. He worked on it almost until the day he emigrated. Kimball had good reason to assign this task to Clayton. He was an extremely busy church leader, and Clayton was not only a good friend but also a better writer and penman. A comparison of the handwriting, spelling, and general grammatical skills of the two clearly shows that Clayton had the advantage.

The history Clayton prepared for Kimball was probably the document that later became "History of the British Mission," which was signed by Kimball, Orson Hyde, and Willard Richards and published in Joseph Smith's *History of the Church* under the date of March 23, 1841. It covered the history of missionary work in England from the time Kimball first arrived in 1837 to April 6, 1840.[32]

This was not the end of Clayton's ghost-writing for Kimball. As the Saints were preparing to leave Nauvoo and at the same time administer the sacred temple ordinances to thousands of people, Kimball asked, or perhaps assigned, Clayton to keep a temple journal for him. By this time Clayton was heavily overworked, but he took on the task anyway. The journal, which Clayton wrote in the first person as if he were Kimball, gives interesting details regarding the hectic activities in the temple between December 10, 1845, and January 7, 1846.[33]

Kimball called on Clayton's talents again as the vanguard company left Winter Quarters in 1847 to go west and scout out the location for the new settlement of the Saints. But Clayton was occupied with many other tasks, such as keeping his own journal; working as assistant to Thomas Bullock, the camp scribe; and keeping track of the distances traveled each day. Kimball, however, asked him again. By May 21 Clayton was well behind in the task, so Kimball suggested that he leave several blank pages, start from the present, and then catch up later. Clayton wrote in his own journal on that day: "He furnished me a candle and I wrote the journal of this day's travel by candle light in his journal, leaving fifty-six pages blank."[34]

Emigrants' Guide. While crossing the plains with the vanguard pioneer company, Clayton kept track of the mileage traveled each day. At first he tried to estimate the distance, but soon, recognizing the inaccuracy of such a method, he suggested to several people that an odometer be attached to a wagon wheel. Frustrated when nothing happened, he finally resorted to measuring the circumference of a wagon wheel and then counting the revolutions as he walked beside the wagon all day. The odometer was eventually constructed, and he got his more accurate count, both going to the Salt Lake Valley and returning to Winter Quarters. Back at Winter Quarters he constructed a table of distances, showing the mileage between various suggested stopping points along the way and indicating that it was exactly 1,032 miles between the two points.

The value of this information for Mormons as well as other overland migrants was immediately apparent, and early in 1848 Clayton was able to get his work published. Titled *The Latter-day Saints' Emigrants' Guide*, the volume provided details for every mile along the way. Each major stream, hill, swamp, or other landmark was listed, along with brief descriptions of what the traveler might find there. The guide helped provide a small income for Clayton, as it was sold to willing Saints as they set out on their unfamiliar journey across the plains. It also served thousands of other pioneers bound for Oregon or California. It was copied, at least in part, by compilers of other emigrant guides and for that reason has been recognized for contributing significantly to the saga of the West.

Letter books. Clayton kept other kinds of records that were not church records but, to some degree, provide insights, at least into the lives of church members. His numerous letter books, now housed in the Bancroft Library in Berkeley, California, are filled with day-to-day business transactions in connection with his work as territorial auditor and recorder of marks and brands. For the most part they are repetitious and dull, but tucked amid the tedium are many personal letters that cast light on topics of concern to both Clayton and the church during the first three decades of the Utah experience.

In addition to all this, Clayton was frequently appointed to take the minutes of conferences and other church meetings.

LOYALTY TO THE PROPHET

William Clayton believed his record keeping was a sacred calling. He also felt called, partly through his writing, to build all the support he could for Joseph Smith and to preserve the most positive image of the prophet as possible. In the process, he wrote of many events that eventually found their way into the history of the church. An account he wrote on September 3, 1842, of an ill-fated attempt by a Missouri sheriff to arrest the prophet illustrates at least one aspect of William Clayton's fierce devotion to Joseph Smith. It appears in *History of the Church*.[35]

The Missouri sheriff and two other men arrived in Nauvoo early in the afternoon of that day. They had planned to arrive during the night, but after they left Quincy they lost their way. Fatigued and "sore from riding," they hitched their horses where they could not be seen and crept quietly to Joseph Smith's home. When they entered they found only John Boynton, for Joseph was dining with his family in another room. They questioned Boynton as to the prophet's whereabouts, but Boynton evaded a direct answer by simply saying that he had seen Joseph early that morning. Meanwhile, Joseph slipped out the back door, hurried through the tall corn in his garden, and soon hid himself in the home of Newel K. Whitney. Emma confronted the officers and permitted them to search the premises, even though they admitted they had no search warrant. Perhaps such a search would delay them, giving her husband more time to make good his escape. Unable to find their quarry, the Missourians left. Later that night the prophet moved to the home of Edward Hunter, where, Clayton wrote, "He [could] be kept safe from the hands of his enemies."[36]

The equally interesting part of this account is Clayton's vivid editorializing, for it demonstrates not only his loyalty to the prophet but also his ire against those who would threaten him in any way. "This is another testimony and evidence of the mean, corrupt, illegal proceedings of our enemies," he fumed, "not withstanding the Constitution of the United States" that included guarantees against unreasonable search and seizure. "Yet these men audaciously, impudently and altogether illegally searched the house of President Joseph Smith even without any warrant or authority whatever. . . . They appeared to be well armed, and no doubt intended to take him either dead or alive; which we afterwards heard they had said they would do; but the Almighty again delivered His servant from the bloodthirsty grasp."[37] Clayton never moderated his words when praising the prophet and denouncing his enemies.

CONCLUSION

Without historians who write the books and articles we read, there would be no Latter-day Saint history. Without the documents of the past, there would be little for the church historian to write about. Without the scribes, secretaries, diarists, and others who created the documents, the stuff from which church history is created would not exist.

At the same time, the nature of history usually reflects the nature and predilections of the historian, as does the nature of the documents on which the historian relies. William Clayton's predilections included his unfailing testimony of the gospel and his loyalty to Joseph Smith. To the degree that his records affect anything in the written histories of the church, those predilections are perpetuated. Most Latter-day Saints will never know his name, but through his contributions they can better understand the man he revered most deeply, the Prophet Joseph Smith. We owe much of our knowledge of early Latter-day Saint history to the work of obscure figures such as William Clayton.

NOTES

1. *History of The Church of Jesus Christ of Latter-day Saints*, ed. B. H. Roberts, 2nd ed. rev. (Salt Lake City: Deseret Book, 1978), 6:409. For a list of all these clerks and their major contributions, see Dean C. Jessee, "The Writing of Joseph Smith's History," *BYU Studies* 11, no. 4 (Summer 1971): 439–73.

2. Tithing and Donation Record, 1844–46, 220–22, Church History Library, The Church of Jesus Christ of Latter-day Saints, Salt Lake City; William Clayton, Nauvoo Journals, January 29, 1845, The Church of Jesus Christ of Latter-day Saints, Salt Lake City.

3. Much of the information in this article was taken from James B. Allen, *No Toil nor Labor Fear: The Story of William Clayton* (Provo, UT: Brigham Young University Press, 2002).

4. See James B. Allen and Thomas G. Alexander, eds., *Manchester Mormons: The Journal of William Clayton, 1840 to 1842* (Santa Barbara: Peregrine Smith, 1974).

5. William Clayton, "History of the Nauvoo Temple," ca. 1845, reproduced as Appendix 2 in Allen, *No Toil nor Labor Fear*, 423. This work is a revised edition, with two added appendices, of *Trials of Discipleship: The Story of William Clayton, a Mormon* (Urbana: University of Illinois Press, 1987).

6. Reproduced in Allen, *No Toil nor Labor Fear*, 73–74; original in Pioneer Memorial Museum, Salt Lake City.

7. Minutes, November 10, 1873, School of the Prophets, Salt Lake City Records, Church History Library.

8. Clayton to the Saints in Manchester, December 10, 1840, as copied by William Hardman, January 26, 184[1], Church History Library.

9. Clayton to William Hardman, March 30, 1842, as quoted in *Millennial Star*, August 1842, 75–76; emphasis in original.

10. The original journal is located at Brigham Young University but has been published as Allen and Alexander, *Manchester Mormons*.

11. It is instructive to compare what Clayton originally wrote with what finally appeared in the published *History*. Such comparisons are included, in parallel columns, in an appendix to my biography of Clayton, *No Toil nor Labor Fear*, 385–413.

12. Clayton, Nauvoo Journal, May 1, 1843.

13. *History of the Church*, 5:372.

14. Stanley B. Kimball, "Kinderhook Plates Brought to Joseph Smith Appear to Be a Nineteenth-Century Hoax," *Ensign*, August 1981, 66–74; Ben McGuire, in FAIR: Defending Mormonism, http://www.fairlds.org/Misc/How_Do_We_Explain_Early_Comments_about_the_Kinderhook_Plates.html.

15. *History of the Church*, 5:393–94; Clayton, Nauvoo Journal, May 18, 1843.

16. The Church History Library has both the published Clayton pioneer journal and the two unpublished volumes from which it was drawn. As noted in the text, the published version ends with Clayton's entry on October 21,

1847; the unpublished version, however, has one more page with entries going through December 5, 1847.

17. *William Clayton's Journal* (Salt Lake City: Clayton Family Association/Deseret News, 1921), 75–76.

18. *William Clayton's Journal*; W. Clayton, *The Latter-day Saints' Emigrants' Guide: Being a Table of Distances, Showing All the Springs, Creeks, Rivers, Hills, Mountains, Camping Places, and All Other Notable Places, from Council Bluffs, to the Valley of the Great Salt Lake* (St. Louis: Mo. Republican Steam Power Press/Chambers & Knapp, 1848).

19. Editorial, *Deseret News*, May 1, 1852.

20. Located in the Edward Hunter Collection, 1816–84, Church History Library.

21. William Clayton to Thomas Bullock, February 5, 1853, Thomas Bullock Correspondence, Church History Library; William Clayton, Diary, August 1852–March 1853, Church History Library.

22. Clayton, Nauvoo Journal, November 30, 1845; *History of the Church,* 7:534–35. The latter entry is based almost verbatim on the Clayton journal except that a few items from the journal are omitted, such as the fact that the participants were dressed in their temple clothing and that they rehearsed the ceremonies.

23. Clayton, Nauvoo Journal, December 7, 1845.

24. *History of the Church*, 6:298–99; Allen, *No Toil nor Labor Fear*, 426–27.

25. Allen, *No Toil nor Labor Fear*, 415–42; "An Interesting Journal," *Juvenile Instructor* 21 (January 15–May 15, June 15–July 1, August 1–October 15, 1886): 23, 47, 60–61, 79, 106–7, 122–23, 141–42, 157–58, 186–87, 202–3, 230–31, 246, 258–59, 281, 290–91, 310–11; George D. Smith, ed., *An Intimate Chronicle: The Journals of William Clayton* (Salt Lake City: Signature Books, 1991), 525–53. The original manuscript of the temple history is housed in the Church History Library.

26. Dean C. Jessee, comp. and ed., *The Personal Writings of Joseph Smith* (Salt Lake City: Deseret Book, 1984), 525–37, 690–91. Additional information on the "Book of Law of the Lord" has also been provided personally by Dean C. Jessee as well as by Alex Smith's "Joseph Smith's Nauvoo Journals: Understanding the Documents," delivered at the annual conference of the Mormon History Association, Casper, Wyoming, May 2006.

27. The entire dictation is recorded in *History of the Church*, 5:107–9, 124–28; Jessee, *Personal Writings of Joseph Smith*, 530–37. *History of the Church*

indicates that Joseph Smith began this dictation on August 16 and continued it on August 22, but Dean Jessee says it was continued on August 23.

28. Jessee, "Writing of Joseph Smith's History," 456.

29. For example, his personal journal entry for Sunday, August 18, 1844, indicates that on that day he was "at the office copying the record of the Kingdom."

30. Clayton, Nauvoo Journal, "Reflections," recorded January 1, 1845.

31. Clayton, Nauvoo Journal, April 11, 1844, records the vote: "Prest J. was voted our P. P. & K. with loud Hosannas." This important entry says much about the goals of the Council of Fifty, but it does not say that Joseph was actually ordained a king. The evidence for such an ordination is still debatable.

32. *History of the Church*, 4:313–21.

33. This journal has been published in Smith, *Intimate Chronicle*, 199–258. Smith calls this a Clayton journal, for it is in Clayton's handwriting. But it was never intended to be thought of that way and, at least in my opinion, should be included in a compilation of Kimball journals rather than Clayton journals.

34. *William Clayton's Journal*, 169.

35. The *History of the Church* does not specifically state that the account quoted here is by William Clayton, but it does indicate that it was written by "the Prophet's secretary." The evidence that leads me to conclude Clayton is the secretary in question is that (1) the first part of the account reflects specifically the idea that Clayton received in the Hollister letter (see D. S. Hollister to William Clayton, September 1, 1842, Church History Library); (2) at this point Clayton was Joseph Smith's scribe; and (3) the language of the account, especially where it denounces the Missourians, is much like Clayton's language in other places. The same heated tone is evident in many of his statements about the Prophet's detractors.

36. *History of the Church*, 5:145–46; George Miller to William Clayton, September 4, 1842, and D. S. Hollister to William Clayton, September 1, 1842, Church History Library.

37. *History of the Church*, 5:145.

5

DEVELOPING A HISTORICAL CONSCIENCE: WILFORD WOODRUFF AND THE PRESERVATION OF CHURCH HISTORY

WHILE the Saints were at Winter Quarters in 1846, an important discussion ensued among the Quorum of the Twelve Apostles. Willard Richards, an apostle since 1840, believed his role as the church historian should take precedence over his other duties, even during the difficult and complex migration west. At stake was whether Richards was still to be funded for his labors by tithing during that trying period. Amid this debate, Wilford Woodruff, a member of the quorum for seven years and a diligent journal keeper, stood up and gave a passionate defense of the office and duty of the historian.

> Elder W. Woodruff said, the subject alluded to by [Richards] was a benefit to the whole Church and kingdom of God. When he heard Joseph Smith preach he could not rest until he

Benjamin E. Park is a graduate student in intellectual history at the University of Cambridge.

wrote it—[He] felt we were living in the most important era of the world, and the people ought to keep a strict eye upon the Historian—[He] felt deeply interested in the books out of which he was to be judged. He rejoiced that the Church had a ready writer and said he felt [Richards] should go to work and save the Church history.[1]

Little did Woodruff know that in less than a decade he would be called as a church historian himself. In the April conference of 1856, he was assigned to the Church Historian's Office, where he would serve as either assistant church historian or church historian for more than three decades. While known for the voluminous journals he kept from 1834 until his death, Woodruff also contributed much to the history of the Latter-day Saints through his activities in these positions. Constant throughout his many years and historical projects was a burning desire to produce a "true and faithful record and history" for God, his ancestors, and his progeny.

This paper charts Woodruff's early experiences in dealing with church history, largely focusing on his historical outlook and early projects.

WOODRUFF AS HISTORIAN

No set of nineteenth-century journals is more important to the preservation of church history than Wilford Woodruff's. As Dean C. Jessee noted, "Beginning shortly after his conversion and continuing to his death in 1898, Wilford Woodruff's day books and journals, comprising thirty-one handwritten volumes, cover almost the entire span of the Church's nineteenth-century history."[2] B. H. Roberts, in his typical flowery language, did not hold back his praise for Woodruff's contribution:

Other men may found hospitals or temples or schools for the church, or endow special divisions or chairs of learning in them; or they may make consecrations of lands and other property to the church, but in point of important service, and in placing the church under permanent obligations, no one will surpass in excellence and permanence or largeness the service which Wilford Woodruff has given to the Church of Jesus Christ in the New Dispensation, by writing and preserving the beautiful and splendid *Journals* he kept through sixty-three eventful years.[3]

Steven C. Harper went so far as to say, "Wilford Woodruff largely made the glasses through which we see the [Latter-day Saint] past."[4] Indeed, Woodruff's journals document many of the most important events in early Mormon history, including the march of Zion's Camp, the "Pentecostal experience" during the months following the Kirtland Temple dedication, and numerous sermons of church leaders.

While the importance of his journals cannot be overstated, many historians have overlooked his other contributions to the preservation of church history.[5] Woodruff served as an assistant to three church historians (George A. Smith, Albert Carrington, and Orson Pratt) from 1856 to 1881, and then acted as church historian himself from 1881 until 1889. During those thirty-three years he accomplished many remarkable feats, including finishing the massive "History of Joseph Smith," working on the often overlooked "History of Brigham Young," compiling biographies for almost every individual called by Joseph Smith to be an apostle, and collecting numerous historical documents from many sources.

Woodruff began to love history as he came of age. Biographer Matthias Cowley wrote that though Woodruff hated to read as a child, he soon came to describe the act of reading as "most exaltant" and "most delightsome." Before joining the church, he had already read "histories of the United States, England, Scotland, Greece, and Rome," as well as the works of Josephus, which were popular during the period.[6] Thus, he came into the church with the importance of historical work already planted in his mind.

Shortly after his baptism, he turned his attention to keeping a historical record of his own. He later recalled that he had "been inspired & moved upon to keep a Journal & write the affairs of this Church as far as I Can [remember]."[7] Elsewhere he reflected on his early awareness of the importance of record keeping:

> I seldom Ever heard the Prophet Joseph, or Brigham Young, or the Apostles teach preach or Prophesy or perform any official act but what I have recorded it in my Journals unless some other persons were recording the same and I Could not feel Easy untill I had accomplished it.
>
> I have written more sacred History of the teaching of the prophets & Apostles & official acts of the Latter day Saints than would make several Testaments as large as the one Handed down to us by the Ancient Apostles. I have kept a Journal of almost Evry day of my life since I have been a member of this Church.[8]

Once he was in the Church Historian's Office, he could acknowledge the significance of his previous record keeping. He felt proud to admit that "a great portion of the Church History has been Compiled from my Journals, & some of the most glorious Gospel Sermons truths & revelations that were given from God to this people . . . Could not be found upon the Earth on record ownly in my Journals."[9] Though he most likely understood the importance of his early journals when he wrote them, he gained added appreciation for them while working as a historian—particularly when dealing with events that were not as thoroughly documented as he would have liked.

A central tenet to Woodruff's historical conscience was his belief that keeping a faithful record was a spiritual obligation. When addressing a congregation in 1857, he stated that Joseph Smith had urged the brethren to keep a true record, and that he was just following counsel.[10] Woodruff felt it was his duty "to keep a journal of my travels that when required I may give an account of my stewardship."[11] Record keeping was part of a collaborative effort with God: "Should we not have respe[c]t Enough to God," he once asked, "to make a record of those Blessings which He pours out upon us and Our official acts which we do in his name upon the face of the Earth?"[12]

While on his mission to Great Britain, Brigham Young remembered Woodruff for spending more time writing in his journal than helping the British Saints.[13] Indeed, Woodruff believed that keeping a faithful history was required for membership in the kingdom of God.

PREPARATION AND APPOINTMENT TO THE CHURCH HISTORIAN'S OFFICE

A few years after settling in Utah, Wilford Woodruff was called as clerk and historian for the Quorum of the Twelve Apostles—the first history-related position he held in Utah. In 1851 a meeting "moved & carried that the Record of the Twelve Apostles be put into the Hands of Wilford Woodruff to keep & record such acts as was necessary."[14] Two years later, he exhorted his priesthood brethren "to keep a Journal & History of their lives for the record & history of this Church & Kingdom will be wanted in a future day. The[re] has been no dispensation on Earth the procedings of which will be more interesting than the one in which we live."[15] In this position Woodruff helped George A. Smith, then church historian, reconstruct events of the past, especially when the facts could be determined by an appeal to his journals.[16]

When Smith was called on a mission to the East in 1856, church leaders found it necessary to appoint someone to pick up Smith's historical work and continue various projects—particularly the completion of the time-consuming and vastly important "History of Joseph Smith." An obvious replacement for the vacancy in the Historian's Office was Smith's former missionary companion and fellow apostle Wilford Woodruff. In Woodruff's summary to the April 1856 conference, he wrote, "All of the Authorities of the Church were presented & received And W. Woodruff was Appointed Assistant Historian was to take charge . . . of the office during the absence of G. A. Smith."[17] His long career as official historian had finally commenced.

One of Woodruff's earliest duties in this new position was to oversee the move into the recently built Historian's Office that fall. As part of this task, he offered the dedicatory prayer for the new building—a prayer that revealed his belief in the sacredness of his calling:

> By virtue of the Holy Priesthood vested in us, in the name of Jesus Christ, we do dedicate [the Historian's Office] and consecrate it unto the Lord our God, and we set it apart that it may contain the holy records of the Church and kingdom of God, and we ask in the name of Jesus Christ that it may be sanctified and holy unto thy name and we pray that we may be inspired by the gift and power of the Holy Ghost, while acting as Historians, or clerks for the Church; and may we keep a true and faithful record and history of thy Church and kingdom, and thy servants and may it be kept in that way

and manner that it may be acceptable un[to] the[e] O Lord and unto thy servants the presidency of thy Church. . . .

And we ask thee to bless us and prosper us in all things, and we pray that thou wilt bring to our remembrance all things which are necessary to the writing of this history. And that papers and documents and all things necessary, may be brought to us, to enable us to compile a right, useful, and proper history.

. . . And bless those of thy servants who are among the nations of the earth and grant that they may be inspired to send an account of their works that we may be . . . enabled to keep a true and faithful record that when we have gone into the world of spirits that the saints of God may be blessed in reading our record which we have kept.[18]

As the prayer demonstrates, Woodruff felt that the keeping and writing of history was a task deserving of divine aid. Just a week earlier, he urged the Saints to keep a record, explaining that "we are living in one of the most important generations that man ever lived on Earth & we should write an account of those important transactions which are takeing place before our Eyes in fulfillment of the prophesies & the revelation of God."[19]

Woodruff once recorded in his journal a prayer that further reveals his belief in the sacred nature of his calling: "I Pray that the Lord will preserve me for a season that I may labour to assist in preserving & keeping a Record of this Church & kingdom & the dealings of God with us & preserve me O Lord from dishonouring my Calling or priesthood but give me faith power & grace to pass through whatever I may be Called to meet."[20] That Woodruff associated failing at his calling with "dishonouring [his] . . . priesthood" shows how seriously he took his responsibilities.

OUTLOOK ON HISTORY AND IMPORTANCE OF PERSONAL RECORDS

The "true and faithful record and history" Woodruff envisioned would need to be as comprehensive as possible. While imploring a fellow Saint to share what he remembered of an important moment in the Mormon past, he explained, "We feel that it is due Joseph Smith and the Church and Kingdom of God, and to all future generations that we embody every act and word in the History of the Last days of the Prophet."[21] Such a history required collaboration between appointed historians and other individuals who kept detailed, accurate records. In a sermon to the church in 1862, Woodruff taught:

> You may say that Historians have handed [the history of nations, kingdoms, and countries] down unto us. But How have Historians obtained materials from which to Compile theire History? I answer From the scribes, reporters, & Journalists who wrote day by day Events as they passed before the[ir] Eyes. And this Class of men forms the foundation of all History and from the[ir] Material, Historians who live hundreds of years after Events transpire will Compile History.[22]

Thus, Woodruff relied heavily on eyewitness accounts. A major thrust of his role as historian was to encourage others to gain a historical conscience—to share his vision of the importance of personal historical records. Even before he was appointed as a historian, he asked the Saints in Bountiful, Utah, if they could "not Count [their experiences] worth recording? Not even make the mark of a pen to leave the Account on record for their children & future generations to read?" He continued, "I say they should. I think the Lord requires this at our hands & it is a Rich & Holy legacy which is Justly due our posterity."[23]

In 1857, while admitting that some view history as "dry and uninteresting," he pleaded with Church members to do their part and write their personal histories: "Evry man should writ a brief history of his life his parentage, His birth his religion when he was baptized & by whom when ordained what to & by whome give a brief sketch of all his missions & of all his offical acts & the dealings of God with him. Then if He was to die & the Historians wished to publish his history they would have sumthing to go by. Many may think this a dry subjet & unimportant but it is not so to me."[24]

Though a historical conscience typically focused on the past, Woodruff held that it also had an eye on the future. "If the[re] was no other motive in view ownly to have the privilege of reading over our Journals & for our Children to read," he reasoned, "it would pay for the time spent in writing it."[25] Woodruff felt the end result of keeping personal records would be a history that future generations, even those outside the church, would cherish.

DOCUMENTING JOSEPH SMITH'S MARTYRDOM

An example of Woodruff's devotion to accurate history comes from his first few months in the Church Historian's Office. After he was called at the April 1856 general conference, he was anxious to get started, writing within a couple of days that "I am about getting in[it]iated into my office as assistant Historian."[26] But the first few weeks were more difficult than he expected. First he came down with a crippling disease that kept him away from the office for several weeks; it was so severe that he couldn't even leave his bed for quite some time. Finally, toward the end of May, he was able to put in his first full day of work. He wrote to George A. Smith, "I am now calculating to devote my time [to the history]."[27]

Before Woodruff's call, George A. Smith, Thomas Bullock, and others working in the Historian's Office had been diligent in "compiling the history of Joseph Smith from April 1st 1840 to his death on June 27th 1844."[28] In May 1856 the only task left to be completed was the account of the Prophet Joseph's last days in Carthage. This was challenging, however, because of incomplete records and historical gaps. On June 24 Woodruff noted in his journal that "we find a great Difficulty in writing the History of Joseph esspecially During the last few days of his life as no one kept a Journal of the same except Dr Richards wrote some but Died before the History was written out."[29] As a result of this problem, Woodruff was left to rely on eyewitnesses who were still living (and still in the church) to help fill in the gaps. Fortunately, he had been working with these eyewitnesses at various times during the previous decade and would continue to do so.

But the use of eyewitnesses introduced a challenge: conflicting accounts. Writing George A. Smith on June 30, Woodruff lamented:

> We are still laboring upon that part of the History, and we almost daily get new statements from men who were directly or indirectly connected with the scenes of the last four days of the lives of the Prophet and Patriarch, and many of these accounts are in direct opposition to each other. We have the statements of John S. Fullmer, Dan Jones, S. Markham, W. W. Phelps, R. Cahoon, A. C. Hodge, O. P. Rockwell, Wm Clayton, D.B. Huntington and others in connection with Dr Richards Journal lying before us, and find they conflict a good deal.[30]

In an attempt to solve this dilemma, Woodruff wrote the person he felt was the most reliable eyewitness to the events leading up to the martyrdom: John Taylor, who was then serving a mission on the East Coast. "We are very busy writing the history of the latter days of Joseph," he wrote to Taylor, "and we have a great many conflicting statements on the subject, which renders it necessary for me to call in the aid of an eye and ear witness to enable me to do justice to it." Woodruff then counseled Taylor to sit down with George A. Smith when he had time and "write out an account of all the circumstances relating to the subject which came under your immediate observation or experience" while in Carthage. Specifically, Woodruff wanted answers to certain questions ranging from whether it was Joseph or Hyrum who requested Taylor to sing "A Poor Wayfaring Man of Grief" the second time, to several questions regarding the handling of the dead bodies.[31]

Another challenge the new assistant church historian evidently experienced was the need to confront growing biases among the Utah Saints. For instance, many viewed Emma Smith, once a celebrated figure within the church, as having been unworthy and unable to follow the Lord's counsel because of her rejection of polygamy and her refusal to move west.[32] A decade earlier, William Clayton had written approvingly about her attempt to prepare a petition for the governor to release the men imprisoned at Carthage. Saints were now trying to make her appear sinister. One of John Taylor's wives, for example, claimed that "Sister Hyrum Smith and herself got a man to draw up a petition to the Governor to restore those men in prison to their wives and children; this was signed by Sister Hyrum Smith; Sister Taylor . . . but when presented to Emma she utterly refused to sign it." This account perpetuated the stereotype that Emma had grown increasingly distant from her polygamous husband. Woodruff was leery of this view and therefore wrote both Taylor and John Bernhisel, another witness to events leading up to the martyrdom, to try to get the facts straight. [33]

What stands out most from Woodruff's experience with the history is his determination to get even the smallest facts right. He clearly sought to "keep a true and faithful record and history of thy Church and kingdom," as he had pleaded in his dedicatory prayer.[34] He felt so confident about the accuracy of the history that he and George A. Smith penned the following postscript to their work:

> The History of Joseph Smith is now before the world, and we are satisfied that a history more correct in its details than this was never published. To have it strictly correct, the greatest possible pains have been taken by the historians and clerks engaged in the work. They were eye and ear witnesses of nearly all the transactions recorded in this history, most of which were reported as they transpired, and, where they were not personally present, they have had access to those who were.

Smith and Woodruff closed with this bold claim: "We, therefore, hereby bear our testimony to all the world, unto whom these words shall come, that the History of Joseph Smith is true, and is one of the most authentic histories ever written."[35]

While historical problems are present in the finished product, especially when measured against contemporary historical methods, the "History of Joseph Smith" is a monument to the dedication of Woodruff and others in creating a faithful, accurate history of the church. Compared with other historical works of the time, these Mormon historians did an exceptional job.[36]

WRITING THE HISTORIES OF THE TWELVE

In 1856, as the writing of Joseph Smith's history was coming to a close, attention was turning to the next historical project. Those working in the Historian's Office decided to write a history of Brigham Young, which involved going back in chronology to cover his birth in 1801 through August 8, 1844, when the Twelve took on the leadership of the church.

Woodruff desired a detailed history of the entire Young family, not just Brigham. To Phineas Young, Brigham Young's brother, Woodruff wrote:

> Will you favor us with a brief sketch of your life, for the church history in connexion with the Young family, name your religion before embracing mormonism, where & when you was baptized, and by whom. Your ordinations, offices, by whom, short synopsis of your missions, with the number baptized, your marriages & children &c. up to Augt. 8. 1844. We have an account of all the family but you, and shall be pleased to have yours by return of mail.[37]

Woodruff also wanted to compile short biographies of every member of the Quorum of the Twelve prior to August 1844. His interest in this project probably stemmed from several factors. First, his role as secretary to the Twelve—a position he held since 1852—kept him interested in the history of the ecclesiastical body. Second, the work was a reflection of the growing importance of the quorum itself, especially where the manuscript dealt with the quorum's rise to authority during the Nauvoo years, which Woodruff had just finished writing about. And finally, the project was a testament to Woodruff's desire to compile a history that was as complete as possible.

At the beginning of February 1857, Woodruff began sending out requests to several quorum members:

> Br. [Amasa] Lyman, the history of the church is now revised and corrected up to Augt. 8 1844 when Prest. Young and the Twelve become the Presidency of the church, at this period

the history will commence, and give a brief account of the parentage, early life, missions and history of each of the Twelve. We would be pleased to have your history at your earliest convenience, say from 8 to 10 pages foolscap. Br. [Charles C.] Rich's history will come in at the date of his ordination and reception into the Quorum.[38]

As he wrote these biographies, Woodruff received plenty of advice from his subjects—it must have been a relief to him after the troubles he had while writing about the last days of Joseph Smith's life. The Church Historian's Office Journal recorded many visits from several apostles who came to the office to review, revise, and correct their histories—most often Brigham Young, who seemed very concerned with how he and his brethren were portrayed in their histories. Luke Johnson, one of the original apostles who fell away but later returned, once spent an evening with Woodruff going over his history.[39] On another occasion, Brigham Young stayed "3+ hours in Compiling his History."[40] In February, Heber C. Kimball had his history read to him and then remarked that "he did not think it full enough."[41] Clearly there were drawbacks to writing about those who had constant contact with the work.

Woodruff's concern for completeness compelled him to reach out to those who had fallen away from the church. Several weeks after he requested help from Amasa Lyman and Charles C. Rich, Woodruff noted in his journal that he "found great difficulty in obtaining any thing for the History of those who had apostitized."[42] For instance, Lyman Wight, an early confidant of Joseph Smith and a Nauvoo-era apostle, became disaffected with Brigham Young and eventually established his own schismatic Mormon settlement in Texas. Though the Utah church had no contact with the wayward Wight, Woodruff hoped to include him in the historical process. On the first day of July 1857, Woodruff wrote Wight:

> I take the liberty of addressing a few lines to you for various reasons, one is for old acquaintance sake and another for the purpose of making a request of you, and upon the subject I will write first, it is this. During the last year I have been engaged in writing the History of the church and especially the History of the Twelve. I am taking up the Quorum from the commencement, have been trying to write your History but I cannot do justice to it at all without your assistance, and on the receipt of this I wish you would write a sketch of your life and forward it to me to this city, name your lineage or forefathers as far back as you can get, with anything you knew about them, and where you was from and when, what your religion was before you embraced the Gospel, where you was baptized and who by and all your ordinations, and by whom ordained—an outline of all your missions.

Woodruff also asked specific questions including whether Wight fought in the War of 1812 and what his recollections were concerning Liberty Jail.[43] Unfortunately, although Wight did send some form of a history, it arrived too late. In June of the following year, 1858, Woodruff wrote him again, explaining that the Utah War had caused "almost universal destruction of all our mail matter" and delayed the delivery of Wight's response. He apologized and told Wight where to find what was published.[44]

These biographies were eventually compiled in books F and G of the Manuscript History of the Church and were published in the *Deseret News* and *Millennial Star*.[45] Woodruff was extremely relieved when the project was finished, writing in his journal that he was "vary thankful that we in a measure are getting through with the History of the Twelve for it has Cost me nearly a years hard brain labor."[46] The project stands as a testament to Woodruff's unflinching desire to fulfill his duties. Historian Howard Searle asserted that together the biographies constituted one of Woodruff's two most significant contributions to Mormon history, the other being his journals.[47]

CONCLUSION

Wilford Woodruff's contributions to the church's history were not lost on his contemporaries. George A. Smith, after enjoying the apostle's assistance in the Historian's Office for four years, claimed that Woodruff "had done more to preserve the History of this Church than any man on the Earth."[48] Eliza R. Snow expressed similar sentiments in a poem she presented to Woodruff in 1857:

> With heart inspired rich matter to indite
> In Zion now your business is to write.
> With skill you wield the ready writer's pen.
> Tis yours to immortalize the deeds of men.
>
> Full many a righteous act and gifted word
> By saints performed—from lips of Prophets heard
> Had sliped mem'ries of Judicious men
> But for the promptings of your faithful pen.
>
> The Church Historians labours to divide
> As his assistant coupled side by side
> You write for Zion whare her Hist'ry known
> Inscribing hers perpetuates your own.[49]

Woodruff believed his historical conscience was a fulfillment of his spiritual promises. He urged the Saints to keep better records, and he strove to consult all available accounts when preparing a "true and faithful record and history" for the entire church. He stressed over minute facts, believing that "every act and word" of the history needed to be recorded. As a result of his dedication, he left behind a body of work that was important in his time and that is priceless today.

NOTES

1. Journal History of The Church of Jesus Christ of Latter-day Saints, December 17, 1846, Church History Library, The Church of Jesus Christ of Latter-day Saints, Salt Lake City. The historical record is silent on the other side of the debate, likely because the narrative comes from Richards's own account. See Willard Richards, Journal, December 17, 1846, Willard Richards Papers, Church History Library.
2. Dean C. Jessee, "Wilford Woodruff: A Man of Record," *Ensign*, July 1993, 29.
3. B. H. Roberts, *A Comprehensive History of The Church of Jesus Christ of Latter-day Saints* (Salt Lake City: Deseret News Press, 1930), 6:355; emphasis in original.
4. Steven C. Harper, "A True and Faithful Record: Wilford Woodruff as Journal Keeper," paper presented at the BYU Church History Symposium, October 12, 2007, copy in author's possession.
5. Howard Searle's excellent dissertation on early Mormon historiography probably gives the most attention to Woodruff's labors as a historian, though it is necessarily limited since his purpose was to describe all historical activities within the first three decades of the church. Howard Clair Searle, "Early Mormon Historiography: Writing the History of the Mormons 1830–1858" (PhD diss., University of California, Los Angeles, 1979). Thomas Alexander's otherwise outstanding biography mentions few of Woodruff's activities in this capacity. Thomas G. Alexander, *Things in Heaven and Earth: The Life and Times of Wilford Woodruff, a Mormon Prophet* (Salt Lake City: Signature Books, 1991).

6. Matthias F. Cowley, *Wilford Woodruff* (Salt Lake City: Deseret News, 1909), 25.

7. *Wilford Woodruff's Journal*, 5:36, March 17, 1857. All quotations from Woodruff's journals come from *Wilford Woodruff's Journal: 1833–1898, Typescript*, ed. Scott G. Kenney, 9 vols. (Midvale, UT: Signature Books, 1983–85). The original journals are located at the Church History Library.

8. *Wilford Woodruff's Journal*, 6:23–24, February 12, 1862.

9. *Wilford Woodruff's Journal*, 5:37, March 17, 1857.

10. *Wilford Woodruff's Journal*, 5:35, March 17, 1857.

11. *Wilford Woodruff's Journal*, 1:3, undated.

12. *Wilford Woodruff's Journal*, 6:24, February 12, 1862.

13. Brigham Young, sermon, April 6, 1857, in *Journal of Discourses*, vol. 4 (Liverpool: F. D. Richards, 1857), 305.

14. *Wilford Woodruff's Journal*, 4:10, February 3, 1851.

15. *Wilford Woodruff's Journal*, 4:200, February 15, 1853.

16. *Wilford Woodruff's Journal*, 4:261, April 20, 1854.

17. *Wilford Woodruff's Journal*, 4:409, April 7, 1856.

18. Journal History, September 15, 1856.

19. *Wilford Woodruff's Journal*, 4:444, September 6, 1856.

20. *Wilford Woodruff's Journal*, 5:86, August 28, 1857.

21. Woodruff to John Bernhisel, June 30, 1856, Church Historian's Office Letterpress Copybook, 1:325, Church History Library; emphasis added. Unless otherwise identified, all letters come from this copybook.

22. *Wilford Woodruff's Journal*, 6:19, February 12, 1862.

23. *Wilford Woodruff's Journal*, 4:358, November 18, 1855.

24. *Wilford Woodruff's Journal*, 5:34, 38, March 17, 1857.

25. *Wilford Woodruff's Journal*, 4:444–45, September 6, 1856.

26. *Wilford Woodruff's Journal*, 4:410, April 15, 1856.

27. Woodruff to Smith, May 28, 1856, 1:299.

28. George A. Smith to Wilford Woodruff, April 21, 1856, Historical Record Book, 1843–1874, p. 218, Church History Library.

29. *Wilford Woodruff's Journal*, 4:424, June 24, 1856. In a letter to John Bernhisel, Woodruff wrote that "this period of Joseph's History is the most difficult to make out as Dr Richards wrote but little, and that in detached sentences, expecting to make it out himself, but died before doing it." Woodruff to Bernhisel, June 30, 1856, 1:325–26.

30. Woodruff to Smith, June 30, 1856, 1:323.

31. Woodruff to Taylor, June 30, 1856, 1:315–20. According to the final history, which relied on John Taylor's response, it was Hyrum who asked Taylor to repeat the hymn. *History of The Church of Jesus Christ of Latter-day Saints*, ed. B. H. Roberts, 2nd ed. rev. (Salt Lake City: Deseret Book, 1978), 7:101. See also B. H. Roberts, *The Life of John Taylor: Third President of The Church of Jesus Christ of Latter-day Saints* (Salt Lake City: George Q. Cannon & Sons, 1892), 135–37. Interestingly, Woodruff also asked Taylor about an event Dan Jones claimed happened the night before the martyrdom: Jones had said: "We were awoke [during the night of the 26th] by heavy treads as of soldiers close by, and heard a whispering under the window 'who shall go in? how many shall go in? &c. they came up stairs to the prison door against which we had taken the precaution to place a chair; hearing us speaking to each other they hesitated, when Joseph called out, 'come on you assassins! we are ready for you and would as willingly die now as at daylight!' Hearing this they returned again." It appears that John Taylor must not have corroborated this detail, since it did not appear in the final history.

32. "Emma Smith is one of the damnest liars I know of on this earth," declared Brigham Young in 1866. Address, October 7, 1866, Brigham Young Papers, Church History Library, quoted in Valeen Tippetts Avery and Linda King Newell, "The Lion and the Lady: Brigham Young and Emma Smith," *Utah Historical Quarterly* 48 (Winter 1980): 82. For the Utah church's assumptions concerning Emma, see Linda King Newell and Valeen Tippetts Avery, *Mormon Enigma: Emma Hale Smith* (Garden City, NY: Doubleday, 1984), 260, 270, 292.

33. Wilford Woodruff to John Bernhisel, June 30, 1856, 1:325; Woodruff to Taylor, June 30, 1856, 1:315–20. Woodruff ended up not mentioning the petition in the final history, likely due to a lack of corroborating evidence. No contemporary accounts speak of Emma signing such a petition.

34. Journal History, September 15, 1856.

35. *History of the Church*, 7:242–43.

36. See Dean C. Jessee, "The Reliability of Joseph Smith's History," *Journal of Mormon History* 3 (1976): 23–46. Most criticisms of the history relate to controversial matters that are not addressed in the work.

37. Woodruff to Young, February 28, 1857, 1:434. Elsewhere, Woodruff gave further details concerning the history of Young's family: "Please also tell

br. Phinehas [Young] that we want a brief sketch of his life as we are compiling a short sketch of each one of the Brothers and sisters of bro. Brigham, their families, their missions, and important events in their lives, all these sketches will be required from your birth till Augt. 8, 1844, when the history of the church becomes the history of Br. Brigham, and takes all his brethren from that date along daily as Joseph's history did." Wilford Woodruff to Orson Pratt, February 28, 1857, 1:433.

38. Woodruff to Amasa Lyman and Charles C. Rich, February 28, 1857, 1:430–31; see also *Wilford Woodruff's Journal*, 5:28, on the same date.

39. *Wilford Woodruff's Journal*, 5:40, March 20, 1857.

40. *Wilford Woodruff's Journal*, 5:84, August 26, 1857.

41. *Wilford Woodruff's Journal*, 5:26, February 23, 1857.

42. *Wilford Woodruff's Journal*, 5:34, March 17, 1857.

43. Woodruff to Wight, July 1, 1857, 1:467.

44. Woodruff to Wight, June 30, 1858, 1:536. The author has not been able to find Wight's response and corresponding history. Woodruff noted that it was "dated Mountain Valley Aug. 4 '57." However, it appears that Wight wrote a long, perhaps polemical history to support his schismatic claims, for it garnered a spirited response from Woodruff, George A. Smith, Amasa Lyman, Charles C. Rich, and two of Wight's nephews who defended Young's claim to authority.

45. Searle, "Early Mormon Historiography," 141. Searle includes useful graphs detailing who wrote which histories (341–42) and where they were published (344–45).

46. *Wilford Woodruff's Journal*, 5:177, March 20, 1858.

47. Searle, "Early Mormon Historiography," 141.

48. *Wilford Woodruff's Journal*, 5:484, August 21, 1860.

49. Eliza R. Snow, "To Elder Wilford Woodruff," November 23, 1857, in *Wilford Woodruff's Journal*, 5:138–39, December 16, 1857.

Robin Scott Jensen

6

Ignored and Unknown Clues of Early Mormon Record Keeping

For the past several years, the Public Broadcasting Service (PBS) has aired a program titled *History Detectives* that follows historians who research viewers' questions. These "detectives" attempt to solve historical mysteries based on intriguing documents, passed-down artifacts, or even family lore. Viewers watch the show's historians effortlessly solve the mysteries by using resources from archives and museums or by consulting outside experts. (As a trained historian, I envy how everything seems to fall into place.)

The show compresses the entire research period into a ten- to fifteen-minute segment, and the culmination of each "case" comes in the final exciting explanation. Yet the show's appeal lies not only in finding out the ultimate answer to each question but

---

Robin Scott Jensen is a documentary editor with the Joseph Smith Papers Project, now housed at the Church History Library in Salt Lake City.

in seeing the process that led to that answer. What could be more exciting than watching historians scouring boxes of documents or going through rolls of microfilmed old newspapers?

In a similar vein, think of this paper as a Mormon *History Detectives* case file. It will analyze three puzzles found in early Mormon record keeping.

UNDERSTANDING MORMON RECORD-KEEPING PRACTICES

First, a short primer on Mormon record-keeping practices and an introduction to ledger volumes will set the background. Early Mormon historians benefited greatly from the sources made available by the record-keeping practices of clerks, scribes, and historians. Before the history-writing efforts in Missouri, which led to the critically important "Manuscript History of the Church," scribes recorded minutes into minute books. Before Oliver Cowdery began what is now known as the 1834–36 history, scribes copied loose letters into a blank book, thereby preserving the letters' contents. Joseph Smith and his scribes and historians could eventually write a history because they had the material from which to draw. Surviving histories either would not exist or would be dramatically different if individuals had not kept administrative, personal, and communal records.

Today, scholars of Mormonism should feel compelled to study early Latter-day Saint record keeping in depth, building upon the critical work of Dean C. Jessee and others who have analyzed the work of early Mormon scribes.[1] An understanding of even the minute details of record-keeping practices can help historians write better history as they recognize why the sources were created and what information can be extracted from these sources.

Such an understanding begins with the records themselves, as they are the most helpful sources in uncovering information about their creation, use, and storage. Supplementary information may come from record keepers' accounts, though at times this information is misleading. A critical backdrop to the early nineteenth-century culture of record keeping is found in comparable contemporary record keeping and in the archival theory of similar record-keeping practices.

THE INTRODUCTION OF LEDGER VOLUMES

An important development in Mormon record keeping occurred when early Mormon scribes began keeping different types of records in bound, blank ledger volumes. The three examples highlighted below come from elements found on or just inside covers of these ledger volumes. Before we consider each example, a short history of the ledger volume in early Mormon record keeping is in order.

Joseph Smith began his own record-keeping practices by writing down scripture. The translation of the Book of Mormon, the recording of his revelations, and his revision of the Bible eventually resulted in hundreds of pages of text. The prophet did not initially write any of this text in a ledger volume. The best available extant sources indicate that the introduction of ledger volumes into Mormon record keeping began in the spring of 1831 with the creation of Revelation Book 1, titled "A Book of Commandments and Revelations."[2] This was followed in 1832 by four more volumes in rapid succession: Revelation Book 2, titled "Book of Revelations" and known more contemporarily as the "Kirtland Revelation Book"; the 1832 history and Letterbook 1, which share the same volume; Minute Book 1, titled "Conference A," also known as the "Kirtland High Council Minute Book";

and Joseph Smith's first journal—the only volume not strictly a twelve-by-eight-inch ledger volume.[3]

Many scholars might see this change in record-keeping material as inconsequential at best. But it was actually a dramatic shift in medium and represented a profound change in how record keeping was viewed.

Recent archival studies have explored the meaning behind the use of record-keeping materials.[4] The act of purchasing, maintaining, and preserving a ledger book as opposed to using loose-leaf paper indicates a desire to keep more permanent records. Current historians consequently can access a tremendous array of primary sources. The manner in which each ledger volume was used also provides valuable information. For instance, unless a volume was damaged in some way, one can easily see if pages are missing. In addition, scholars can estimate the amount of usage by surveying the wear and tear of a volume.

A thorough analysis of records—including an examination of how they were kept, what they were kept in, and why they were kept—provides information and raises questions that can lead to a better understanding of a record's historical context. This paper does not analyze the provenance historiography—or evolving interpretations surrounding the provenance—of early Mormon manuscripts, nor does it anticipate future scholarship historians might explore. Instead, it reveals how a greater understanding of the records created by early Latter-day Saints can provide a window into Joseph Smith's thinking as well as that of other early church leaders.

The examples that follow will help uncover information about the creation, usage, and repurposing of three record-keeping "cases." Like the previously mentioned PBS show, this paper not only gives some intriguing answers to the puzzles presented here but also shows the strategy and importance of the analytical journey itself. Therefore, conclusions are purposefully drawn out, arguments are tentative, and evidence is presented at a fairly slow pace. These examples are not meant to be exhaustive, nor are the solutions typical of document analysis. Rather, they underscore the necessity of carefully studying the sources. Not all documents have hidden meanings under the ink, but all share a story to those willing to search. An improved understanding of the documents helps sharpen the focus on the facts, which leads to a more accurate reconstruction of history.

CASE #1: POSSIBLE BOOKKEEPING NOTATIONS

In the inside front cover of many ledger volumes used by early Mormon clerks, an opaque notation appears in pencil—apparently unrelated to the content of the volume (see figure 1). The following are examples of these notations ("|" indicates a new line):

- "c c/i | pep" (could be transcribed "pe/=") (from Revelation Book 2)
- "c = c/i | i/=" (from JS Letterbook 1)
- "c c/i | pep" (from Minute Book 1)
- "i/n[?] | 12/=" (from the Quorum of the Twelve Minute Book)
- "c/i" (from the Far West and Nauvoo Elders Certificates book)
- "c u/d | i/=" (from the Egyptian Alphabet volume)
- "c o/i | u/i" (from the Kirtland Elders' Quorum Minute Book)[5]

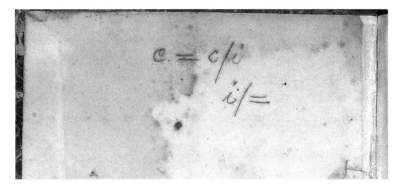

Figure 1. A notation found on the inside front cover of Joseph Smith's first letterbook. A similar notation is found in several other bound volumes. (Joseph Smith, Letterbook 1, Joseph Smith Collection, Church History Library.)

As can be seen in the examples, commonalities throughout the notations are the prevalent use of *c*, *i*, and the slash mark (/). The differing notations are related both in their makeup and style. Upon reflection, the notations appear to be a set of archival markings due to their fairly prominent placement, their temporary nature (written in graphite), and their obscurity—as if they were linked to an unknown, database-like cataloging system. Exactly what the notations' letters and symbols meant is currently lost to this generation.

The theory that archivists made these notations at a later date loses merit when the single Community of Christ volume, the Kirtland Elders' Quorum Minute Book, is taken into consideration. As far as can be determined, this volume was at no time in the custody of The Church of Jesus Christ of Latter-day Saints in Utah or even in Nauvoo.[6] Its notations, therefore, may have appeared soon after the volumes were begun (some of these records were updated into the 1840s and beyond), or, due to their prominent position, the notations may have been added to the volumes before the volumes were even inscribed by the original user.

Comparing the notations and attempting to decode their meaning forces a deeper analysis. Most of these volumes appear to have been begun in the early 1830s.[7] The relatively narrow time frame for the creation of these volumes may indicate that the books were purchased or otherwise acquired during a similarly narrow window of time. This conclusion seems more plausible when the creation of the notations is taken into consideration: a short period of time would likely result in similar, across-volume notations. If the volumes were purchased over a five-year period, for instance, it is less likely that a similar notation was created either before the volumes were inscribed or early in the process.

The terse notations might compare loosely to early forms of bookkeeping or accounting terms, but at the same time, no obvious meaning can be deduced from any guidebooks of the period.[8] If the notations are indeed somehow related to accounting terms, they may have been a regional or personal adaptation of those terms—perhaps a single storekeeper's notations now lost to history.

A significant clue to this mystery—which seems to hint at a storekeeper's notations—comes from another volume with a similar notation: the John Whitmer Daybook, begun around the same time as most of the other volumes.[9] The notation near the beginning of the volume reads "c-d/= 75 cs" (see figure 2). If the "cs" (the reading may be "cts" with the *t* uncrossed) is a shortened form of *cents*, this notation seems to buttress the theory that these unknown markings may have been an effort to mark the book before purchase—with the price, for instance. This does not preclude the possibility that it might also be a storekeeper's notation indicating the type, format, or quality of the volume.

Unless a new source or notation is discovered, or unless new insight on nineteenth-century record-keeping practices is gained,

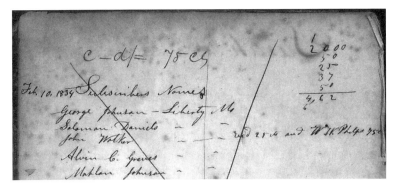

Figure 2. A notation made on the inside front cover of the daybook kept by early Latter-day Saint John Whitmer. This notation provides a clue to the meaning of similar notations written on multiple volumes at about the same time. (John Whitmer, Daybook, Church History Library.)

historians may never know the exact meaning of the notations in the volumes. One can assume, however, that these volumes were purchased or created within a short window of time—indicating that these volumes are a grouping in the early Mormon record-keeping story.

CASE #2: ALPHABETIC ARRANGEMENT

The second "case" is an alphabetic puzzle found on the covers of seven volumes throughout the collection of the Church History Library. Each cover is adorned with a letter (or letters) of the alphabet:

- A (Letterbook 1; begun in 1832)
- A | B (Revelation Book 2; begun in 1832)
- A | C (Minute Book 1; begun in 1832)
- D (Joseph Smith's 1835–36 Journal)
- F (Joseph Smith's 1832–34 Journal)
- G (Joseph Smith's March–September 1838 Journal)

- H (Missouri Teachers Quorum Minute Book; begun in 1834)[10]

Note the absence of the letter *E* and the nonchronological arrangement of the volumes. Three books of documents seem to be grouped first—letters, revelations, and minutes. Three journals then seem to be grouped together, but as volume *E*—if it ever existed—is missing, this may or may not be a grouping of journals.

The alphabetic collection is not a comprehensive grouping of volumes containing historical documents or all of Joseph Smith's journals. Revelation Book 1 contains no letter on its cover, nor does Letterbook 2.[11] The Missouri Teachers Quorum Minute Book appears to be alone among quorum records with a letter assigned to its cover. The covers enclosing the Kirtland Elders' Quorum Minute Book and the Quorum of the Twelve Minute Book are devoid of any letters.[12] Two volumes, Revelation Book 2 and Minute Book 1, have two letters on the front cover, both bearing an *A* and then bearing a *B* and a *C* respectively. On some volumes, the letter is the only thing gracing the cover. For most,

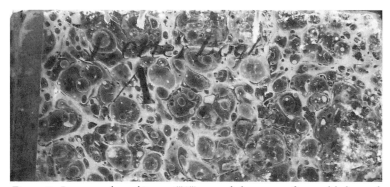

Figure 3. Letters such as this one ("A") graced the covers of several ledger volumes, providing a hint about their later use. (Joseph Smith, Letterbook 1, Joseph Smith Collection, Church History Library.)

however, the letter or letters seem to be part of a title or positioned around an already-existing title (see figure 3). These notations do not appear to predate the use of the volumes as Mormon records.

That these letters were used as a classification system seems clear. The style of several letters is quite similar, and the grouping of the journals seems to be somewhat methodical—although the absence of the letter *E* might indicate a nonjournal volume amid that genre (which is the case, as we will see shortly).

Due to the similar style of some of the letters, it seems likely that the letters were written at the same time, meaning that the alphabetical system was started after the latest volume was created in 1838—well after many of these volumes were complete. Had the volumes been lettered shortly after their creation or while they were being used (presumably indicated by an ordered lettering system—in other words, earliest records with earlier letters of the alphabet), the ordering would have suggested either an anticipation of a system of recall or filing, or a system that was already in place for office needs. The fact that no system was in place is not surprising considering the limited nature of early 1830s record keeping and the nonsystematic way of handling records during the nineteenth century. This attempt to identify volumes largely out of use by 1838 with an alphabetic lettering system indicates a method of storage or secondary use.

Record managers today will understand this record life cycle: the records were no longer actively used by church clerks and instead became archival records, or records preserved for a use other than their primary purpose. A system of storage or secondary use suggests that the volumes were repurposed and were assembled, identified, and stored according to this later need. Such a need arose out of the history-writing effort in Nauvoo.

In 1838 Joseph Smith continued his multiyear effort of creating a history by writing an autobiography that would fill six large manuscript volumes when it was completed well after his death.[13] Initially the history consisted of dictation from memory, interspersed with the occasional revelation as copied from the 1835 Doctrine and Covenants. Beginning in 1843, scribes Willard Richards and William W. Phelps dramatically changed the format of the history—namely, by copying into the history many more documents from earlier records, thereby transforming a memoir into a documentary-history effort.[14] The inevitable need to compile and classify such earlier documents for ease of reference, use, and cross-reference would have arisen at this time.

This reconstruction is more than just conjecture. Fortunately for the droves of people clamoring for a better understanding of Mormon record keeping, a document exists that sheds light on this alphabetic lettering system. Revelation Book 2 served its primary purpose as a register of copies of revelations dictated by Joseph Smith. Half of the volume was left blank, however, and Richards and Phelps used a few blank pages at the end of the volume to record their notes on the history-writing effort in Nauvoo. They provided this explanation for the purpose of the notes: "Material facts left out of the history of the church are noted here that they may be brought in. in their place."[15]

As Richards or Phelps discovered documents not incorporated into the history, they would record that document in their notes, with the volume and page number if the document was found in a manuscript volume. The abbreviations they used when referring to the cited manuscript volumes took the form of an alphabetical system of assignment. What is more, the document description allows one to independently determine the letters they assigned to each volume; it confirms the letters found on the covers. In addition, the notes cite the missing *E* volume, which, based upon a comparison of the document cited in the notes, turns out to be Minute Book 2. Minute Book 1, with its dual letters of *A* and *C*, is referenced in the historical notes Phelps and Richards compiled as *C*. It is possible the *A* was added at a later time when the understanding of *C* was lost, or perhaps the *A* was added first and revised to *C*.[16]

Minute Book 2 as volume *E* reinforces the concept that this system of letters was put in place and inscribed on the volumes after 1838. Minute Book 2, also known as the Far West Record, was not created until 1838, when Ebenezer Robinson copied earlier records of minutes from John Whitmer.[17] Assigning *E* to a volume created in 1838 before *F*, which was created in 1832, again indicates the nonchronological nature of the classification system. No obvious reason exists why the scribes did not inscribe a letter on the cover of Minute Book 2. The differences between all the volumes in this group are many, but Minute Book 2 is the only volume bound in full leather. However, other Nauvoo-era volumes bound in full leather have writing on the cover, providing proof enough that scribes were willing to inscribe upon this type of volume.

An important insight into this alphabetical classification system is the manner in which early church historians compiled the history. It appears that Nauvoo-era historians took a survey of the documents in the church's possession and adopted a secondary use for the volumes as historical records. The notes the Nauvoo historians created indicate which volumes Richards and Phelps were scouring in 1843 to supplement the history already written. Their view of an imperfect history ("Material facts left out of the history of the church are noted here") should warn current historians who might assume the early portions of the history are without error. (For instance, the fact that the historians did not have access to early conference minutes of the church explains why some dates and other details are wrong in the manuscript history.)[18] Current historians should also be aware of the volumes double-checked for inclusion in the history. Because Revelation Book 1—a source that provides many early revelation dates—is not found in the list of volumes on the notes, nor does it appear to be used in the early or later history portion, adjustments should be made to the dates of early revelations found in the manuscript history that contradict the dates found in Revelation Book 1, based on careful research and comparison of other primary sources. The manuscript history is of great importance, but this case underscores how historians can better identify potential historical fallacies by determining the sources that the compilers consulted.

CASE #3: TOPICAL CLASSIFICATION OF OLD TESTAMENT TERMS

Finally, this paper will discuss an example of a Mormon-scripture-related project which, had it been completed, likely would have out-scaled any other theological project during Joseph Smith's lifetime. This project not only would have offered tremendous insight into the theological cosmology of church leadership but would have shaped early Latter-day Saint hermeneutics on multiple facets of the religion. As it stands, it provides limited but important insight into the development of Mormon theology. The project is virtually unknown by anyone today, however, and only scant remnants of it exist from three ledger volumes not traditionally known as being part of the project. One reason for the project's obscurity is the obscurity of the clues left bchind. Historians who concern themselves only with the content rather

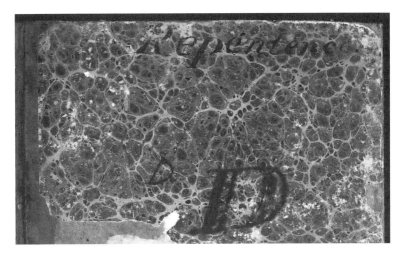

Figure 4. Gospel topics such as this one ("Repentence") were written on several volumes used by early Latter-day Saints. Clues to their meaning are found inside this and other volumes, as well as in loose pages found at the Church History Library. (Joseph Smith, 1835–36 Journal, Joseph Smith Collection, Church History Library.)

than the context of the records reinforce this challenge. One must remember to view these documents not just as they are today but as they were used from the first day they were created.

Three ledger volumes display gospel-related words on the covers (the front and back of two volumes and the front cover of one). The words are featured prominently at the top of each cover, giving the appearance of titles. The three volumes, with their gospel-related topics, are currently known as the following manuscript books (see figure 4):

- Joseph Smith, 1835–36 Journal ("Repentence" and "Sabbath Day")
- A ledger volume of the Egyptian Alphabet ("Faith")

- Kirtland Elders' Quorum Minute Book ("Second Comeing of Christ" and "Gift of the Holy Ghost")[19]

If document specialists had been left with only the words on the covers, little could be determined about the meaning behind these topics. Upon opening the books, however, it becomes apparent that the first page of each volume is related to the words on the cover. Two of the three volumes include scriptural passages relating to the word on the front of the volume (the third volume—the Egyptian Alphabet volume—is missing these initial pages). Notations such as "Scriptures relating to the Gift of the Holy Ghost" directly tie the scriptural citations to the gospel topic.

For instance, the front cover of Joseph Smith's 1835 journal bears the term "Repentence" and the back cover uses the term "Sabbath Day." Opening the front cover of the volume, one finds seven lines of "Scriptures relating to Repentine" (see figure 5).

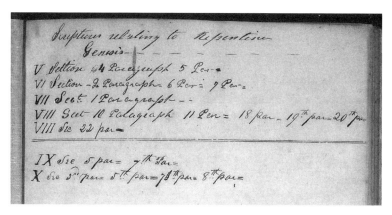

Figure 5. A list of scriptural citations was created for nine gospel topics such as this one ("Repentence"). The volume was later also used as Joseph Smith's 1835–1836 journal. (Joseph Smith, 1835–36 Journal, Joseph Smith Collection, Church History Library.)

The back cover opens to a page containing "Scriptures relating to the Sabbath day," which includes six lines of scriptural references.

All three volumes carry numbers in addition to the gospel-related terms. The minute book has the number *3*, the journal displays the number *9*, and the Egyptian Alphabet was numbered *10*. The similar nature of the ink characteristics and positioning of the numbers on the volumes suggest that the numbering is related to the gospel terms. If the volumes were numbered sequentially, at least ten volumes would have been created as part of this scripture-related project. The 1835 journal ("Repentence" and "Sabbath Day") might indicate that the volumes were arranged alphabetically according to topic. However, the Kirtland Elders' Quorum Minute Book has "Second Coming of Christ" and "Gift of the Holy Ghost" on its covers, not in any obvious order.

Besides the three ledger volumes that bear scriptural terms, three looseleaf pages in the Joseph Smith Collection and one grouping of thirty-six pages that later made up the 1839 draft history—all at the Church History Library—include similar scriptural references. These pages cite scriptures relating to four different terms: "Covenants," "Baptism," "Priesthood after the order of Aaron," and the "order of the High Priesthood." The three sheets appear to have been cut or torn from a ledger volume, but they seem to have come from makes of paper that are different from each other as well as from the volumes in the set. Thus, evidence exists that two to three other ledger volumes might have existed in this work. The thirty-six-page grouping, however, indicates that material other than blank books was used. The extant manuscripts provide a total of nine topics, with scriptural citations likely having been created for all nine topics. (As mentioned, the Egyptian Alphabet volume is missing its initial pages, but citations likely existed.)

What are the scriptures cited? Many of the citations come from "Genesis," but, as we shall see, this is not a simple collection of Old Testament citations. Several unusual characteristics give us clues. As opposed to citing the scriptures by chapter and verse— standard practice then as now—the references in these volumes are to section (normally with roman numerals) and paragraph number. Additionally, and perhaps most significantly, the scriptural references patterned after a particular gospel topic do not match the scripture cited in the King James Version of the book of Genesis. In essence, those attempting to use these gospel topical guides would not find any scriptures to which the index purports to direct them. Something else is going on. Even a novice in Mormon studies would recognize why the Latter-day Saint biblical citations do not match the King James Version of the Bible— the Mormons are citing the Joseph Smith Bible revision.

A single sentence on a one-page document provides the critical clue in determining the purpose of these biblical topical indexes: "This day commenced classifying the different Subjects of the Scriptures and reweving the same," signed by "F. G. Williams, Scribe," and dated "Kirtland the 17th July 1833."[20]

The summer of 1833 was an important time in the development of Mormon scripture. On July 2, 1833, two weeks before the date of the statement above, Joseph Smith and Frederick G. Williams finished the revision of the Bible. The revision was the prophet's effort to restore the many important truths in the Bible that he believed had been lost through mistranslations.[21] An attempt to index, arrange, or "classify" the newly revised Bible according to gospel topics would have been a natural outgrowth of that completed project.

Because many of the scriptural citations make reference to the book of Genesis, one would assume that the revision of the Bible manuscript dictated by Joseph Smith would provide the meaning of the citations. However, a comparison of the scriptural citations with the extant manuscripts of the Old Testament revision Williams would have had in his possession reveals a few problems.

Part of the difficulty comes in not knowing the manuscript or chapter/verse system used. Neither Old Testament manuscript 1 nor 2 was originally broken up into paragraphs or verses but was instead created in long sections with chapter breaks. Shortly after the completion of the manuscript, different sets of chapter or section numbers and paragraph or verse numbers were inserted into Old Testament manuscript 2. It seems likely, then, that Williams used this second manuscript, which contained the added chapters/sections and verses/paragraphing. It is unclear who added the several sets of chapter numbers, but it is clear that Williams did not add them.[22]

This poses a problem with finding the scriptures intended for citation. For instance, when looking at scriptures related to the topic of the Sabbath day, the first reference ("Section 3 Paragraph 1") matches up with the third series of inserted paragraph or verse numbers in the Old Testament manuscript 2 (there is no numerical heading for this chapter/section), which discusses God's resting on the seventh day following the creation period. However, the second reference ("IX Section," paragraphs 22–26) does not exist under the latest added headings in the manuscript, chapter 9 having no original paragraphs or verses. Chapter 9, which seems to correlate with the added paragraph numbers, only goes up to paragraph 15. Not until chapter 4 (later changed to chapter 7) do we find verses matching the cited verses, which contain references to Sabbath-day theology. Here, Enoch, in his great vision of the heavens and the earth, discovers that the earth will finally rest for a thousand years when the Savior returns.[23]

Williams's citations do not match the original or inserted chapter/ section numbering found on the extant manuscript. The inserted verse/paragraph numbers, however, do match if one ignores the numbers of the chapters. In other words, if one assumes a new section or chapter begins when the verse numbers recommence at 1, Williams's citations correlate with the manuscript.

The discrepancies between Williams's section numbers in the scriptural citations when compared to any extant manuscript might be explained by introducing a nonextant manuscript into the scenario. As scribe for this classification system, Frederick G. Williams may have compiled the ledger volumes as he was creating a new, second copy of the Old Testament manuscript— perhaps incorporating all redactions in preparation to publish it. He also may have indicated the section numbers on a separate manuscript and used the existing paragraph numbers on the extant manuscript. It is possible to determine for all the citations the likely paragraph and chapter numbers for the current Bible revision, allowing for insight into the theological implications of the newly finished Bible revision (see appendix to this chapter).

Incredibly, as many as ten volumes full of scriptural citations from Joseph Smith's Bible revision were attempted as a major scribal project as early as 1833. Such an ambitious work was never completed, but this particular failed ambition was not an isolated incident in Mormon record keeping; never-finished projects were common. For example, Oliver Cowdery never completed the history he began in late 1834. In Joseph Smith's first diary, many more days went unrecorded than recorded.

With two topics per ledger volume, a total of about twenty topics may have been used, and potentially more volumes or loose compilations begun. While twenty topics may sound meager for a search of scriptures, a lean topical approach to the scriptures is consistent with at least two contemporary works of biblical analysis. For instance, *The Biblical Analysis; or A Topical Arrangement of the Instructions of the Holy Scriptures* by J. U. Parsons breaks the Bible into twelve topics, which are further broken into subtopics.[24] *A Topical Question Book* contains forty lessons on various biblical topics.[25] Had the Mormons truly been creating a topical guide to the Bible revision, a breakdown of around twenty topics with various subtopics would have fit into a larger pattern of biblical study for the time. Perhaps this could best be thought of as a prototype of the seven "section" lessons on only one gospel topic, later published in the 1835 Doctrine and Covenants as the "Lectures on Faith." A series of lectures on twenty topics would have been a tremendous theological undertaking for any organization, but especially for the fledgling church.

Taken together, these three volumes served an entirely different and lofty purpose before the use of the individual volumes took over. These volumes were initially intended to be a collection of gospel topics but were retooled as a minute book, a Joseph Smith journal, and a volume on the Egyptian language. Other volumes were possibly used for different purposes or were simply discarded. Historians who focused on the final purpose of these volumes actually missed a critical understanding of their original purpose.

CONCLUSION

This paper is not meant to be a comprehensive description of cover-related record-keeping practices, nor are the cases discussed here intended to represent Mormon record keeping in general. Rather, these cases provide a new way of looking at Latter-day Saint sources. Historians should not focus on only the content of these sources. This approach hides many important clues that give insight not only into the sources themselves but into Mormon record keeping and Mormon thought. Instead, historians should also analyze how documents were created, why they were created, and how they were later used. Doing so can only improve their scholarship.

APPENDIX

The scriptural citations found in two ledger volumes, three loose pages, and a thirty-six-page grouping all contain Genesis references with section and paragraph numbers in roman numerals. The similarities between the verses inserted into Old Testament manuscript 2 and the references in the ledger volumes and loose pages allow scholars to identify the modern citation. The references are based on each new paragraph or run of paragraphs, not on section numbers. All roman numerals have been changed to Arabic numbers.

Joseph Smith, 1835–36 Journal, Joseph Smith Collection, Church History Library

Repentance

Section	Paragraph	Modern Reference
5	4–5	Moses 5:5b–9
6	2	Moses 5:14–15
6	6–7	Moses 5:21b–27
7	1	Moses 6:1
8	10–11	Moses 6:23–30
8	18–20	Moses 6:49–54
8	22	Moses 6:56b–57
9	5	Moses 7:9–10
9	7	Moses 7:12–13

Section	Paragraph	Modern Reference
10	3	Moses 8:16–17
10	5	Moses 8:20–21
10	7–8	Moses 8:23–26

Sabbath Day

Section	Paragraph	Modern Reference
3	1	Moses 3:1–3
9	22–26	Moses 7:54–66

Egyptian Alphabet Ledger Volume, Church History Library

Faith

The page where the scriptural references would have been written is no longer in the volume, but some of the original wet ink transferred to the opposite page. While it is impossible to tell what was in all of the scriptural citations, the beginning of a word—probably *Scriptures*—is seen on that page, with possibly an *F* and a *G*.

Kirtland Elders' Quorum Minute Book, Community of Christ Library-Archives

Second Coming of Christ

Section	Paragraph	Modern Reference
9	23–26	Moses 7:58–66

The following group of scriptures is found several pages into the Kirtland Elders' Quorum Minute Book and does not have a heading. This seems to be a second copy of the scriptures related to the topic "Gift of the Holy Ghost," found at the back of the volume.

Section	Paragraph	Modern Reference
Unknown	Unknown	
Unknown	Unknown[26]	
8	11[27]	Moses 6:25–30
8	19–20	Moses 6:51–54
8	23–24	Moses 6:58–61
8	26–27	Moses 6:63–68
9	11	Moses 7:21–27
10	7	Moses 8:23–24

This small section of scriptures is found several pages into the Kirtland Elders' Quorum Minute Book and does not have a heading. Sections 1, 6, 8, 9, and 10 (the highest section number of any of the scriptural references) are the only sections with paragraph numbers this high.

Section	Paragraph	Modern Reference
Unknown[28]	16–19	

Gift of the Holy Ghost

Section	Paragraph	Modern Reference
2	1	Moses 2:1–2
5	5	Moses 5:9
8	1	Moses 6:7
8	11	Moses 6:25–30
8	19–20	Moses 6:51–54
8	23–24	Moses 6:58–61
8	26–2	Moses 6:63–68
9	11	Moses 7:21–27

Three loose leaves, Joseph Smith Collection, Church History Library

Baptism

Section	Paragraph	Modern Reference
8	19–20	Moses 6:51–54
8	23–24	Moses 6:58–61
8	27	Moses 6:64–68
9	6	Moses 7:11
10	7	Moses 8:23–24

Priesthood after the Order of Aaron

Section	Paragraph	Modern Reference
1	9	Moses 1:15b–16
3	9–10	Moses 3:19–20
3	12–13	Moses 3:23–25
4	6–8	Moses 4:14–19
4	12	Moses 4:26–27
5	1–6	Moses 5:1–11
6	1–2	Moses 5:12–15
6	5	Moses 5:18–21a
6	7	Moses 5:26–27
8	1	Moses 6:7

Order of the High Priesthood

Section	Paragraph	Modern Reference
1	1	Moses 1:1–2
1	3–14, 16–25	Moses 1:3b–42
2	1	Moses 2:1–2
2	8	Moses 2:26–27
3	8	Moses 3:18
4 [6][29]	1–2	Moses 5:12–15

Section	Paragraph	Modern Reference
4 [6]	13	Moses 5:41–42
4 [6]	20	Moses 5:58–59
7	1–2	Moses 6:1–6
8	1–11	Moses 6:7–30
8	13–16	Moses 6:35–46
8	19–20	Moses 6:51–54
8	22–27	Moses 6:56b–68
9	1–13	Moses 7:1–34
9	21–22	Moses 7:53–57
10	4	Moses 8:18–19
10	7	Moses 8:23–24

Thirty-six-page grouping in 1839 history draft, Church History Library[30]

Covenants

This document contains some material not found in the book of Moses in the current Pearl of Great Price. Differences or important distinctions between the King James Version and the Joseph Smith Bible revision manuscript are noted in endnotes.

Section	Paragraph	Modern Reference
9	20–21	Moses 7:49–53
9	28	Moses 8:2
10	12	Genesis 6:17–18[31]
11	5	Genesis 9:1–3[32]
11	8–11	Genesis 9:8–17[33]

NOTES

1. Dean C. Jessee, "The Writing of Joseph Smith's History," *BYU Studies* 11, no. 4 (Summer 1971): 439–73; Howard C. Searle, "Early Mormon Historiography: Writing the History of the Mormons, 1830–1858" (PhD diss., University of California, Los Angeles, 1979).

2. See Robin Scott Jensen, Robert J. Woodford, and Steven C. Harper, eds., *Manuscript Revelation Books*, facsimile edition, vol. 1 of the Revelations and Translations series, *The Joseph Smith Papers*, ed. Dean C. Jessee, Ronald K. Esplin, and Richard Lyman Bushman (Salt Lake City: Church Historian's Press, 2009). A ledger volume may have been used to record the conference minutes begun in June 1830. The current version of these minutes, however, is likely a copy of a copy of the original, and thus one cannot know for certain. The pattern of Mormon record keeping in general—and minute-taking specifically—would hint that the minutes were possibly kept on loose pages that were copied into a ledger volume—likely by John Whitmer sometime after 1833. The current version of these minutes is available in "The Conference Minutes and Record Book of Christ's Church of Latter Day Saints," also known as the Far West Record or Minute Book 2, found at the Church History Library, The Church of Jesus Christ of Latter-day Saints, Salt Lake City (hereafter CHL). Minute Book 2 is a record book created in 1838 that copies an earlier, nonextant record.

3. This paper uses the nomenclature of the citations found in *The Joseph Smith Papers*. Kirtland Revelation Book (also known as Revelation Book 2), Revelations Collection, ca. 1831–76, CHL; Joseph Smith, Letterbook 1, Joseph Smith Collection, CHL; Kirtland High Council, Minutes, December 1832–November 1837 (also known as Minute Book 1 or Kirtland High Council Minute Book), CHL; Joseph Smith, 1832–34 Journal, Smith Collection.

4. See, for instance, James M. O'Toole, "Between Veneration and Loathing: Loving and Hating Documents," in *Archives, Documentation, and Institutions of Social Memory: Essays from the Sawyer Seminar*, ed. Francis X. Blouin Jr. and William G. Rosenberg (Ann Arbor: University of Michigan Press, 2006), 43–53; Mark A. Greene, "The Power of Meaning: The Archival Mission in the Postmodern Age," *American Archivist* 65 (Spring/Summer 2002): 42–55; Sue McKemmish, "Evidence of Me," *Archives and Manuscripts* 24

(May 1996): 28–45; Tamara Plakins Thornton, *Handwriting in America: A Cultural History* (New Haven, CT: Yale University Press, 1996).

5. Revelation Book 2, Revelations Collection; Smith Letterbook 1, Smith Collection; Minute Book 1; Quorum of the Twelve Apostles, Record, February–August 1835 (also known as Quorum of the Twelve Minute Book), CHL; Far West and Nauvoo Elders Certificates, 1837–38, 1840–46, CHL; "Grammar & A[l]phabet of the Egyptian Language," Kirtland Egyptian Papers, ca. 1835–36, CHL; Kirtland Elders' Quorum Minute Book, Community of Christ Library-Archives.

6. Personal e-mail correspondence with former Community of Christ archivist Ron Romig, February 11, 2009.

7. The only exception is the Far West and Nauvoo Elders Certificate volume that seemed to have commenced in 1836. This does not preclude the clerks from owning the volume in the early 1830s and simply not using it until 1836.

8. For instance, see Lyman Preston, *Preston's Treatise on Book-keeping: or, Arbitrary Rules Made Plain: in Two Parts* (New York: Robinson, Pratt & Co., 1842); James H. Coffin, *Progressive Exercises in Book Keeping, by Single and Double Entry* (Greenfield, MA: A. Phelps, 1836).

9. The John Whitmer Daybook was passed down through family members until it recently was acquired by the Church History Library. This separate provenance adds further weight to the argument that these notations were made before or shortly after the volumes' initial use.

10. Smith Letterbook 1, Smith Collection; Revelation Book 2, Revelations Collection; Minute Book 1; Joseph Smith, 1835–36 Journal, Smith Collection; Joseph Smith, 1832–34 Journal, Smith Collection; Joseph Smith, March–September 1838 Journal, Smith Collection; Teachers Quorum Minutes, December 1834–December 1845 (also known as Missouri Teachers Quorum Minute Book), CHL.

11. "Book of Commandments and Revelations" (also known as Revelation Book 1), CHL; Joseph Smith, Letterbook 2, Smith Collection.

12. Kirtland Elders' Quorum Minute Book; Quorum of the Twelve Minute Book.

13. See Jessee, "Writing of Joseph Smith's History"; Searle, "Early Mormon Historiography."

14. An interesting yet undocumented theory places many of these original volumes in the possession of William W. Phelps after his excommunication in 1838. After he returned to fellowship in the church, and especially after he

moved to Nauvoo, a dramatic surge in the use of primary sources for the history occurred, which would be explained by the return of these important documents. An alternative explanation for the increased use of primary documents would simply be a difference in historical approaches by the various scribes who worked on the history. The author is indebted to archivist Christy Best for the theory involving William W. Phelps.

15. See Jensen and others, *Manuscript Revelation Books*, 659. See also 410.

16. Jensen and others, *Manuscript Revelation Books*, 658–65; Minute Book 2, Smith Collection.

17. "The record [kept by Whitmer] was subsequently obtained . . . and brought to our house, where we copied the entire record into another book, assisted a part of the time, by Dr. Levi Richards." Ebenezer Robinson, "Items of Personal History of the Editor," *Return* 1 (September 1889): 133. Minute Book 2 is in the handwriting of Robinson and Richards, as Robinson recollects. The copied manuscript makes anachronistic reference to the 1833 publication of the Book of Commandments, indicating Whitmer copied from earlier minutes and added some commentary. Synopsis of a meeting on January 1, 1831, Minute Book 2, p. 2, Smith Collection.

18. See, for example, the minutes of conferences held on June 9, 1830; September 26, 1830; and June 3, 1831; and the (mis)remembering of those dates in the Manuscript History. Minute Book 2, pp. 1–4; Manuscript History of the Church, 1838–56, pp. 41, 54, 118, CHL.

19. Smith, 1835–36 Journal, Smith Collection; "Grammar & Aphabet of the Egyptian Language," Kirtland Egyptian Papers; Kirtland Elders' Quorum Minute Book.

20. Frederick G. Williams, note on scriptural references, Smith Collection.

21. A one-sentence description of the Smith Bible Revision does not do justice to the complexities and historiographical and theological implications of this important manuscript in early and current Mormon thought. A reproduction of the entire manuscript with important historiographical updating is available in Scott H. Faulring, Kent P. Jackson, and Robert J. Matthews, *Joseph Smith's New Translation of the Bible: Original Manuscripts* (Provo, UT: Religious Studies Center, Brigham Young University, 2004). Robert J. Matthews, *"A Plainer Translation": Joseph Smith's Translation of the Bible, A History and Commentary* (Provo, UT: Brigham Young University Press, 1975) is still the best work on the subject, but commentary in Kent P. Jackson,

The Book of Moses and the Joseph Smith Translation Manuscripts (Provo, UT: Religious Studies Center, Brigham Young University, 2005) and H. Michael Marquardt, *The Four Gospels According to Joseph Smith* (Longwood, FL: Xulon Press, 2007) is important to consult.

22. For instance, the heading of current Genesis 11 was originally inscribed as "Chapter IX," but a *13* and an *11* were both added at a later time. Faulring and others, *Joseph Smith's New Translation*, 634. Several of Williams's citations do not match either the original chapter designation or the inserted chapter or paragraph numbers.

23. This is currently Moses 7:54–66.

24. J. U. Parsons, *The Biblical Analysis; or A Topical Arrangement of the Instructions of the Holy Scriptures. Adapted to the Use of Ministers, Sabbath School and Bible Class Teachers, Family Worship, and Private Meditation* (Boston: William Peirce, 1837).

25. Joseph Banvard, *A Topical Question Book, on Subjects Connected with the Plan of Salvation, Arranged in Consecutive Order; with Hints for the Assistance of Teachers. Designed for Sabbath Schools and Bible Classes* (Salem, MA: John P. Jewett, 1843).

26. Wax covers the first two lines of the scriptural citation.

27. Wax covers part of this line; there could be more than eleven paragraphs.

28. Wax covers part of this line.

29. All paragraph numbers for section "IV" are on the same line. There is no paragraph 20 in section 4 or 5; Williams likely intended to write "VI."

30. See Dean C. Jessee, ed., *The Papers of Joseph Smith*, vol. 1 (Salt Lake City: Deseret Book, 1989), 255.

31. The Joseph Smith Bible revision manuscript adds some detail to the current verses in Genesis with respect to covenants: "But with thee will I establish my covenant, even as I have sworn unto thy father Enoch, that a remnant of thy posterity should be preserved among all Nations." Faulring and others, *Joseph Smith's New Translation*, 626.

32. The heading to this portion of the Joseph Smith Bible revision manuscript states in part: "The covenant which God made to Noah." Faulring and others, *Joseph Smith's New Translation*, 629.

33. The Joseph Smith Bible revision manuscript reads (angle brackets indicate insertions in the text):

"And God spake unto Noah, & to his Sons with him Saying, & I, behold, will establish my covenant with you which I made unto your Father Enoch concerning your seed after you. And it shall come to pass, that evry living creature that is with you of the fowl, & of the cattle, & of the beast of the Earth that is with you, which shall go out of the Ark Shall not altogether perish; Neither shall all flesh be cut off any more by the waters of a flood; Neither shall there any more be a flood to destroy the Earth; And I will establish my covenant with you, which I made unto Enoch Concerning the remnants of your posterity. [9] And God made a covenant with Noah And said this shall be the token of the covenant I make between me & you. And for every living creature with you for perpetual generation & I will set my bow in the cloud. And it shall be for a token of a covenant between me & the Earth. And it shall come to pass, when I bring a cloud over the Earth, that the bow shall be seen in the cloud; And I will remember my covenant which I have made between me & you for every living creature <of all flesh>. And the waters Shall no more become a flood to destroy all flesh, & the bow shall be in the cloud; & I will look upon it, that I may remember the everlasting covenant which I made unto the father Enoch; that, when men should keep all my commandments; Zion should again come on the Earth, the City of Enoch which I have caught up unto myself. [10] And this is mine everlasting covenant <that I establish with you> that when thy posterity shall embrace the thruth And look upward; then Shall Zion look downward. And all the Heavens shall shake with gladness. And the Earth shall tremble with Joy; & the general assembly of the Church of the first born, shall come down out of Heaven. And possess the Earth And shall have place untill the end come. [11] And this is mine everlasting covenant which I made with thy father Enoch. And the Bow shall be in the cloud. And I will establish my covenant, unto thee which I have made between me & thee for evry living creature of all flesh that shall be upon the Earth. And God said unto Noah This is the token of the covenant, which I have established between me & thee, For all flesh that shall be upon the Earth." Faulring and others, *Joseph Smith's New Translation*, 630–31.

7

ENLARGING THE MEMORY OF MORMONISM: HISTORIAN ANDREW JENSON'S TALES FROM THE WORLD TOUR, 1895–97

O N March 26, 1895, Danish-American historian Andrew Jenson filled out a U.S. Department of State passport application in the presence of his plural wife, Emma. He was hopeful that the First Presidency and Quorum of the Twelve Apostles would approve his petition to personally visit all non–North American Latter-day Saint missions and local units to gather historical data.

Andrew Jenson's passport form provides twenty-first-century observers with the basic biographical details of his life: He was born on December 11, 1850, in Torslev, Denmark. As a young boy with his parents, Jenson and his family immigrated to Utah in 1866—a move clearly motivated by their conversion to Mormonism. He became a naturalized U.S. citizen in 1873. Because

---

Reid L. Neilson is managing director of the Church History Department of The Church of Jesus Christ of Latter-day Saints.

photographs were not attached to nineteenth-century American passports, Jenson provided the required personal physical description: age—forty-four-years old; stature—five feet, seven inches; forehead—regular; eyes—hazel, sometimes gray; nose—aquiline [hooked]; mouth—ordinary; chin—rounded; hair—light brown; complexion—fair; and face—oval. To complete the statement, "I intend to return to the United States . . . ," Jenson wrote, "in 1897 or 1898."[1] Regardless of what Emma may have thought of her husband's pending lengthy journey, he was eager to go.

Weeks later, Andrew Jenson received word that the church leadership had authorized his global fact-finding mission.[2] The intrepid Dane departed from Salt Lake City on May 11, 1895, and did not return to the "City of the Saints" until June 4, 1897. Over the course of his twenty-five-month circumnavigation of the world, Jenson passed through the following islands, nations, and lands, in chronological order: the Hawaiian Islands, Fiji, Tonga, Samoa, New Zealand, the Cook Islands, the Society Islands, the Tuamotu Islands, Australia, Ceylon, Egypt, Syria, Palestine, Italy, France, Denmark, Norway, Sweden, Prussia, Hannover, Saxony, Bavaria, Switzerland, the Netherlands, England, Wales, Ireland, and Scotland.[3]

Jenson's global tour was an unprecedented adventure in Latter-day Saint history. In fact, no member of the First Presidency or Quorum of the Twelve had ever visited the isles of the Pacific (with the exception of Hawaii) or the continents of Asia and Australia. As the South African Mission (1865–1903) was then closed and the Japan Mission (1901–1924) had not yet opened, Jenson became the first church member to visit all the existing non–North American Latter-day Saint missions since the Mormon evangelization of the Pacific basin frontier commenced in the 1840s.

A portrait of President Joseph F. Smith with Andrew Jenson and Oluf Andersen taken while President Smith was visiting the Scandinavian Mission, of which Jenson was president. (Courtesy of Church History Library.)

The purpose of this paper is not to detail Jenson's travels abroad but rather to sketch out the events and forces that propelled the historian on this fact-finding mission and to suggest several enduring legacies of his experiences. Jenson's world tour was a watershed event in Mormon history. After sixty-five years of persecution and decades of exile in the American West, the church was emerging from the shadows of plural marriage, theocracy, and isolationism and adopting a new identity as part of the American mainstream and global Christianity. In fact, while Jenson was abroad, the Territory of Utah would gain American statehood. Up to that point, as historian Richard E. Turley Jr. has pointed out, the Church Historian's Office, which sponsored Jenson's two-year journey, had largely been focused on chronicling the history of Brigham Young and the Mormon colonization of the Great Basin Kingdom. "By the end of the century, a great opportunity existed to document and preserve the history of the Church throughout the world," and Jenson would single-handedly jump-start the office's transition from a provincial to a global worldview.[4]

Jenson's success abroad would also solidify and elevate his employment status to full-time in the Church Historian's Office. And Jenson's tour of the borderlands of Mormonism would later enable him to compile the *Encyclopedic History of the Church*, with entries on every important place in the Latter-day Saint past. While visiting the missionary outposts of Mormonism in Polynesia, Australasia, the Middle East, and Europe, Jenson trained local Latter-day Saint clerks in proper record-keeping procedures and would, in time, help formalize and standardize Mormon history-writing standards.

ENLARGING THE MEMORY OF MORMONISM

The idea to tour the church's non–North American missions seems to have been the culmination of Jenson's years of hard work domestically. In 1889 he began a series of visits to local church units to collect ecclesiastical and pioneer records. During these outings Jenson gathered information from whatever official records he could find as well as personal writings from the early settlers. A letter from the church historian informed stake presidents and bishops of Jenson's task and encouraged them to cooperate. This official endorsement proved useful and ensured that Jenson traveled in relative comfort.[5]

Jenson often took the opportunity to address local congregations on the importance of record keeping. In the span of a little more than five years, he visited practically every stake and ward of the church in Idaho, Utah, Nevada, Arizona, Colorado, Mexico, and Canada, as well as important historical sites in the eastern United States. By March 1895 he had completed his assigned task on behalf of the Church Historian's Office. Over the next few weeks he resumed his work of indexing a history of Joseph Smith that had been published in the church's British *Millennial Star* and drafting a history of the apostle Charles C. Rich and some of his associates.[6]

That April, Jenson prepared a report of his activities for his file leader Franklin D. Richards, church historian and president of the Quorum of the Twelve Apostles. He informed Richards that he had now visited all North American stakes and most of the wards, branches, priesthood quorums, and auxiliaries that had existed since the 1830 organization of the church. Jenson had traveled almost forty thousand miles on behalf of the Church Historian's Office in the process. "In all my travels, public discoures [*sic*] and private conversation I have endeavored to follow your instructions to the letter," he wrote. "I find that a thorough reform in record-keeping throughout the stakes of Zion is necessary; the public Church records, in almost every instance, are kept in a very imperfect manner; hundreds of the original records kept in older wards years ago have been lost entirely, and others are found in the hands of private individuals and parties who have no right to them whatsoever." Jenson further noted to Richards that he had made it a point of his visits to instruct local leaders: "I have given suggestions to clerks, recorders and others as to what ought to be written and what might be left unwritten. My instructions have generally been well received by all concerned, and as a rule I have also been well received personally and treated with due kindness."[7]

Church leaders were impressed with Jenson's North American labors, and after much discussion they determined to send him on an extended fact-finding mission around the world. (It is interesting to note that while the First Presidency and Quorum of the Twelve Apostles debated the merits of such a journey into early April, in anticipation of their decision Jenson had secured his passport by late March.) As an official representative of the Historian's Office, Jenson was expected to replicate his domestic labors abroad so that he would have enough materials to later write histories of all the church's missions, districts, and branches.[8]

Jenson spent the balance of April 1895 fulfilling his family and ecclesiastical responsibilities in anticipation of his projected two-year absence. He baptized his daughter Eleonore Elizabeth in the Salt Lake Tabernacle basement font and witnessed the birth of his son Harold Howell. Jenson also moved his historical materials, personal papers, and books from Rosenborg Villa, his home in southern Salt Lake Valley, to his residence a few miles north. "I took the documents to my new study in the second story of my 17th Ward home, and for several days I was busy arranging the papers in the respective shelves and pigeon holes which I had provided," he wrote.[9] Concerned that Jenson was not paying the proper attention to his family, especially his newborn son and wife Emma, who had just endured childbirth, Elder Richards encouraged his ambitious employee to curtail his history-gathering activities until his departure. "I advised Andrew Jensen [*sic*] not to go to San Pete but visit & bless his family till his long journey," Richards noted in his diary.[10]

Saturday, May 11, 1895, was the day scheduled for Jenson's departure. "My folks packed my valises and lunch basket, and everything being ready, I called the family into the library, where I united with them in earnest prayer," he recorded in his autobiography. Jenson then gave priesthood blessings to his two wives, children, and in-laws. "In blessing and praying with the family we were all melted to tears and the spirit of God was with us."[11]

Late that afternoon he left his home and made his way with family and friends to the Union Pacific Railway station in Salt Lake City. At 5:20 p.m. his train pulled out, bound for Ogden, Utah, and from thence, the Pacific Northwest and British Columbia.[12] From the deepwater Canadian port of Vancouver, he crossed the Pacific Ocean by steamer, arriving in Honolulu, Hawaii. He remained in Hawaii for two months, touring the branches and districts of the Hawaiian Mission. Jenson next boarded a steamer heading to Suva, Fiji, although the isles of Melanesia hosted no Latter-day Saint congregations or missionary outposts. After the Fijian Islands he toured the Samoan Mission, at the time comprising the island nations of Samoa and Tonga.

New Zealand was next on his itinerary. In a matter of weeks Jenson came to love the Maori Latter-day Saints and their devotion to the gospel. From New Zealand he traveled east to the Society Islands and French Polynesia. Here, in the region of Mormonism's earliest venture into the Pacific world in 1844, he stayed for nearly two months. Next he went to Australia, where he met with the members and missionaries of the Australasian Mission. Afterward Jenson made his way to the Middle East via the Indian Ocean. After Cairo and Jerusalem, he made a circular tour of Europe. He collected Latter-day Saint historical data from England, Denmark, Norway, Sweden, Germany, Switzerland, the Netherlands, Wales, Ireland, and Scotland.

JENSON'S TALES FROM THE WORLD TOUR, 1895–97

Jenson kept meticulous records during his global adventure. Not only was he gathering history; he was making it himself. Before leaving Utah he arranged to have the editors of the Church-owned *Deseret Weekly News* serialize his travelogue letters. Jenson hoped that Latter-day Saints in Utah would take an interest in his journey and catch the vision of proper Mormon record keeping.

His first letter, written on May 13, 1895, from Portland, Oregon, was published two weeks later on June 1 under the series title "Jenson's Travels."[13] Over the next year Jenson drafted regular letters chronicling his adventures in places that most Latter-day Saints would never have the means, time, or reason to visit personally. He penned his eightieth and final letter to his *Deseret Weekly News* readers during the summer of 1896, but it was not published until February 19, 1898, one and a half years later. "The letters have been written under many difficulties, quite a number of them on ship board, when my fellow passengers would be wrestling with seasickness or idling away their time in the smoking parlors, playing cards or other games," Jenson explained. "The last sixteen communications, which have not been dated, were mostly written on board the steamer Orotava, on my voyage from Port Said, Egypt, to Naples, Italy, but not submitted to the editor of the 'News' till after my return home, June 4, 1897."[14]

He concluded his travelogue by expressing hope that his two years abroad on behalf of the Historian's Office would lay the foundation for future historical studies of global Mormonism.

"During my mission I circumnavigated the globe, traveled about 60,000 miles, preached the Gospel on land and on sea, whenever I had the opportunity, and gathered a great deal of historical information, which I trust will prove beneficial and interesting when it is prepared hereafter and incorporated in the history of The Church of Jesus Christ of Latter-day Saints of the Nineteenth century."[15]

In addition to his published correspondence, Jenson also chronicled his movements and activities in an almost-daily journal, a habit he had begun decades earlier as a young man. While his voluminous handwritten diaries remain unpublished in the Church History Library, the Danish-American historian did excerpt and print entries spanning his life as the *Autobiography of Andrew Jenson* in 1938, just three years before his death. Jenson devoted 161 pages (227–388) of autobiographical text to his 1895–97 world tour, or about 24 percent of the entire book. A careful comparison of the two published accounts reveals that Jenson likely used his more detailed letters as the basis for his corresponding journals. Jenson's serialized letters total more than 210,000 words, while his parallel *Autobiography* passages total about 98,000 words. There is significant overlap between the two records, although "Jenson's Travels" ends in July 1896, when he departed from the Holy Land to tour the church's missions in Europe. Fortunately, Jenson's *Autobiography* supplies the details of his final nine months in Europe as well as his homecoming in America. Reading all of "Jenson's Travels" together with Jenson's non-overlapping *Autobiography* sections provides readers with a fascinating account of his adventure.[16]

Jenson's personal writings offer twenty-first-century readers a unique window into the Latter-day Saint past, as well as life around the world at the end of the nineteenth century. Each of his letters and *Autobiography* entries provides a snapshot of a particular place and time, as Jenson describes in great detail daily life and worship for native Latter-day Saints in their homelands. In terms of studying "lived religion," few sources come close to the scope of Jenson's writings.

In addition, Jenson tells the story of missionary life in the church's non–North American evangelism outposts. From his letters and journal one learns that Mormonism was experienced somewhat differently by Euro-American elders and sisters and their native charges. Jenson also sheds light on the relationship between Mormon and non-Mormon missionaries in various lands as they competed for new converts, especially commenting on the strained relationships between the representatives of The Church of Jesus Christ of Latter-day Saints and the Reorganized Church of Jesus Christ of Latter Day Saints in the Pacific. He offers historical overviews of the settlement and colonization of each land and isle he visits, together with a précis of subsequent Mormon beginnings.

Always resourceful, Jenson relied on interviews with church members, missionaries, leaders, former members, other religionists, locals unconnected with religion, government officials, librarians, museum curators, newspaper editors, site docents, and anyone else whose ear he could bend. For more than two years he often worked sixteen hours a day, gathering materials to take back to Utah in his capacity as a professional (meaning paid) historian and amateur anthropologist, ethnographer, sociologist, and geographer.

While Jenson's published letters and *Autobiography* offer details about the public historian, they are silent about the inner man. Jenson was quick to reveal his feelings about race, place, and space around the world, yet he was hesitant to disclose his thoughts on his family, friends, and coworkers. His writings are littered with references to his continual bouts of seasickness on the oceans, but they lack entries about homesickness for his children and wives back in Utah. Between May 1895 and June 1897 he made almost no mention of his relations. One notable exception occurred when his wife Emma traveled to Europe for a surprise meeting. Jenson devoted just a handful of sentences to their reunion, and then Emma again disappeared from his narrative. Another anomaly occurred months later when he asked the Lord in prayer if he should remain in Europe or return to Utah. Jenson wrote that he was delighted when he felt impressed to go home. Yet readers are left wondering if he was more excited to be reunited with his babies or his books, his family or his files. He noted after his train pulled into the Salt Lake City depot, twenty-five months after he left for Vancouver, "I soon caught sight of my wives, Emma and Bertha, and four of my younger children, namely, Minerva, Eleonore, Eva and Harold. They gave me a hearty welcome." Yet that same day he went back to work unpacking his boxes and preparing his files for further historical duties.[17]

A number of reasons might account for Jenson's lack of transparency in his personal writings. To begin with, Jenson knew that whatever he wrote would soon appear in print in one of Utah's largest newspapers, the *Deseret Weekly News*, and eventually in a memoir. He was mindful that the eyes of church leaders and laity were following him as he circumnavigated the globe. Thus, everything he wrote was filtered and packaged for general Latter-day Saint consumption. Moreover, he knew that failure abroad would likely curtail domestic opportunities in the future. Jenson wanted Latter-day Saints at home to view him as competent and courageous, especially as he was spending church funds. He wanted to be seen as in control of his surroundings, mission, and emotions. And it appears that Jenson was: he never noted even fleeting moments of self-doubt or discouragement. Yet it is also possible, given his past strained relationships, that some of his coworkers in the Historian's Office were silently rooting for his failure, jealous that he could undertake such a journey while they remained fettered to their desks in Salt Lake City.

Another possibility for the lack of private detail in his writings was that Jenson was having the adventure of a lifetime and did not suffer from bouts of homesickness or feelings of inadequacy. He seemed to treat his world tour like all the other extended missionary labors for which he was set apart. Aside from seasickness and shifting weather, Jenson experienced few trials in his travels. He appeared willing to endure anything for the cause of Mormon history writing—it was both his vocation and his avocation. Furthermore, life on the road was simple: he had to worry only about food, transportation, housing, and record keeping. Back in Utah, he had to juggle his work, church, and family commitments. He was constantly being pulled in multiple directions. But for two years he was left alone to his passion for history.

Jenson also enjoyed the celebrity of touring the church's missions as an official representative of the church leaders. Back at church headquarters, he was merely an overworked and underappreciated clerk in the Historian's Office with an uncertain future and minimal stipend. But "traveling through the West and the nation, working with bishops, stake presidents, and mission presidents and staying in their homes, he was treated very much like a General Authority," historian Louis Reinwand points out. "Almost invariably, he was given an opportunity to speak in local wards, and was often called upon to speak in stake conferences."[18] Mission presidents, branch presidents, and local members did their best to accommodate his wishes and make his visits comfortable. Even non-Mormon heads of state and captains of industry in Hawaii, Tonga, Samoa, and French Polynesia agreed to be interviewed by him. Feasts and meetings were held in his honor, especially in the Pacific Isles. Perhaps Jenson rarely complained in his personal writings because there was not much to fuss about.

Jenson returned to Utah and church headquarters on June 4, 1897, twenty-five months after saying good-bye to his loved ones. He had traveled nearly 54,000 miles over land and sea by steamship, schooners, boats, trains, carriages, and *jinrikisha* (rickshaws), and on the backs of horses, camels, and donkeys. In addition to his historical labors, he accomplished much church work. He delivered more than 230 sermons and discourses, baptized two converts, confirmed eleven new members, blessed six children and eight adults, ordained four men to the priesthood, set apart one sister, and blessed many who were sick. Jenson further logged that he had enjoyed great vigor despite his arduous schedule: "In all my travels I enjoyed good health considering that I had been subject to so many changes in climate and diet, and returned home well satisfied with my labors. I worked hard and was in this respect perhaps more zealous than wise, for I often stuck to my task 16 hours a day."[19] Weeks after his return, Jenson shared tales of his world tour from the pulpit in the Salt Lake Tabernacle.[20]

LEGACY OF JENSON'S WORLD TOUR AND HISTORICAL LABORS

What was the heritage of Jenson's expedition to Mormonism abroad? How did his two-year fact-finding mission help shape the balance of his life and the Latter-day Saint historical enterprise? To begin with, Jenson's history-gathering prowess secured him a full-time position at home in the Historian's Office, something his previous labors failed to accomplish. On October 19, 1897, four months after his return, the First Presidency called Jenson as assistant church historian, a position he had sought for years. He was sustained by church members at the following general conference in April.

The significance of this formal calling to Jenson personally and the church institutionally cannot be overstated. It provided Jenson and his family with financial security, professional respect, and ecclesiastical support. In return, Jenson devoted the next four decades of his life to the gathering and writing of Mormon history. "Andrew Jenson's contributions to Latter-day Saint historical literature seem almost incredible, especially in the light of his background," Reinwand writes. "At each stage in his career Jenson exhibited a rare dedication and resourcefulness. His limitless energy and ambition—his capacity to endure, even to enjoy, the drudgery of historical research and writing—made it possible for this otherwise unpromising convert-immigrant to become one of the foremost historians of the Latter-day Saints."[21]

During his sixty-five-year career, which began in 1876 and ended in 1941, Jenson was constantly in the harness of Mormon history. He was the "author of twenty-seven books, editor of four historical periodicals, compiler of 650 manuscript histories and indexes to nearly every important historical manuscript and published reference work, zealous collector of historical records, faithful diarist, and author of more than five thousand published biographical sketches," according to historians Davis Bitton and Leonard J. Arrington. "Jenson may have contributed more to preserving the factual details of Latter-day Saint history than any other person. At least for sheer quantity his projects will likely remain unsurpassed. Jenson's industry, persistence, and dogged determination in the face of rebuffs and disappointments have caused every subsequent Mormon historian to be indebted to him."[22] It would be almost impossible—and quite irresponsible—to write on nearly any aspect of the Latter-day Saint past without first reviewing and referencing Jenson's historical spadework.

The eventual publication of the *Encyclopedic History of the Church* was a second major legacy of Jenson's global fact-finding mission. The *Encyclopedic History* is a condensed version of Jenson's mission, district, stake, ward, and branch manuscript histories. Having visited nearly every local unit and historical site of the church, Jenson was uniquely qualified to compile such a reference work. He gathered much of the material he used for the many non–North American entries during his 1895–97 world tour. "On my extensive travels I have collected a vast amount of historical information, by perusing the records and documents, which have accumulated in the various stakes of Zion and the respective missionary fields. And also by culling from private journals and interviewing many persons of note and long experience in the Church," Jenson reported to Richards upon his return in 1897.

I have also sent and brought to the Historian's Office hundreds of records from foreign missionary fields, which were not needed abroad any more, and many more such records which I packed for shipment in different places can be expected here soon with returning Elders. My notes being gathered under different conditions and under many difficulties—often hurriedly—need careful compilation and arrangements before they can be used for history. They, however, constitute the foundation and outline for histories of nearly every stake, ward, branch, quorum, association, etc., of the Church, in its gathered state, and of every mission, conference, branch, etc., abroad, from the organization of the Church to the present time.

At the same time, Jenson admitted to Richards that it would "require years of patient toil and labor" to shape these primary source materials into accessible narratives.[23]

Over the next several decades, Jenson would personally shoulder that load as he labored to chronicle the rise and spread of Mormonism around the globe. When it was completed, the *Encyclopedic History* was first serialized in the *Deseret News*. Officially endorsed by the Corporation of the President of The Church of Jesus Christ of Latter-day Saints, it was published in 1941—Jenson's first work copyrighted by the church. "With the publication of the *Encyclopedic History of the Church* I feel that my life's work is nearly done, so far as the writing of books and historical articles are concerned," he wrote in the volume's preface in March 1941. "I shall soon pass on to the great beyond, leaving behind a great work yet to be done and plenty of able men and women to do it. I have done my best to contribute to the history of the Church, covering the first century of its existence, but a greater work will be done by future historians as the Church grows."[24] Jenson died that November, just months after his final book came off the Deseret News Publishing Company press in Salt Lake City.

A third major legacy of Jenson's world tour was the subsequent improvement and standardization of Mormon record keeping. Recall that in April 1895, while the First Presidency and Quorum of the Twelve Apostles were still debating whether to send him abroad, Jenson reported to Elder Franklin D. Richards on his North American history-gathering efforts thus far and pointed out the sorry state of domestic church documentation. His disheartening report may have been the catalyst that prodded church leaders to send him around the world to gather and preserve Mormonism's global past.

Jenson's worst fears concerning the state of local records abroad were realized as he toured the church's non–North American missions and witnessed firsthand the deplorable state of their preservation. In June 1897 he again reported to Richards, this time on his findings in the Pacific Islands, Australasia, the Middle East, and Europe. "In some of my previous reports I have referred to the very imperfect state of our records as kept of late years throughout the Church," Jenson wrote. "I would earnestly recommend a thorough reformation in regard to record keeping. There is a lack of system and uniformity throughout the Church, and in the recording of ordinance work, and in the making of minutes and rolls, statistical reports, annual reports, etc., etc. Each mission, stake and ward seems to have its own peculiar system, or no system at all; and until regular forms and blanks are furnished from headquarters for use throughout the entire Church, this irregularity must necessarily continue."[25]

As assistant church historian, Jenson oversaw the creation, dissemination, and collection of standardized forms and reports used by all church missions and local units. During much of the twentieth century, all the church's missions were responsible for sending in annual historical reports, including detailed statistics to the Church Historian's Office, where Jenson toiled.

POSTSCRIPT

Through his own hard work and the seeming hand of Providence, historian Andrew Jenson found his niche as a laborer in the cause of Mormonism. He pursued the goal of collecting and writing comprehensive, accurate, and useful histories of the church with a rare passion. Acquiring, documenting, and publishing church history was not purely a scholarly or historical pursuit for him—the untiring Danish-American believed it was a spiritual labor with eternal ramifications.

While visiting early church history sites in 1888, Jenson and his companions Edward Stevenson and Joseph S. Black encountered a number of Mormon schismatic groups. Stevenson shared with Jenson a principle that Joseph Smith had taught him in Nauvoo: "Where the true Church is, there will always be a majority of the saints, and the records and history of the Church also."[26] Jenson apparently took this counsel to heart, for thereafter he believed that the legitimate Restoration movement would possess the physical history of Mormonism. He devoted his adult life to enlarging the institutional memory of the church and protecting what he considered to be the sacred records of the final dispensation.

Jenson preached the importance of record keeping in his many sermons and general conference addresses. "If it had not been for the writers . . . who belonged to the original Church, what would the doings of Christ mean to us?" Jenson asked the Latter-day Saints on one occasion. "And if somebody had not recorded the many other beautiful sayings of Christ and his apostles, what would we have known of the ministry of Christ and of his apostles? We would merely have had some vague ideas handed down by tradition that would lead astray more than lead aright."[27] In other words, if not for the writers and historians of past dispensations, there would be no sacred history in the form of Hebrew and Christian scripture. The same would hold true in this dispensation, he often taught, if church members failed to keep contemporary ecclesiastical and personal histories.

Jenson had a sense of cosmic foreordination as a latter-day historian. Reflecting on the idea of "noble and great ones" chosen in the premortal life to perform specific tasks, he speculated on his own fortune:

> For 4000 years I had perhaps been keeping a record of what had taken place in the spirit world. The Lord having chosen me to become a historian kept me waiting these many years from the time Adam and Eve were placed in the Garden of Eden. Then about 86 years ago (earth time) the Father of my spirit came to me and said: My son you have kept a faithful record of your brothers and sisters (my sons and daughters) who have been sent down to earth from time to time and now it is your turn to go and tabernacle in mortality. . . . At length I found myself as the Danish-born Andreas Jensen who later became universally known as the Americanized Dane Andrew Jenson the historian. Lo here I am on hand to do the work unto which I was appointed.[28]

This sense of destiny, coupled with an unmatched work ethic and passion for history, shaped Jenson's life and work. One merely needs to search the Church History Library catalog for works by Jenson to get a glimpse of his labors.

Global Latter-day Saint history *is* church history. Church members need to realize that much of their most interesting history took place abroad. They must remember that the "restoration" of the gospel occurs every time a new country is dedicated by apostolic authority for proselyting. In other words, the original New York restoration of 1830 was in many ways replicated in Great Britain in 1837, Japan in 1901, Brazil in 1935, Ghana in 1970, Russia in 1989, and Mongolia in 1992. Mormon historians need to refocus their scholarly gaze from Palmyra, Kirtland, Nauvoo, and Salt Lake City to Tokyo, Santiago, Warsaw,

Johannesburg, and Nairobi. Non–North American stories need to be told with greater frequency and better skill.[29]

In this sense, Jenson was a man ahead of his time. In the final years of the nineteenth century, the workhorse of the Church Historian's Office had the foresight and willingness to dedicate two years of his life to documenting the global church and its membership. As Louis Reinwand points out, "Jenson played a vital role in keeping alive the ideal of a universal Church. He was the first to insist that Mormon history include Germans, Britons, Scandinavians, Tongans, Tahitians, and other national and cultural groups, and that Latter-day Saint history should be written in various languages for the benefit of those to whom English was not the native tongue."[30] Back in 1895, when Jenson completed his passport application in anticipation of his two-year world tour, he likely had little inkling of the far-reaching effects his fact-finding mission would have on his life and on Mormon history.

NOTES

1. Andrew Jenson, passport application, March 26, 1895, in *U.S. Passport Applications, 1795–1925* (online database), http://search.ancestry.com/search/db.aspx?dbid=1174. Important sources on Jenson's life and labors as a historian of Mormonism include *Autobiography of Andrew Jenson* (Salt Lake City: Deseret News Press, 1938); Louis Reinwand, "Andrew Jenson, Latter-day Saint Historian," *BYU Studies* 14 (Fall 1973): 29–46; Keith W. Perkins, "Andrew Jenson: Zealous Chronologist" (PhD diss., Brigham Young University, 1974); and Davis Bitton and Leonard J. Arrington, *Mormons and Their Historians* (Salt Lake City: University of Utah Press, 1988), 41–55.

2. I consciously use the term *global* rather than *international* when referring to The Church of Jesus Christ of Latter-day Saints around the world. *Webster's Third New International Dictionary* defines *global* as "of, relating to, or involving the entire world" and *international* as "of, relating to, or affecting two or more nations." Historically, the term *international church* has described

Mormonism beyond the borders of the United States, which privileges American members: the leaders and laity living in the Great Basin are assumed to be at the center while everyone else is relegated to the periphery.

3. *Autobiography of Andrew Jenson*, 386–87. My forthcoming documentary history will chronicle Jenson's entire journey. Reid L. Neilson, ed., *Tales from the World Tour: The Letters and Journal of Andrew Jenson, 1895–1897*. The Religious Studies Center at Brigham Young University has generously supported the research and editing of this documentary history.

4. Richard E. Turley Jr., "Gathering Latter-day Saint History in the Pacific," in *Pioneers in the Pacific: Memory, History, and Cultural Identity among the Latter-day Saints*, ed. Grant Underwood (Provo, UT: Religious Studies Center, Brigham Young University, 2005), 148.

5. *Autobiography of Andrew Jenson*, 193–94, 387.

6. *Autobiography of Andrew Jenson*, 227–28, 387.

7. *Autobiography of Andrew Jenson*, 227–28.

8. *Autobiography of Andrew Jenson*, 228. In subsequent years these presiding quorums discussed the idea of sending other church leaders and representatives abroad. In an April 1896 meeting of the Quorum of the Twelve Apostles, Francis M. Lyman proposed that at least one apostle should annually visit each of the Church's non–North American missions. "He favored a trip around the world at least once a year by one of the Apostles," one attendee noted. "He felt the Apostles should be in a position from personal knowledge through visiting our missions to be able to report their condition correctly to the Presidency of the Church." Minutes of the Quorum of the Twelve Apostles, April 1, 1896, Anthon H. Lund Collection, typescript in Quinn Papers, Yale University Library. Moreover, Heber J. Grant, as a junior apostle, contemplated touring the missions of the Pacific on several occasions, including while serving in Japan as mission president between 1901 and 1903. Ronald W. Walker, "Strangers in a Strange Land," in *Qualities That Count: Heber J. Grant as Businessman, Missionary, and Apostle* (Provo, UT: Brigham Young University Press, 2004), 249; Gregory A. Prince and Wm. Robert Wright, *David O. McKay and the Rise of Modern Mormonism* (Salt Lake City: University of Utah Press, 2005), 358. The First Presidency also encouraged and financed an exploratory tour of China by two enterprising missionaries—Alma Taylor and Frederick Caine—on their way home from Japan in 1910 to determine whether they should resume the evangelization of the Chinese. See

Reid L. Neilson, "Alma O. Taylor's Fact-Finding Mission to China," *BYU Studies* 40, no. 1 (2001): 177–203.

9. *Autobiography of Andrew Jenson*, 228.

10. As cited in Perkins, "Andrew Jenson: Zealous Chronologist," 155–56.

11. *Autobiography of Andrew Jenson*, 231.

12. *Autobiography of Andrew Jenson*, 231.

13. "Jenson's Travels," *Deseret Weekly News,* June 1, 1895.

14. "Jenson's Travels," *Deseret Weekly News*, February 19, 1898.

15. "Jenson's Travels," *Deseret Weekly News*, February 19, 1898.

16. Jenson published his own account in Danish as *Jorden Rundt: En Rejsebeskrivelse Af Andrew Jenson* [Around the World: A Travelogue of Andrew Jenson] (Salt Lake City, 1908). I am in the process of editing and annotating both "Jenson's Travels" and relevant portions of his *Autobiography* in preparation for publication.

17. *Autobiography of Andrew Jenson*, 386.

18. Reinwand, "Andrew Jenson, Latter-day Saint Historian," 38.

19. *Autobiography of Andrew Jenson*, 386–87.

20. See "Sunday Services," *Deseret Weekly News*, July 3, 1897.

21. Reinwand, "Andrew Jenson, Latter-day Saint Historian," 46.

22. Bitton and Arrington, *Mormons and Their Historians*, 41.

23. *Autobiography of Andrew Jenson*, 388.

24. Andrew Jenson, *Encyclopedic History of The Church of Jesus Christ of Latter-day Saints* (Salt Lake City: Deseret News Publishing, 1941), iv; emphasis added.

25. *Autobiography of Andrew Jenson*, 388.

26. *Autobiography of Andrew Jenson*, 153.

27. Andrew Jenson, in *Ninety-Seventh Semiannual Conference of The Church of Jesus Christ of Latter-day Saints* (Salt Lake City: The Church of Jesus Christ of Latter-day Saints, 1926), 54–59, as cited in Paul H. Peterson, "Andrew Jenson Chides the Saints," *BYU Studies* 39, no. 1 (2000): 198.

28. As cited in Perkins, "Andrew Jenson: Zealous Chronologist," 248.

29. Reid L. Neilson, introduction to *Global Mormonism in the Twenty-first Century*, ed. Reid L. Neilson (Provo, UT: Religious Studies Center, Brigham Young University, 2008), xv.

30. Reinwand, "Andrew Jenson, Latter-day Saint Historian," 45.

Ronald K. Esplin

8

MODERN EFFORTS TO PRESERVE CHURCH HISTORY

TODAY I spend my time immersed in the Joseph Smith Papers, a major documentary editing enterprise. Editing and publishing documents is a key thrust of the Church History Department and has been for its predecessors. Indeed, the pioneer Church Historian's Office grew out of the effort by Joseph Smith and his assistants, especially Willard Richards, the church historian, to compile a history using available documents, a labor that produced the text of the multivolume *History of the Church*. These early historians used Joseph Smith's journals to help connect these documents and provide a narrative thread to the history.

I have been both a witness to and a participant in the church's documentary editing and other record-keeping efforts of the past generation and a half. These activities have prepared the way for

Ronald K. Esplin is managing editor of the Joseph Smith Papers Project, now housed at the Church History Library in Salt Lake City. He was director of the Joseph Fielding Smith Institute for Latter-day Saint History at Brigham Young University for nearly sixteen years.

the Joseph Smith Papers Project and for future endeavors, which may include the papers of other church leaders. I wish to share some of my experiences with these efforts.

History of the Church Archives

In 1972, the newly called church historian, Leonard J. Arrington, selected Davis Bitton and James B. Allen to be assistant church historians. Bitton wrote an article in 1983 called "Ten Years in Camelot: A Personal Memoir,"[1] which accurately described the decade under Arrington's direction as an idyllic time of excitement, discovery, access, openness, wonderful exchange, and great relationships with scholars both within the church and outside of it. Many people fondly remember Bitton's article. Unfortunately, however, the "Camelot" designation obscures as much as it reveals by implying that darkness descended after those ten years. That did not happen. Nor did the Arrington period arise out of a wasteland: important developments preceded it and laid a foundation for both the Arrington years and what we do today.

I would argue, in fact, that there is no better time to be a historian of the Latter-day Saint experience than today. We have more resources, opportunities, encouragement, and support than we have ever had. But the "ten years in Camelot," of which I was part, were important. I want to discuss those years and what we did in the 1970s to try to understand and reassemble Joseph Smith's and Brigham Young's papers, initiatives that can be understood only by looking at Arrington's predecessors.

In a sense, all the work I do today—and the ten years or more that I spent working on Brigham Young's papers, as well as the further research I still intend to do—rests on the shoulders of people such as Willard Richards, an early church historian and recorder who kept most of Joseph Smith's journals during the Nauvoo era and penned many other important records, and Thomas Bullock, a chief assistant. Working imperfectly and in challenging circumstances, they left a legacy of records that allow us to understand our past better than most communities can. One example of the limitations: those who are preparing for publication the journals Richards kept for Joseph Smith in Nauvoo quip that they will never forgive Joseph Smith for selecting a doctor as his scribe. Although Willard could write legibly, when he was trying to take dictation or capture the spoken language of a discourse, his handwriting often deteriorated into a nearly illegible scrawl. Nevertheless, he contributed to the richness of our documentary heritage, both by creating important records and by gathering up and preserving documents. In 1845 and 1846, Richards, Bullock, and others oversaw efforts to gather all the church's records and box them up for the journey across the plains.

Although Joseph Smith launched his expansive history in Nauvoo and the early years were completed before his death, the project was not finished until more than a decade later in Utah. In fact, work on the history continued several years after the death of Willard Richards in 1854. After Richards's premature death, other luminaries held the office of church historian and, with associates, labored in the Church Historian's Office in early Utah; these included George A. Smith, Wilford Woodruff, and Orson Pratt. Once they had completed the history of Joseph Smith, they and others in the Church Historian's Office went on to compile a comparable chronological collection of papers for the Brigham Young period, a pattern that continued with the manuscript history of John Taylor after Brigham Young died in 1877.

Given the priority of these histories, it is not surprising that a major work of the Church Historian's Office in the nineteenth century was to collect documents and organize them chronologically. By the late nineteenth century, after the Church Historian's Office had finished the histories (which eventually metamorphosed into a slightly different product called the Journal History), they began figuring out how to answer other kinds of questions from their rich holdings. They consequently ended up rearranging many of the holdings, initially filed mainly chronologically, into subject files. So, for example, if a letter from Brigham Young was about Cedar City, it went into the Cedar City file. If it was about Mountain Meadows, it went into the Mountain Meadows file.

The hiring of new professional staff in the 1960s and 1970s created the opportunity to improve the care and organization of the records, beginning with Joseph Smith's and Brigham Young's documents. Twentieth-century innovations in copying and indexing provided options earlier historians lacked. The wonders of electronic scans and electronic filing, for instance, offer possibilities undreamed of in the nineteenth century, permitting the same document to simultaneously "reside" in different research files. Earlier historians had fewer options for filing and organization. During his lifetime, Brigham Young's approximately thirty-five thousand incoming letters were filed chronologically (or chronologically by correspondent). To facilitate accessing them topically, later staff reorganized thousands into subject files, ignoring a cardinal principle of modern archivists to preserve original order. So what would these later archivists, with new professional tools, do?

THE PROFESSIONALIZATION OF THE ARCHIVES

Some have pointed to Jeffery O. Johnson's arrival in the old Church Historian's Office in 1969 as the beginning of the professionalization of the archives. That professionalization is crucial to everything I do today and much of what we want to do as a church in understanding our heritage. Jeff, however, points to Dean C. Jessee's arrival in November 1964. Indeed, Dean may have been the first person in the Church Historian's Office who already had professional training in history or manuscripts when he was hired.[2] Dean had worked in Brigham Young University's Special Collections, had earned a master's degree in church history from Brigham Young University, and was teaching seminary. He didn't have formal training as an archivist at the time, but he was arguably the first to get a vision of what an archive ought to be and how we ought to treat our records. By February 1971, he and Jeff, along with Max J. Evans, helped lay a foundation for professional archives that revolutionized how we handle records in the church.

The story of Dean's hiring is worth telling. While he was doing regular research in the archives of the Church Historian's Office, he wondered about the possibility of gaining employment there. When he asked, he was directed to Earl E. Olson, a long-time employee in the office and a grandson of the great pioneer assistant church historian Andrew Jenson. Earl said there was indeed an opening and encouraged Dean to seek an interview with Elder Joseph Fielding Smith, the church historian.

When Dean was ushered into Joseph Fielding Smith's office, Elder Smith, engrossed with the papers on his desk, did not immediately look up or engage him in conversation. Thought Dean, "How do I get his attention? I really want this job!" Finally they had a short conversation, one Elder Smith concluded somewhat abruptly: "You look like a very nice young man, but we don't have an opening. Good day."

A day or two later Earl called Dean and asked for a report. Dean explained that he had visited with Elder Smith as instructed, only to be told that there was no opening. "There is an opening," Earl insisted. "Let's try again!" This time the result was better. "Well, we have work to do," Elder Smith agreed, and perhaps Dean could join the staff.

Somewhat apologetically, staff members told Dean that he would have to work at one of four desks in "the cage"—the very place where many of the most important records were housed! There, inside this big steel cage, surrounded by Joseph Smith's and Brigham Young's papers and other important documents, Dean happily settled in and began his work.

It would be five years before Jeff Johnson, the second professionally trained staff member hired to work with manuscripts, came aboard. Two years later, in 1971, and some months before Arrington was appointed church historian in early 1972, the third professional, Max J. Evans, was hired as a cataloger when a slot opened with the death of assistant church historian A. William Lund.

Until his death in 1971, Lund served as a primary gatekeeper of the records. When I began work with the newly organized Church Historical Department in 1972, I heard numerous Brother Lund stories. The thrust of them was that the researcher first had to secure Lund's reluctant permission to look at the records, and then figure out how to make research notes and benefit from use of the records—even though Lund never warmed up to the idea that scholars should be so intimately involved with the manuscripts.

Beginning in the early 1970s, then, Max and Jeff, assisted by Dean and soon joined by others, oversaw a full professionalization of the archives—a professionalization that prepared the way for the success of Leonard Arrington and the History Division and for everything we do today, including our work on the

Joseph Smith Papers Project. I had the wonderful opportunity of spending five of my ten years at the Historical Department in the archives being mentored by Jeff and Max, who helped me understand both the state of our collection and the archival principles upon which we could make it better.

Interestingly, one of the projects Jeff and I worked on together in the 1970s was a Joseph Smith project. Jeff did the first professional organization of the Joseph Smith collection and prepared the first register. I then wrote the brief historical and biographical introduction for that register. And now, more than thirty years later, Jeff has returned to the department after fourteen years as the Utah state archivist, and I am back after twenty-five years at Brigham Young University. We are both working on the Joseph Smith Papers Project.

In the mid-1970s, Max Evans left the Historical Department to become assistant state archivist of Wisconsin. Subsequently he returned to Utah to become director of the Utah State Historical Society, and he later served as the executive director of the National Historical Publications and Records Commission (NHPRC). Operating under the National Archives, this commission plays an important role in American documentary editing, certifying projects like the Joseph Smith Papers, and funding many such projects. Max returned to the Church History Department in February 2008 after five years with the NHPRC. He and several other pioneers who helped professionalize the archives more than a generation ago—myself included—are now back at the end of their careers.

As noted, one of the important challenges the professional staff faced in the 1970s stemmed from the fact that records had been organized and reorganized by several generations of earlier lay archivists. Emphasis on provenance, chain of custody, original order, and other archival principles guided these new professionals. Provenance has to do with when a document was created, why it was created, and who created it. Chain of custody has to do with where the document has been over the years. Each document raises questions: Do we know the history of the item? Do we know who created it and when? Is there a clear chain of custody? Is the document included in early inventories?

In the 1980s, many were taken in by Mark Hofmann's forgeries. If individuals had paid close attention to the provenance, as an archivist might, perhaps fewer would have been deceived. Looking at these "newly discovered" documents not as a historian but as an archivist, Jeff Johnson felt that they never fully agreed with the already known historical record, nor did the known provenance of Hofmann forgeries conform to what he, as an archivist, expected.

The provenance of most documents in the Church History Library is reasonably clear. Early inventories and other records demonstrate that many of them have been in the custody of the church since the mid-nineteenth century. Therefore, when we publish them as part of the Joseph Smith Papers Project, or any future project, we can do so with confidence that these are genuine historical documents. Even so, we often go to considerable length to carefully research their creation, their chain of custody, and all the other factors that can help us authenticate them.

Original order is also important. Even though collections often come into the archives without the kind of systematic, carefully thought-out order one might hope for and some order may have to be supplied, an archivist prefers to preserve the original order as closely as possible. However, as we have now seen, after decades of use for various purposes, an "original order" for many of the items in the Church Archives no longer existed. What remained were many clues and some general sense of what a few of the collections once were. There was no way to return to an original order of the past, but reassembling important collections in a logical and usable order that resembled earlier use and order made sense. Doing so for the Brigham Young Collection became a major focus of my work in the archives during the 1970s.

MY ROAD TO THE CHURCH HISTORICAL DEPARTMENT

Allow me to explain the circumstances that led me to the Church Historical Department in 1972 and fostered my personal interest in Brigham Young, his life, and his papers. I studied at the University of Virginia in Charlottesville—Mr. Jefferson's university—for my master's degree. My full intention when I went to Virginia was to complete an MA degree and then return to the West to write a dissertation on Brigham Young. I have since tried to recover where that expectation came from, but cannot, though I know it was very much a part of my perspective as I studied history at UVA. It was not by chance that I associated there with professors who were specialists in biographies of early American figures, especially Bernard Mayo, who had written a prize-winning biography of Henry Clay.[3]

It was with more than passing interest, then, that I encountered while at Virginia a recently published (1969) biography of Brigham Young titled *The Lion of the Lord*.[4] Written by Stanley P. Hirshson and supported by a prestigious national fellowship, this had the appearance of being a work of serious scholarship, but I soon discovered serious flaws. After spending a short time in the Church Historian's Office in Salt Lake City, Hirshson felt less than welcome and grew impatient with the slow pace of gaining access to materials, and so he left. At first discouraged about the prospects of completing his study, he found in New York City a treasure trove of materials on Brigham Young and early Utah that revived his spirits. Can you imagine what it was? It was the New York Public Library's collection of newspaper accounts about Utah and the early church, written by Brigham Young's enemies. Hirshson wrote a biography based on those accounts. The book is a wonderful index to the New York Public Library collection of generally critical newspaper reporting, but it is not a good guide to the life and personality of Brigham Young. My future work on Brigham Young, I vowed, would be informed by the sources closest to him, and not based on secondhand accounts of his critics.

Another event that related to my time at the University of Virginia, even though it occurred several years later, also underscored my conviction that proper use of the best sources is essential to good history. In 1974 Fawn Brodie, who had earlier written a biography of Joseph Smith that drew criticism from Latter-day Saint scholars because of her selection and use of sources, published her biography of Thomas Jefferson.[5] It was interesting for me to watch from afar the reaction of University of Virginia professors, well-versed on Jefferson and sometime defenders of his legacy, as they challenged her methodology in writing about him. Earlier, they would not have understood or accepted the reasoning of Latter-day Saint scholars who tried to point out the same flaws in her writing about Joseph Smith; now, thoroughly grounded in the sources for the study of Jefferson, they understood the shortcomings of Brodie's work.

In 1970 I left the University of Virginia, degree in hand, to pursue my PhD in history at Brigham Young University. I was committed, as I noted, to doing a dissertation on Brigham Young. A year and a few months after I enrolled, Leonard Arrington was called as the church historian, and the Church Historian's Office was reorganized into a modern Church Historical Department with a History Division (for research and writing), an Archives Division, and a Library Division. The scene was set for what would become a pivotal turn in my own career.

In the spring of 1972 the newly organized Historical Department was looking ahead to later in the year when its substantial collections of books, manuscripts, and records would be moved from the Church Administration Building—which for decades had housed the First Presidency, the Quorum of the Twelve, and the Church Historian's Office—to the east wing of the new Church Office Building. James B. Allen, my dissertation adviser, had just been called as assistant church historian in January. Knowing of my commitment to research Brigham Young and of the desire of the church historian, Leonard Arrington, to understand a cache of Brigham Young–era records before the move, Jim arranged to get us together. At the luncheon where we got acquainted, Leonard made me an offer I could not refuse. In essence, he asked: "Will you come to Salt Lake this summer and go through some Brigham Young papers? Nobody knows what they are, how they got there, or why they are there. We need to know about them so that we can catalog them and get ready for the move."

I was already under contract with the Church Educational System to teach in California, where I would be responsible for a couple of small, part-time institutes. But I thought that going through the papers in the basement of the Church Office Building would be an amazing way to spend the summer, an opportunity to get into the original records and begin serious work on Brigham Young.

Most of the manuscripts, including many Brigham Young documents, were then housed in the Church Historian's Office on the third floor of the Church Administration Building. The records I was assigned to review, however, were in a basement storage room filled with ductwork, with books and papers crammed into all the crevices of the window well and around the ductwork from floor to ceiling. The room was interesting, but what it contained made it even more so. Every morning I would go into the quaint third floor space so long occupied by the Church Historian's Office, say hello to Dean Jessee, Jeff Johnson, and others who were there, and then make my way to the basement.

Let me digress for a moment about doing research back in those days. Though Professor Hirshson had not felt welcome, many other scholars had. In 1972 I daily found Robert J. Woodford in the cramped reading area doing the seminal work on the Doctrine and Covenants that became his dissertation.[6] Edward Leo Lyman was there many days, working on what became his dissertation and later his book, *Political Deliverance*.[7] People who were truly dedicated could do great work in the old Church Historian's Office. As a young scholar in the 1940s, long before he became the church historian, Leonard Arrington was given sage advice by an old hand at research in the incomparable collections of the Church Historian's Office. Rather than getting discouraged, he was counseled, "Just keep going in until you're part of the woodwork, and eventually you will be able to see anything you need to!" Arrington's deeply researched, richly detailed dissertation was eventually published by Harvard University Press as the impressive *Great Basin Kingdom*.[8]

Stanley Hirshson was just wrong. He was impatient. He expected to have everything made available to him the first day he walked in the door. One could do great work, but it required patience and diligence.

Even a patient Leonard Arrington, however, had not gained access to the materials in the basement overflow storage, and no one was certain what was there. Soon, and day after day, I found myself going through fascinating records, most of them from the Brigham Young era. Among the things I uncovered were massive ledger books, some of which said on the spine, "Trustee in Trust" or "Brigham Young Sr." Brigham Young's office was the economic center of Utah Territory. Books labeled "Trustee in Trust" were for church-owned businesses; books labeled "Brigham Young Sr." were for companies that Brigham Young oversaw more directly. These ledgers, stacked in piles and seemingly untouched for decades, had the potential to reveal the economic life of early Utah, the foundation of which was a system based on scrip and trust, not coin. Historian Ronald G. Watt, whom the department hired in the early days of professionalization, retired in 2008 but has since returned as a missionary with an assignment that includes finalizing the cataloguing of those impressive ledgers—and better understanding their uses.

Another interesting discovery I made in that basement relates to the mail system. The early Saints accused the government of tampering with the mail during the Utah War in 1857 and 1858. As I sorted these basement papers I found copies of the correspondence of Alfred Cumming, who in 1857 traveled west to replace Brigham Young as governor. If the United States government tampered with the Latter-day Saints' mail, apparently, in turn, the Saints had access to the mail of the governor-to-be. I also found materials that had to do with the confrontation between the federal government and early Utah officials in the 1850s that led to the Utah War.

For example, in 1852 U.S. president Millard Fillmore insisted that Brigham Young answer a string of charges from his critics. Fillmore had been a friend to Brigham Young and Utah, and the Saints reciprocated: Brigham Young designated Fillmore in

Millard County as Utah's territorial capital. But eventually the political cost of keeping Brigham Young in office caused President Fillmore to accede to the critics to the extent that he asked Brigham Young to formally answer the charges of those critics as published in the *Congressional Globe*, the *Congressional Record* of the day. The result was a hundred-page manuscript written by Brigham Young's clerks, with Willard Richards apparently taking the lead. In that manuscript, the clerks, speaking for Brigham Young, answered the charges point by point, either with facts or with hyperbole. The manuscript begins by saying:

> For me to attempt to prove a negative, on the general tenor of said Report, made up of hearsays and declarations, without a shadow of testimony on the affirmative, would be as extra judicial as it was for Don Quixote to perpetuate his war fame at the battle of the windmill; or as it was for the giant Kill-all to load a hundred and twenty four cannon to the brim to shoot a musquito. Cash for cash, and credit against credit, I therefore make my explanations in the coin I receive, simple declarations, with this difference, i.e. between coin counterfeit and true.[9]

The letter then responded to the charges as enumerated in the *Globe*.

This was a fascinating document, one hundred pages written in the name of the president of the church to the president of the United States, though we never could find proof that it had been finalized and sent because the document does not appear to be among Millard Fillmore's papers.

One of the charges listed in the *Congressional Globe* was that, according to Judge Perry E. Brocchus, President Young had said, "Zachary Taylor is dead and gone to hell, and I am glad of it."[10] Zachary Taylor was a recently deceased president of the United

States. Brigham Young responded that he hadn't said any such thing. Instead, it was his counselor, Heber C. Kimball—and Kimball had added that if Brocchus felt the statement was in error, Brocchus could check when he himself went to hell.

In the official response from Brigham Young's office, President Young's clerks represented their leader as saying, "If Judge Brocchus does not find 'General Taylor in hell when he gets there,' it may be incumbent on Elder Kimball to acknowledge a false prophecy; but how is he to be convicted before hand? . . . If to prove the thing, [Brocchus] is disposed to go to hell forthwith, if he don't find his friend Taylor there, I will be responsible that Elder Kimball will acknowledge his error. But if it prove true, the Revd Elder [Brocchus] will have to foot the bill, and get out of hell the best way he can."[11]

This is not the only thing in Brigham Young's papers that suggests both that his office staff employed humor to deflect criticism and that they enjoyed such humor. When it was proposed that Utah was guilty of gross crimes and misdemeanors because of plural marriage, Brigham Young's clerks created an official-looking affidavit acknowledging that Utah was guilty and affirming that, as punishment, the entire territory should be declared a federal prison. Anyone not guilty under the forthcoming act, they said, should vacate the premises forthwith.[12]

Clearly that summer of 1972 got us into a number of interesting records. These were not the heart of the Brigham Young collection; that came later. But they were important, and this gave us a glimpse into significant records that had not yet been mined by other historians.

Several times a week during that summer, I would give a report to Leonard Arrington on what I had found and we would discuss its significance. Leonard was probably even more delighted than I was to learn of all these wonderful documents.[13] There was so much to sort through that I could not review it all before my summer fellowship was to expire. Naturally, Leonard did not want the work to stop, so he approached me with a proposition. "You haven't finished. I hired you to do a job, and it's not done. You can't leave." I responded that I had a contract to teach with Seminaries and Institutes in southern California, had already arranged for movers, and therefore, "I can't *not* leave!" He went away a little dejected, only to return to the topic two weeks later. "I've talked to Joe J. Christensen, the associate commissioner of church education, and he says you can stay. Now will you stay?" So I stayed, and not just for a year or two, either.

REASSEMBLING BRIGHAM YOUNG'S COLLECTION

In November 1972, the entire historical collection was successfully moved from the Church Administration Building to the new Church Office Building. Staff accomplished this by pushing carts loaded with books and manuscript boxes from the lower level of the Church Administration Building through the underground parking plaza and into the east wing, where the treasures got new homes on the third and fourth floors. Once settled into our new home, we finally had the opportunity to try to reestablish the Brigham Young collection. I remember joking with other archives staff members that when we were done we would dedicate a room to the tens of thousands of pages of sources Stanley Hirshson never used in his biography of Brigham Young—huge letterpress copy books, each with a thousand or more outgoing letters, tens of thousands of telegrams and incoming letters, many journals, massive account books, and a large number of other documents.

Our challenge was to go through the department's holdings, especially the subject and chronological files, and to pull together the documents that had once been part of Brigham Young's office. I spent about half of my ten years at the Church Historical Department searching through the nineteenth-century collections and looking for letters to and from Brigham Young, along with anything else that had been created by or once cared for in his office.

Many clues besides the words "Dear President Young" helped us figure out what was and was not his. Endorsements and other file notations were enormously helpful, but so were such things as a small registry of materials created by Evan Green, who for a time worked in the president's office. Among other items, we found a filing index that showed how the pigeonholes in the church president's writing desk had once been labeled. Several presidents whose papers I came across had a "crank file" for strange, off-the-wall letters. In Brigham Young's case, he received a number of letters from "Elijah," which went into the crank file, although his office didn't call it that. The filing list says, "Balderdash. See Trash." They had a pigeonhole labeled "Trash" for letters that did not merit response or follow-up.

Eventually we were able to reassemble much of the collection that was once housed in President Young's office. The notations on the various records, such as filing notations on the back of documents, helped us to identify something as belonging to Brigham Young's office, and once those materials were reassembled, it was possible to better understand both the notations and the filing system. We had no illusions that we knew the original order of the documents, although in some cases we had a pretty good idea. Why does that matter? It is important because records provide more information if they are reviewed in context. We can then learn how records relate to other records, how they were used, and how they were filed.

That project involved a massive effort. When I left to go to Brigham Young University in 1982, Christy Best continued the work. There may still be a few loose ends, but it is nevertheless a wonderful collection, and we have it because of the dedication that generations of record keepers displayed in preserving and protecting those documents.

DOCUMENTARY EDITING
EFFORTS SINCE THE 1970S

The work of Dean C. Jessee, Jeff Johnson, Max Evans, and later successors such as director of the Church Archives Steven R. Sorensen created the kind of archival foundation required for the success of larger-scale documentary editing projects like *The Joseph Smith Papers*. Similarly, the research on Joseph Smith done over a lifetime by historians such as Richard L. Anderson, Ronald O. Barney, and Larry C. Porter has laid a scholarly foundation. The two together make possible the publishing of a comprehensive edition of *The Joseph Smith Papers*.

When Dean Jessee started working in the cage in 1964, he realized immediately that the church had a magnificent collection of Joseph Smith materials, and almost from that beginning he had a vision of what must eventually be done with them. In 1943, the two hundredth anniversary of the birth of Thomas Jefferson, historian and editor Julian P. Boyd launched the nation's first fully professional and modern project of documentary editing— the publication of *The Papers of Thomas Jefferson*. Boyd and his assistants labored until 1950 gathering and preparing materials before they published the first volume, but volumes started to appear with some regularity thereafter (nineteen volumes in print by 1974). The volumes available by the time Dean Jessee started at the Church Historian's Office in 1964 provided him with a vision for what he hoped one day to see done for the papers of Joseph Smith.[14] As Boyd was doing for Jefferson, as Leonard W. Labaree was doing for Benjamin Franklin (an edition I relied heavily on when I wrote my master's thesis),[15] and as still others were doing for John Adams and George Washington, so Dean hoped that the Church Historian's Office might one day do for Joseph Smith. This became his vision.

When Leonard Arrington was called as the church historian in 1972, out of all the employees in the Church Historian's Office (soon to be reorganized into the Historical Department of the church), he selected Dean Jessee to become the first full-time historian in the newly organized History Division, the division charged not with collecting and preserving the records but with using them. He invited Dean to find the right documents and help get them into print.

Although Dean was most interested in Joseph Smith, for a variety of reasons it became clear that for publication he should start with a collection he also cared about and had previously done work on: the letters of Brigham Young to his sons. In 1974 that collection was published in what was called the Heritage Series, copublished by the Church Historical Department and Deseret Book.[16] Dean then resumed his work on Joseph Smith's papers. He published seminal articles that extended our understanding of the records kept by and for Joseph Smith[17] while also getting several important documents into print. This work continued at Brigham Young University when, in 1982, Leonard became the director of the Joseph Fielding Smith Institute for Church History instead of the church historian and director of the History Division of the Church Historical Department.

In 1984 Dean Jessee published *The Personal Writings of Joseph Smith,* the first of his several volumes of Joseph Smith documents.[18] To celebrate this landmark publication, we had a small gathering on the BYU campus. Jeffrey R. Holland, president of the university, and a number of other campus leaders attended the event. I remember saying, in effect, "This changes the landscape. Stanley Hirshson could write about Brigham Young without using his papers. But after this, you can't write about Joseph Smith without using his papers." That was not an accurate prophecy. The first edition of Joseph Smith's personal writings sold tens of thousands of copies among Latter-day Saints and even more when it was reissued in 2002, but the volumes did not equally penetrate the library and academic markets where historians and writers could easily access them. Eventually we understood that we had to do something more ambitious.

That more ambitious initiative was first conceived of as an edition of nine or ten volumes, perhaps with an index and a reference volume, to bring the total number of volumes to a dozen. By that time, Leonard had retired and I was serving as director of the Smith Institute. Although I made certain that Dean had student help and all the support and encouragement we could muster, it was still mainly a one-man effort to publish the papers of Joseph Smith. Blessed with talent and energy, Dean published two volumes in the late 1980s and early 1990s before, for a variety of reasons, the third volume stalled. Dean continued his efforts to get his arms around the whole corpus of Joseph Smith documents, but the publishing was at a standstill.

By the late 1990s it became clear that we needed an even bigger project—and that Dean Jessee could not do it alone. By the summer of 2000, an ambitious plan had been prepared as a collaboration between the Church Historical Department and

BYU, with the editors to be drawn mainly from Brigham Young University professors: Grant Underwood, Richard L. Jensen, and William G. Hartley of the Smith Institute; Alexander L. Baugh, Steven C. Harper, and Andrew H. Hedges from Religious Education; and David J. Whittaker from the Lee Library.

In June 2000 Barbara Oberg, one of Julian Boyd's successors as the editor of *The Papers of Thomas Jefferson*, spent a couple of days with us at Brigham Young University and at the Church Archives. Later some of our people visited her operation at Princeton. These exchanges helped us prepare for a larger and more professional project. Richard L. Bushman, professor of history at Columbia and a member of the board of the Hay Papers, also contributed enthusiasm and expertise. By early 2001, with the endorsement and assistance of Richard E. Turley Jr., managing director of the Family and Church History Department, we were ready to seek official authorization from church leaders to publish all of Joseph Smith's papers in the church's possession.

By March 2001 we were also ready for an unusual meeting with Utah businessman and philanthropist Larry H. Miller. Larry had long been interested in history, and he often used history in his teaching—whether he was addressing executive MBA students at BYU, the senior executives of his companies, or the young people he taught in church assignments. He did the same when he spoke to the civic or church groups he was often invited to address. Ironically, however, Joseph Smith had never been the subject of any of his talks until the fall of 2000. Then, on three different occasions between November 2000 and January 2001, he felt prompted to change his topic at the last minute to speak about Joseph Smith.

Larry popularized a phrase that has become something of an informal motto among Joseph Smith Papers personnel: "How many coincidences does it take before you realize it's not a co-incidence?" Unbeknownst to Larry, at the time he was prompted to talk about Joseph Smith, we were working to launch the Joseph Smith Papers Project. Unbeknownst to us, in early 2001 Larry had experienced his first-ever encounter with the personal papers of Joseph Smith during a presentation of the original documents by Ron Barney of the Church Archives. Larry had simply at-tended the presentation with a friend, David Brown, who with his wife was preparing to serve a mission in Kirtland, Ohio, but it was an experience that Larry could not get out of his mind. All this was context for a meeting in early March 2001, ironically in the same east wing conference room where Larry had weeks before first seen the manuscripts. Forever after Larry called this the "meeting of the three Rons and a Steve"—Ron Esplin, Ron Walker, Ron Barney, and Steve Sorensen.

I was director of the Joseph Fielding Smith Institute at the time, and Ron Walker was the institute's director of research. Ron had said to me, "Now, you give him the pitch and tell him what it's all about. You can sell that better than anybody, but you can't close; you'll be too timid. You need me to get in there and close the deal." So Ron Walker jumped in at the end and boldly announced, "This is the church's Manhattan Project," a charac-terization Larry never forgot, "and it will take at least $100,000 to make a dent in it." Larry thought for a minute and then said, "How about $125,000 a year for the next three years?" He told us later that he had known then that that initial sum was just a down payment—and that he was convinced we had no clue how much money this was going to take. Ultimately, he provided us with an endowment, the annual income of which dwarfs that first com-mitment. Were it not for the Millers' generosity, we could not do what we do today with a staff of archivists, historians, and editors working together on Joseph Smith's papers.

We also learned later how Larry's encounter with the documents had prepared him for our meeting. Instead of a quick tutorial on Kirtland history, Ron Barney used original documents to vividly explain several crucial episodes in the life of Joseph Smith and the history of the early church. That "show and tell" with Ron Barney was the first time history buff Larry had even thought about the original manuscripts, and it changed his life and eventually ours. Larry left the archives that day knowing in his heart that there was something he was supposed to do with the documents. He soon called Ron Barney and said, "We've got to talk!" He made a follow-up visit with Ron that seemingly resolved nothing. "There's something here that I'm supposed to help with. Do you know what it is?" he asked Ron.

"No," Ron responded, but he went on to speak about various ongoing projects. Sitting on a filing cabinet in Ron's office was a copy of volume 3 of the Papers of Joseph Smith, still unpublished, which I had asked Ron to read as part of our effort to get the book back on track. Ron pointed to the volume and talked about Dean Jessee's work. Then Larry left, still puzzled.

The next time Larry visited Ron Barney, he was animated. "I know what I'm supposed to do!" he told Ron. "I know too," insisted Ron, and they then shared their insight that it had to do with Dean Jessee's work. Their conversation that day deepened Larry's conviction that he was supposed to help with the Joseph Smith Papers, which set the stage for the "meeting of the three Rons and a Steve."

At that meeting in March 2001 we told Larry that an expanded Joseph Smith Papers project was not yet approved. "We think we'll get approval, but it has not yet come. There is still some risk involved." He chuckled and said that he knew a little about risk. "I think I can handle that." In April 2001 we received official approval from the First Presidency and Quorum of the Twelve Apostles to publish all of Joseph Smith's papers. In June, a number of church leaders (Elders Neal A. Maxwell, Jeffrey R. Holland, and Henry B. Eyring of the Quorum of the Twelve, and Elders Bruce C. Hafen and D. Todd Christofferson of the Seventy) along with BYU president Merrill J. Bateman (also of the Seventy) met at BYU with project personnel to officially launch the Joseph Smith Papers Project.

Since that time we have built a staff and moved the entire project to the Church History Department in Salt Lake City—and next to the historical documents we are publishing. Although much of the day-to-day work can be accomplished with colored scans of the original documents, having access to the originals as needed and being able to look at the documents together in context has been a great blessing. Some of the work we have since done could not have been accomplished at BYU, leading us to realize again that for historians and archivists who are doing intensive work on the early history of The Church of Jesus Christ of Latter-day Saints, no place on earth is better than the church's own archives.

THE NEW CHURCH HISTORY LIBRARY

I had hoped that the new Church History Library might be known as the Church Archives, because for me that is the heart of the department, but I must agree that "Church History Library" is more inviting. That is the approach today: come learn our history, your history. Jeff Johnson rescued a brass plaque from the old Church Historian's Office that for years stood above the door into the holdings, a plaque that said, "Library. No admittance."

In contrast, today's wonderful new library will stand as an invitation to all to come in and explore the rich heritage that is the history of the Latter-day Saints.

The remarkable collection of documents found in the Church History Library owes much to Willard Richards and his successors; to the custodians of the nineteenth and early twentieth century; to the pioneers of professionalization—Dean Jessee, Jeff Johnson, Max Evans, and Steven Sorensen—and to the many professionals who care for the collection today. The combined efforts of all these individuals and many others allow us to protect this heritage, learn from it, and finally, today, to make more of it easily accessible to more people. Increasingly, researchers and writers everywhere will have access to this treasure trove of documents that have been carefully preserved by dedicated individuals and are now housed in the secure, climate-controlled storage vaults of the Church History Library.

NOTES

1. Davis Bitton, "Ten Years in Camelot: A Personal Memoir," *Dialogue: A Journal of Mormon Thought* 16, no. 3 (Autumn 1983): 9–20.
2. Predating both Dean Jessee and Jeffery Johnson was a professional librarian, Janet Jenson, who had a master's degree in library science from Brigham Young University.
3. Bernard Mayo, *Henry Clay: Spokesman of the New West* (Boston: Houghton Mifflin, 1937).
4. Stanley P. Hirshson, *The Lion of the Lord: A Biography of Brigham Young* (New York: Alfred A. Knopf, 1969).
5. Fawn Brodie, *Thomas Jefferson: An Intimate History* (New York: W. W. Norton, 1974).
6. Robert J. Woodford, "The Historical Development of the Doctrine and Covenants," 3 vols. (PhD diss., Brigham Young University, 1974).

7. Edward Leo Lyman, "The Mormon Quest for Utah Statehood" (PhD diss., University of California, Riverside, 1981); Edward Leo Lyman, *Political Deliverance: The Mormon Quest for Utah Statehood* (Urbana: University of Illinois Press, 1986).

8. Leonard J. Arrington, "Mormon Economic Policies and Their Implementation on the Western Frontier, 1847–1900" (PhD diss., University of North Carolina, 1952); Leonard J. Arrington, *Great Basin Kingdom: An Economic History of the Latter-day Saints, 1830–1900* (Cambridge: Harvard University Press, 1958).

9. Brigham Young to the President of the United States, June 11, 1852, Brigham Young, Office Files, Church History Library, The Church of Jesus Christ of Latter-day Saints, Salt Lake City.

10. "Utah Territory: Report from the Secretary of State," *Appendix to the Congressional Globe*, new series, vol. 25 (Washington, DC: John C. Rives, 1852), 85.

11. Young to the President of the United States, June 11, 1852, Young Office Files.

12. Citizens of Utah to the President of the United States, "Burlesque Petition," Young Office Files.

13. Ronald K. Esplin, "Documents and Dusty Tomes: The Adventure of Arrington, Esplin, and Young," *Journal of Mormon History* 25, no. 1 (Spring 1999): 103–12.

14. *The Papers of Thomas Jefferson*, ed. Julian P. Boyd, 36 vols. (Princeton, NJ: Princeton University Press, 1950–2009).

15. *The Papers of Benjamin Franklin*, ed. Leonard Woods Labaree and William Bradford Wilcox, 39 vols. (New Haven, CT: Yale University Press, 1959–2008).

16. Dean C. Jessee, ed., *Letters of Brigham Young to His Sons* (Salt Lake City: Deseret Book, 1974).

17. For example, see Dean C. Jessee, "The Reliability of Joseph Smith's History," *Journal of Mormon History* 3 (1976): 23–46; Dean C. Jessee, "Return to Carthage: Writing the History of Joseph Smith's Martyrdom," *Journal of Mormon History* 8 (1981): 3–19.

18. Dean C. Jessee, ed., *The Personal Writings of Joseph Smith* (Salt Lake City: Deseret Book, 1984).

Ronald O. Barney

9

A GENERATION OF CHURCH HISTORY:
A PERSONAL VIEW

I HAVE been asked to describe my personal experience with the
acquisition, preservation, and distribution of Latter-day Saint
history while working in the Church Historical Department, now
the Church History Department. I have spent more than half my
life there. My primary intent is not to present an autobiography,
though I will say a few things about my integration into Mormon
history and something regarding my early and minor connection
to the preservation and study of Latter-day Saint history. But my
main purpose is to say something about the business of ensuring
that what has gone before us is not forgotten.

Preserving our Mormon past, our heritage as the surviving
manifestation of the restoration of Jesus' gospel in the last days—
indeed, preserving our identity—to me seems about as important

*Ronald O. Barney is an archivist and historian in the Church History
Department of The Church of Jesus Christ of Latter-day Saints and associate
editor for the Joseph Smith Papers Project, now housed in the Church
History Library in Salt Lake City.*

as anything we can do to perpetuate our faith. I've been disappointed that those who concur with this thinking appear to be in the minority of our culture, though I am optimistic for the future for a number of reasons.

My paper is divided into two parts: the autobiographical sketch and some points about important advances in the church's efforts to preserve and share its history.

1. MY STORY

I began working in the Church Archives after finishing coursework for a master's degree in history at Utah State University. My wife and I, then having a couple of small children, decided to wait for two or three years before we reentered the doctoral chase, and an opportunity presented itself that we believed would temporarily fit into our plan. A chance meeting with Ronald G. Watt, at the time a manager in the Church Archives, led to my employment with the church.

I had known Ron Watt for several years because I had done research at the Church Historical Department while working on an undergraduate history degree at Weber State College. Ron invited me to apply for an open position in the Church Archives. I had not finished writing my thesis at the time but decided to apply anyway. I wasn't hired. But within a few days another position opened, and I became a church employee on Halloween day, 1977.

I knew something about the Church Historical Department at the time because of the research in Mormon history I had done there as an undergraduate. The man who first introduced me to the Church Archives was a Weber State University history professor named Donald R. Moorman. Moorman was a colorful man, not a Latter-day Saint, who boasted to his students about his expertise concerning Brigham Young as well as his outsider/insider connection to the Church Archives. (I was, however, suspicious of him early on when, one day in a Utah history class, he bet there wasn't one student in the class who could tell the difference between margarine and butter. Now, I know my way around butter!) There was a charm about Don Moorman. With impish delight, he would play upon his unusual surname every chance he got by declaring to his students that his next son would be named Jack.

Don Moorman scheduled his classes so that every Friday he could travel to Salt Lake City to visit the east wing of the Church Office Building, the location of the Church History Department from 1972 to 2009. Moorman was given access to the papers of Brigham Young and spent years reading them and taking notes. He planned to write the definitive biography of Brigham Young, whom he brashly professed to understand better than anyone else living.

I have surmised that his ambition was to produce a work about the second Latter-day Saint prophet with more veracity than Stanley P. Hirshson's book *The Lion of the Lord: A Biography of Brigham Young,* published by Alfred A. Knopf in 1969—a volume poorly received in Utah history circles. But the enormity of the task, I think, finally sidetracked Moorman into working on a book about Camp Floyd, a volume that his colleague Gene Sessions finished after his death.

I appreciated Don Moorman's efforts to involve his students in hands-on, primary research. He regularly invited students to join him at the Church Archives on Fridays, and I was one of the few who accepted the invitation. He had promised me a good experience, and I looked forward to my first visit to the Church Historical Department. That particular Friday morning Dr. Moorman took me to the east wing of the Church Office Building, showed me the Church Library, and then took me to the second floor, where he proudly introduced me, one of his students, to the people who manned the public service area of the department—in particular, to the man who supervised the archives search room, a place I would later supervise myself.

As Don buoyantly marched off to his designated domain, an area reserved for him to work on the Brigham Young papers, I was interviewed by the supervisor. He asked me what I wanted. I explained that I had a senior paper to write and thought I would do something on polygamy. He told me that topic was forbidden, and I would have to choose another topic. I therefore received my introduction to church archival protocols at the time.

My interest in Mormon history didn't come from Weber State's history department. I had walked the streets of Nauvoo and explored the Carthage Jail in the late 1960s as a young missionary when there still seemed to be an innocence to those sacred places.

Upon returning from the Northern States Mission, head-quartered in Chicago, I enrolled at Weber State, located a few miles east of where I had grown up. It was at the LDS institute of religion located just north of the Weber State campus, where I became a student of Mormon history. Initially Eldon L. Haag and then Kenneth W. Godfrey pulled me into the study of early Mormonism. Because of questions I had about Joseph Smith, Eldon Haag—who taught an institute class called "Joseph Smith: His Life and Teachings"—had me read Klaus J. Hansen's *Quest for Empire*, the first piece of scholarly Mormon history I ever read.[1] Ken Godfrey encouraged me to tackle the Political Manifesto of 1896 instead of polygamy for my senior paper. This resulted in an essay that included my first oral history interview, a compelling discussion for me, with one of apostle Moses Thatcher's family members, who shared the domestic view of some difficult matters of that period. Another institute teacher, Joseph C. Muren, who later became a member of the Second Quorum of the Seventy, introduced me to a thoughtful study of anti-Mormon literature. These were the good men who nudged me toward what later became my professional encounter with serious Mormon scholarship.

I ended up spending far too much time in the institute library, which distracted me from my music major across the street at the college. Eventually I changed my major to history and scrambled to obtain the credits I needed to graduate in that discipline. By the time I left Weber State, I knew I wanted to study Mormon history. As a result of my loitering at the institute, I departed there with more hours of religion than any other institute student at that time. In fact, I did a lot better at the institute than I did at the college—not something to brag about, but in the long run it proved to be the lodestar that defined my career and, more important, shaped my thinking about the faith upon which I rely and in which I believe.

From Weber State my wife and I moved to Logan, where I began to work on a master's degree at Utah State University, ostensibly in American history. But outside my rudimentary study of historical methodology and historiography, I admit that Mormon history consumed the remainder of my attention and affection. In the small orbit in which I lived at the time, there was a palpable excitement about the study of Mormon history and its inextricable partners, Utah and western regional history.

I spent my wonderful first year at Utah State among a group of bright, enthusiastic students, though only a couple of them were interested in Mormonism. Especially significant for me was what I learned about historiography and historical inquiry as it applied to the study of Mormonism and to Latter-day Saint history. But perhaps the most important thing I experienced at the university, where S. George Ellsworth and Charles S. Peterson were my primary instructors, was the encouragement to understand the literature of Mormon history and those who produced that literature.

It started this way. Besides his duty as professor of history at Utah State University, George Ellsworth was also the editor of the *Western Historical Quarterly*, even back then a substantial historical journal. Professor Ellsworth had been teaching at USU since the 1950s, after receiving his PhD in the late 1940s from the University of California–Berkeley, earned, in part, from his doctoral dissertation on early Mormon missionary work.

During my second year at USU I received an assistantship wherein I worked as what is now called the Graduate Editorial Fellow—I was a member of the small editorial staff of the *Quarterly*. I screened submitted manuscripts and compiled the titles of recently published articles for publication in the journal.

One day Professor Ellsworth handed me something somewhat unrelated to my job: a stack of papers that he said were the returns from a survey he had solicited in 1976 from members of the Mormon History Association (MHA), then an organization about a dozen years old. He had asked over a hundred members of the MHA, the majority of the leading academic scholars and students of the history of Mormonism at the time, to identify and then rank the top ten books and articles ever written about Mormon history, Utah history, or both. He received a healthy number of responses and asked me to compile the data—something he could have easily done, but he forced the exercise on me.

That duty became a turning point for me, I suppose. I became exposed to the thinking of many of the most prominent Mormon scholars of that generation, many of whom explained in the questionnaire why they had made the choices they did. I determined to read those publications. My entire career thereafter has been based upon that platform of historical writing.

While I intended to work only a couple of years for the church before reapplying to school, I never did receive my terminal degree, though several times I tried to leave church employment and return to school. Instead, my dreams of academia fading as the years passed, I became an archivist with on-the-job-training in the Church Archives. At the time the most visible face of institutional church history was the History Division, led by Leonard J. Arrington and a fresh generation of professionally trained historians. They were making an impact on Mormon studies in an unprecedented manner.

2. ADVANCES IN CHURCH HISTORY

While the History Division was producing history, ultimately leading to its transfer to Brigham Young University as the Joseph Fielding Smith Institute for Latter-day Saint History, there was also a Library-Archives Division maturing into professional competence. This latter group was composed primarily of people with advanced degrees in history and library training. And in the popularization of an expanding archival discipline in America, training in strategies, techniques, and procedures provided our people with many of the skills and training to elevate our competence to a professional level. Over the years I found that this group of skilled and committed folks, my colleagues, gained unusual insight into the history of Mormonism.

Almost by definition, the people who gather and collect the documentation, who arrange and describe the materials, who catalog and create finding aids of the historical records that they process, become competent in understanding the records for which they care. By virtue of the very process of carefully preparing a document or collection for public or institutional access, the archivist becomes an authority on sources—sometimes the most informed authority on the records. Good history requires perspectives and expertise from both historians and archivists; indeed, it requires a combination of those who gather and prepare the sources for consumption and those who provide context and interpret the records through their writing.

The archival side of the equation generally receives less attention, but we cannot overstate the importance of the archivists' contribution in cultivating the ground for the history to blossom. I credit the leaders of the Church History Department and what was once identified as the Church Archives Division for seminal innovations that may appear routine today but that are hardly so.

In particular I want to note the contributions to church history of the late director of the Church Archives, Steven R. Sorensen, with whom I worked for thirty years. (Steve died in May 2009 of pulmonary fibrosis after a long and enervating ordeal.) As part of his training while obtaining history and library science degrees from Brigham Young University in the 1970s, he learned the rudiments of archival practice and administration at the Harold B. Lee Library's Special Collections. Soon after he joined the staff at the Church Archives in 1980, he envisioned what was required to improve the manner in which the church gathered and cared for its historical records. His initial assignment in the Church Historical Department, which may have seemed mundane, proved to be of great consequence to the church's archival future.

It was an exciting time. Regularly released documentary discoveries of a remarkable nature rose above water-cooler chatter in the archives to capture newspaper and magazine headlines. Mormon history had never received so much widespread attention and scrutiny.

But there were side effects from this elevation of attention to the Mormon past. What could be termed "tabloid history" often substituted for traditional historical procedures in the 1980s. This was a time when there existed unprecedented access to the church's archival collections, which, along with fantastic finds from private dealers and collectors, created an undisciplined frenzy as otherwise unknown history wonks debated the legitimacy of Mormonism in symposia, conferences, and periodicals. Of course, a few seasoned scholars offered balance and urged caution in the atmosphere of uncertainty, but the movement acquired such proportion that the most reasonable voices were often the faintest to be heard. It took the murders of two people in Salt Lake City in October 1985 to downshift the media's and the Mormon historical community's accelerating momentum to more reasonable stasis. The fallout from this era lingered for years.

In the early years of this period, absent the glare of attention and notoriety, Steve Sorensen and his colleagues cataloged the church's local unit records—the minutes and other documentation created by the branches and wards, the districts and stakes, and the missions—equipping him with the foundation of what became his almost unprecedented understanding of the church's archival collections. Now, I do not want to give the impression that the advancements within the Church Archives were all of Steve's making. That simply was not true. Some very good people for a very long time had accomplished many things upon which church archivists built thereafter. Steve entered an arena where others had performed nobly for several generations.

After four years of cataloging church-owned records—in other words, arranging and describing the church's enormous manuscript archival collection—Steve supervised the church's archival cataloging division for two years before becoming the supervisor of archives research in 1986. His domain was the department's archives search room, the point of entry for patrons who accessed the church's collections. The reading room was on the second floor of the Church Office Building's east wing. There, in a glass-enclosed office in the center of the search room, Steve interviewed the scholars and other researchers who applied to use the Church Archives.

He had a two-tiered purpose while conducting the interviews. First, he recognized his responsibility to ensure that church-produced and church-owned records were made accessible in a proper manner by qualifying those who used the archives. And second, his business was to help the scholars and patrons understand the broad scope of what was available to qualified researchers. What followed was the creation of an environment of professionalism where finding aids and the archives catalog actually fostered research, be it scholarly or genealogical, for those who applied to use the church's collection. Having researched records in dozens of repositories from the East to West coasts, many of them with Steve, I can confidently say there were few parallels in the other repositories—government, university, or private—to the proficient manner in which Steve supervised our research facility.

Steve was appointed director of the Church Archives in 1989, and over the course of the next sixteen years he implemented a number of innovative strategies and procedures that advanced Church History Department objectives for the future. For example, he fostered a collection development plan to acquire records in several regions of the world, including Latin America, Eastern Europe, Africa, and Asia. Though other Historical Department employees had earlier initiated numerous ground-breaking efforts to gather Mormon history worldwide, such a calculated strategy had not been enacted by the church since the days of Andrew

Jenson. These church ventures have blossomed into an enlarged global vision that will significantly impact the history of Mormonism in the future.

Other measures of consequential magnitude were simultaneously applied. The couple of items I am going to mention may not seem like much, even to academic folks. There is little glamour in what I am going to describe. And in light of the several other successes achieved by church archivists through the years, these developments lack the spotlight-quality of highest achievement. But it is just for that reason that I am going to note them. To me they seem especially important because they helped fashion the future of church history, and because they will help the church manage its remarkable collection for succeeding generations.

A new cataloging system. We in the Church History Department have had difficulty in helping patrons understand that the purpose of the Family History Library is different from that of the Church History Library. Unlike the Family History Library, which seeks to make its records as widely available as possible, our intent is, first, to ensure the proper management of the church's collection, and second, to create an environment where the church's records will foster the study of Latter-day Saint history and heritage. I state this to give context to two Church History Department achievements I wish to note: the advance from paper-based finding aids and cataloging procedures to a new electronic cataloging system and the improved management of church records. I address these matters because I perceive a widespread misunderstanding of how the church administers its records. Plainly stated, the church has been accused of archival tactics rooted in deceit and intrigue because it carefully administers access to the records in its keeping.

Just a few years into my employment, department leaders enacted an initiative to stride forward in the administration of the church's records. In the early 1980s, most American record repositories still administered the cataloging and accessibility to their collections, including their finding aids, the same way they did in the previous generation. Since then the archival tool kit has expanded considerably, allowing repositories to manage their records in ways that previously were not possible. The leaders of the Church History Department seized the opportunity. The size of the church's considerable collection, described by some as huge and unwieldy, precluded the intellectual control required to properly administer the records. How could an organization, in light of public demand, properly administer access to its records when the vast scope of the documents prevented the institution from knowing the content of its own collection?

Church archivists, assisted by technological tools, thereafter implemented a program and process to obtain the previously elusive intellectual control of the church's records that included these features: an overall description of each collection with an accession and cataloging number to track the collection, the provenance of the record's origin, the scope of its content, and its size and physical condition. The new catalog entry for each collection also included information, such as the names and locations of people and events, to make the content of the collection more useful for church purposes and more accessible to research.

Some of this work, of course, had been performed in rudimentary fashion in years past. But the limitations of a paper-based cataloging system severely hampered the management of such an enormous collection. Once this advancement in strategy and technology was implemented, information about a collection could be searched electronically at any given moment. It was, I believe, an exciting advance in church history, allowing the church to move forward with confidence in administering its records.

But even with the advances in technology, the work required to do this was enormous. Much imagination, experimentation, and deliberation were required to determine how to best manage the limited resources available in money and personnel to efficiently handle the daunting task. But through all of this effort, our capable staff developed procedures to process the church's archival records from the time of their acquisition to the completion of cataloging and intellectual control to their eventual housing in the archives. Simultaneously, the records held by the church for generations—the dreaded backlog of unprocessed material— were finally brought under control through the new system. It was a watershed achievement for the church's archival staff. Because of this initiative, every archival collection now acquired by the Church History Department receives initial cataloging markers that track the document through the whole cataloging process. While no one on our staff would argue that we are omniscient about the church's archival collection today, because of this significant, lengthy, and labor-intensive effort the church has a good understanding of what it has and how to administer it.

Management of church records. This leads to a discussion of another milestone: the improved management of church records. The church has taken a lot of heat through the years regarding the administration of its archives. Because the church restricts access to some records, it has been accused of fearing its history, hiding its past, and covering up misdeeds. I remember well the uproar in the early 1980s when a distinguished local history professor claimed in a public forum that he had received insider information indicating that the Church Archives was closed. One of the local newspapers picked up the story, and in no time at all the rumor spread. The church, the account revealed, had closed its archives because it feared its own past, suggesting it couldn't handle historical scrutiny. (A quarter of a century later, perhaps a residual sentiment of this erroneous perception remains.)

Later, one of my colleagues told me he was likely the one who triggered the story because of a remark he made to the professor, though what he said, he told me, was not at all what the professor reported. My colleague had divulged that the History Department was implementing a new process for defining what records could be made public and what materials the church was not obliged to release.

Indeed, such a process was devised to clarify the archivists' understanding of the church's records. This was not a covert operation. Most other reputable repositories in the United States, public and private, have devised classification systems to assist them in managing their holdings.

Church History Department leaders and staff settled upon an intuitive, understandable, and defensible method of classifying church records and accessibility. This gave the department the ability to administer church records with confidence based upon knowledge rather than hesitancy resulting from a lack of information. As a result of the process, many records became more accessible, while others, primarily created for administrative use on a local or general church level, were restricted from public access.

Three types of records are restricted: (1) Records containing private information—for example, documentation about a living person, such as a church membership record, an application for missionary service, or a record of a financial donation to the church. Privacy matters are of concern in the modern world, and all responsible repositories try to respond accordingly. (2) Records containing sacred information, such as specifics regarding the church's temple ceremonies or other particulars relating to temples. (3) Records containing confidential information—that is, information generated in confidential settings, or records intended to be conveyed only in confidential circumstances. This includes church headquarters department records, material about local unit disciplinary matters or other priest-penitent-type documentation, and security matters relating to church members or facilities. The church makes no apology for restricting access to these records.

A significant portion of the church-owned records in the Church History Library is accessible to the public. The records that generally fit this status include not only several hundred thousand photographs and audio and visual records but also many diaries, journals, letters, reminiscences, memoirs, and local unit records of public meetings that contain no private, sacred, or confidential information.

In my judgment, it is important to understand one last thing about the church archival collection and how the church does business with its records. The public must recognize that in several ways the Church History Library is unlike many other academic repositories, especially institutions like university libraries. Most university libraries, for example, divide their collection of printed books, periodicals, and other printed materials from the manuscript or non-published collections they administer. The latter grouping, usually called the university special collections, involves the library function that houses and administers the manuscript collections determined by the university to fit its specialization or emphasis, such as the American Indian or Western Americana materials at a university in Western America. Here one may find diaries, photographs, correspondence, and other similar types of documentary records, and sometimes rare printed materials.

Still another collection of materials in the university library may be described as the archives, where the university's own institutional records are housed. Here one might expect to find university council and committee records, presidential papers, and the like. Often these institutional materials, because they were created in confidential, nonpublic settings, are not open to the public. The public generally expects that the manuscripts and rare books in a university's special collections will be accessible, while recognizing that the university's institutional materials are kept from public scrutiny for understandable reasons. Many business organizations operate in the same manner—their institutional records are kept confidential.

The Church History Department has large collections of all three types of records described above: a print collection, a manuscript collection, and an archival collection. The reference desk in the new Church History Library is the point of entry for all of them. The archival collection—in other words, the church-produced records that contain private, confidential, and sacred information—will generally not be accessible to the public. Thus, when the church's institutional records are restricted from access, even though the vast majority of the special-collections-type records are readily available, an unwarranted reputation of restriction and closure may be applied to the Church Archives. My personal experience over the past generation is that the staff try to make most of the special-collections-type material as accessible as possible.

A new era in church history. In closing, I want to say something about changes in the department that encourage me very much. I see these changes as an eyewitness, and they are worth noting. Because they are unfolding gradually, far too gradually for some people in our anxious and hurried times, I perceive that people do not realize the revolutionary nature of what is happening in the Church History Department.

The church historian and recorder, Elder Marlin K. Jensen, and the assistant church historian and recorder, Richard E. Turley Jr., have created and direct, with hands-on involvement, an unprecedented publication program to present church history to the church and to the world. Some of these efforts are well known. The Mountain Meadows Massacre project, which has been so well received; the Joseph Smith Papers Project, the rollout of which is just beginning but which portends a paradigm-changing impact upon the study of the Prophet Joseph and the early church; and the creation of the Church Historian's Press, abundantly pregnant with possibilities, are just the most visible evidences of what I believe will be a remarkable advance. It is also the case that, while outside my area of direct observation and participation, the church's other historical properties—including the Church History Museum and the church historic sites—will illustrate the commitment of the church to preserving and presenting its remarkable heritage to church members and to the world. These advances—combined with a new state-of-the-art Church History Library building; the management of the church's records by a competent, well-trained staff; and a growing recognition that our remarkable heritage and legacy are born of our memory of the past—foster the optimism that I envision for church history's future.

NOTE

1. Klaus J. Hansen, *Quest for Empire: The Political Kingdom of God and the Council of Fifty in Mormon History* (East Lansing: Michigan State University Press, 1967).

Though the general church office buildings are located in Salt Lake City, The Church of Jesus Christ of Latter-day Saints is not an "American" religion but rather a diverse, worldwide church with members scattered across the globe. (Courtesy of Brent R. Nordgren.)

10

DOING THE IMPOSSIBLE: DOCUMENTING THE WORLDWIDE CHURCH

IN 1987 Dennis B. Neuenschwander was called to preside over the newly created Austria Vienna East Mission, which comprised Central, Southern, and Eastern Europe and the Middle East. Soviet domination, though waning during those days of glasnost and perestroika, was still in effect. Travel through the mission was difficult, and basic necessities that would support missionaries—such as food, reliable medical care, and a communication infrastructure—were hard to find. Feeling as if he was facing an impossible task, President Neuenschwander asked Elder Russell M. Nelson how serious the church was about missionary work in this vast area. Elder Nelson replied, "The Lord is master of the unlikely, and he expects the impossible."[1]

Matthew K. Heiss is a member of the global support and training division at the Church History Library, The Church of Jesus Christ of Latter-day Saints.

I sometimes feel we are facing a similarly impossible task in the Church History Department.

The department is required to document an ever-expanding worldwide Latter-day Saint population. Currently there are more than thirteen million church members in 177 countries, territories, and protectorates.[2] These Latter-day Saints speak many different languages, have had varying opportunities for education, and live in diverse economic circumstances; therefore, their record-keeping capabilities are uneven. Nevertheless, a record of their stories and history is essential "for the good of the church, and for the rising generations" (D&C 69:8).

To capture and preserve their experiences, the Church History Department will have to rely on nonprofessional and volunteer helpers living in local congregations throughout the world who have a vested interest in their local Latter-day Saint history.

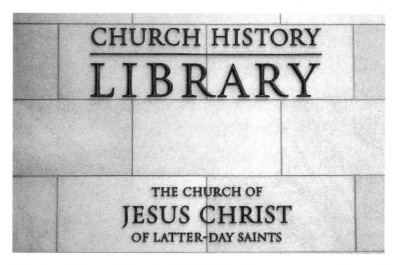

The Church History Library in Salt Lake City houses a massive collection of church history artifacts that can be accessed by the general public. (Courtesy of Brent R. Nordgren.)

The task will require priesthood leader endorsement, basic instructions for people at various education levels, and a reliable technical infrastructure.

In this paper I will describe where we have been and where we are going in terms of documenting global church history. For me, this is a unique opportunity to put a mark in the sand and see what we can accomplish in the next few years.

EVOLUTION OF THE CHURCH HISTORY DEPARTMENT

In a Church History Department meeting, assistant church historian Richard E. Turley Jr. and Steven L. Olsen, then the managing director of the Church History Department, briefly described the history of the department by discussing four different and necessary eras:

1. Clerical era
2. Professional era
3. Collaborative era
4. Global era

Their presentation was informative and culminates, as you can see, with a global focus. Here is a brief summary of what they said.

The first era, clerical, began on the day the church was organized: April 6, 1830, when the Lord declared that "there shall be a record kept" (D&C 21:1). Church historians such as Willard Richards and Joseph Fielding Smith, as well as capable assistants such as B. H. Roberts, wrote the history of the church. The staff of the Historian's Office supported those efforts.

The professional era began when the church started hiring library, archives, and museum professionals who had training in and a love for history. These professionals helped the department implement nationally accepted standards of cataloging, expand its collection efforts, and automate its finding aids.

The collaborative era began when Steve Olsen was asked to be managing director of the department. Steve knew the department could not move ahead significantly, especially in gathering the history of the global church, without partnering with the leaders of the church and other church departments.

The collaborative efforts of the Church History Department improved significantly when Elder Marlin K. Jensen was called and sustained as the church historian and recorder in the April 2005 general conference. It had been sixteen years since the church had a functioning historian and recorder.

Today the Church History Department is poised to enter the global era in a systematic and sustainable way. The question naturally arises: why focus on the global church now? Here are four possible answers; there may be more.

First, if the Church History Department does not begin to document the global church, the department will become increasingly irrelevant to the majority of Latter-day Saints. Most church members have a limited personal connection to nineteenth-century church history. While they know about the foundational events of the Restoration that define all Latter-day Saints, the majority of members today do not trace their ancestry in the church back to the nineteenth century. Instead, most members are pioneers in their own families, having joined the church during the last half of the twentieth century.

Consider this interesting comment made by President Gordon B. Hinckley:

> In 1936, 68 years ago, one of the secretaries to the Quorum of the Twelve told me what a member of the Twelve had told her. She said that in the coming general conference there would be

announced a program which would come to be recognized as even more noteworthy than the coming of our people to these valleys as pioneers. . . .

I wondered back in those days how anything the Church did could eclipse in anyone's judgment the historic gathering of our people to these western valleys of the United States. That was a movement of such epic proportions that I felt nothing could ever be so noteworthy. But I have discovered something of interest in the last short while.

We receive many prominent visitors in the office of the First Presidency. They include heads of state and ambassadors of nations. . . . In our conversations not one of these visitors mentioned the great pioneer journey of our forebears. But each of them, independently, spoke in high praise of our welfare program and our humanitarian efforts.[3]

It is crucial that we document contemporary issues such as our humanitarian efforts, the Perpetual Education Fund, small temples dotting the earth, and church growth in foreign lands. These issues have immense relevance to many, if not most, of our brothers and sisters around the world.

Second, historically speaking, the current era is one of the greatest in the history of the Lord's kingdom on earth. The church has grown significantly since it was first organized. On the day Gordon B. Hinckley greeted the public as president of the church, he said, "The most serious challenge we face, and the most wonderful challenge, is the challenge that comes of growth . . . but what a remarkable and wonderful challenge that is."[4]

What a time to be a historian and to be able to document the church's "most serious" and "most wonderful" challenge!

A third reason for the department's focus on global church history is this: if the department does not begin to systematically document the worldwide church by acquiring and preserving records, others will fill this vacuum. This is not entirely a bad thing; clearly we need to partner with others. But I firmly believe the church should assume the leading role in this work so that it can maintain a focus on remembering the great things of God and on witnessing to the truth of the Restoration. These should be the guiding principles for this documentation effort—not someone's private agenda.

And finally, we will begin the systematic documentation of the global church because we are ready to do so. I base this statement on two critical factors: (1) A few members of the Church History Department staff have spent the past two decades learning how to document the global church. We have traveled extensively and experienced much of the church's wonderful diversity. We are now ready to introduce sustainable history-gathering programs for the entire church. (2) Technology has finally enabled us to better document the global Latter-day Saint experience. I will address this subject following a brief review of our past efforts throughout the world.

HISTORY OF DOCUMENTING THE GLOBAL CHURCH

Preserving global history is not a new endeavor for the Church History Department. Early on, Andrew Jenson traveled the earth as a one-man documentation machine. Beginning in 1891, he went on several "missions," as he called them, to visit nearly every Latter-day Saint settlement in the Rocky Mountains, from Mexico to Canada, all of the historic sites of the Restoration, and finally "all the missions and conferences and nearly every important branch of the Church in the entire world."[5] Ah, those were the days!

In the 1970s a few History Department employees—Gordon Irving and Richard Jensen in particular—traveled to Mexico, South America, and Western Europe, where they recorded interviews with church members. After these trips ended in 1977, fourteen years passed before the Church History Department staff ventured out into the world again. In 1991 a few department employees began doing fieldwork in places such as France and Finland, Mongolia and Malawi, Russia and Romania, Tonga and Thailand, Korea and Kiribati, and many other nations. All of these important efforts have provided a solid foundation and a deeper knowledge of the challenges and possibilities facing the Church History Department.

As I share with you a brief history of these pioneering efforts, I must also pay tribute to a man who had an inspired vision of what the department could do: Steven R. Sorensen. Almost twenty years ago, Steve realized it was critical for the department to gather records from congregations worldwide and from people whose stories would provide insights into the manner of life, faith, and works of church members across the globe. Steve's vision, combined with the trust he gave a few of us, has prepared us to take the next step.

What was the catalyst for our renewed global documentation efforts? In my opinion, there were three important events:

In June 1985 the Freiberg Germany Temple, the only temple ever to exist behind the Iron Curtain, was dedicated. Several years later Elder Russell M. Nelson wrote: "In retrospect, it is evident that the influence of that temple has been immeasurably great. The spiritual radiation from that temple deserves much credit for the changes that have occurred. This house of the Lord was the pivot point around which all good things subsequently seemed to turn."[6] One of those "good things" was the reinstitution of world-wide collecting projects by the Church Archives.

As mentioned, Dennis B. Neuenschwander was called to open the Austria Vienna East Mission in July 1987 and was given responsibility for all of Central, Southern, and Eastern Europe, and the Middle East. This enabled us to document the beginnings of the church in nations that were once behind the Iron Curtain.

In November 1989 the Berlin Wall came crashing down. We could now capture the voices, memories, and records of church members who had lived in East Germany—members of whom President Thomas S. Monson had spoken in some of his general conference addresses. With the demise of communism, these faithful Latter-day Saints could now speak for themselves without fear of reprisal.

In 1991 two fairly new Church Archives employees, Jeffery L. Anderson and I, flew to Germany, where we recorded the oral histories of the East German Latter-day Saints who survived four decades behind the Berlin Wall. For the first time in many years, the Church Archives was capturing the story of Latter-day Saints throughout the world in their own language and within their own context. And some of the stories were truly remarkable.

Henry Burkhardt, the man who presided over the East German congregations, described what it was like to be a target of the infamous Stasi, the East German secret police. He knew spies were in the branches and said he would rather have a faithful church member reporting accurate and harmless information than a person with an ax to grind giving the Stasi false and damaging information.[7]

These early trips led other staff members to travel throughout the world. Armed mostly with tape recorders and later with digital recording devices, they were charged with the responsibility of helping to capture the story of the global church.

Between 1991 and 2005, Church Archives staff members visited sixty-three countries. The department's oral history collection almost doubled, going from 2,390 interviews in 1991 to nearly 4,700 oral histories in the short span of fourteen years. Most of these interviews came from Saints outside the United States.

Why oral history? Sometimes people ask me, "Why did you primarily seek oral histories during these international trips?" There are two main reasons.

First of all, oral histories are easily transportable. It was simpler to carry a recording device, batteries, and tapes than to acquire large quantities of records in the field and carry them back to Salt Lake City. A few of us would fill suitcases with records, but mostly we focused on gathering stories through oral history.

We dreamed of the day when we could capture records in the field, microfilm or digitize them, send the films or images to the archives in Salt Lake City, and leave the original documents in the hands of their owners. But during those early years, the technology and other factors were not in place to make this possible in a systematic way.

Second, we used oral history because we learned that while every member of the church may not be a record keeper, everyone has a story to tell. Some of the people we met, especially in Africa, the Philippines, Polynesia, and Eastern Europe, did not live in record-keeping societies. Illiteracy and poverty prevent people from recording and preserving their stories in ways that are common in the Western world. Once in Nigeria, my coworker and I held a focus group to learn about local record-keeping capabilities. We learned about a generational dividing line: Many people in their forties were the first literate members of their families.

Their parents, some of whom were Latter-day Saints and still lived in villages, were unable to read and write. We also learned it is nearly impossible to preserve documents in the typical Nigerian home. Termites and humidity wreak havoc with records.

In Russia and Bulgaria we learned from a series of focus groups that there is another type of generational dividing line. Younger people who grew up in the glasnost and perestroika era were more likely to keep personal records than their parents were. Older members of the church still feared the possibility of the KGB confiscating personal records and using them to hurt people.

As enjoyable as oral history was, we were also well aware that we were not using a perfect documentation tool. We learned that oral history has its limitations. One quick example of this:

In May 1995 I was in St. Petersburg, Russia, recording oral histories with some of the first Russian Mormons. St. Petersburg was the last leg of my three-week trip. I had already worked in Kiev, Ukraine, and Moscow, where I had recorded many oral histories, most of which were in Russian. I had studied three years of Russian at the University of Utah and was feeling pretty comfortable asking questions and then listening to responses I could only partially understand. Sometimes voice intonation and body language alerted me that it was time to ask the next question. I felt confident I was getting the gist of all the stories.

I always asked about each person's conversion experience. I wanted to know how each person received her or his testimony. This was a question I had already asked countless Russian and Ukrainian Latter-day Saints.

In St. Petersburg I interviewed Alexei Akimov, one of the earliest converts in Russia, having been baptized in January 1991. At the appropriate time in my interview I asked him, "Как вы обрили свое свидетельство?" which I thought meant, "How did you receive your testimony?"

In English Brother Akimov kindly said that I had just asked him, "How did you shave off your testimony?" The Russian words for "have found" and "shaved off" are the same except for one vowel. I now wonder how many other Russians and Ukrainians I asked about their shaving habits when I thought I was asking about their conversions.

I have framed that page of the transcript from my interview with Brother Akimov. I keep it on my wall as a constant reminder of my own limitations and of the need for locals to be engaged in documenting their own history.[8]

The church is flat. Another radical change has altered the course of our documentation efforts, making it possible to gather records in a way that was not imaginable twenty years ago. We have entered a new era with brave new possibilities. What was that change?

The world and the church suddenly became flat. I am referring to the phenomenon documented by Thomas L. Friedman in his book *The World Is Flat.*[9]

Digital capabilities, cheap electronic storage, and the ability to send large electronic files across the Internet are revolutionizing our documentation efforts. Now, instead of having to bring all records to Salt Lake City for microfilming, we can have records scanned in the field and then transferred electronically to the Church History Department. My coworker Clint Christensen has started a pilot program in Mexico to do just that.

A larger question now looms on the horizon: How should the Church History Department implement a worldwide program of acquiring, preserving, and making available church history records that will bless the lives of Latter-day Saints?

LESSONS FROM THE HISTORY
OF THE CHURCH

I believe Latter-day Saint history offers the Church History Department an inspired paradigm for systematically documenting the global church. I am referring specifically to the recent developments in church governance. I don't take credit for these ideas; they are based on chapter 44 of Bruce C. Hafen's biography of Elder Neal A. Maxwell, *A Disciple's Life*.[10]

Four principles will guide our department in expanding our efforts worldwide:

1. A focus on core values
2. Delegation
3. Decentralization
4. Strategy

First, let's look at how these principles apply to the development or evolution of church governance.

A focus on core values. Referring to some changes that were occurring in the early 1980s, Elder Hafen wrote, "The movement of the Twelve toward being a council of generalists was further accelerated by a globalization process across many cultures that required more emphasis on the church's general core values rather than on particular programs."[11]

It is interesting that around this time, the leaders of the church introduced the church's core values as a three-fold mission. In 1981 President Spencer W. Kimball said, "My brothers and sisters, as the Brethren of the First Presidency and the Twelve have meditated upon and prayed about the great latter-day work the Lord has given us to do, we are impressed that the mission of the church is threefold: To proclaim the gospel . . . ; To perfect the Saints . . . ; To redeem the dead."[12] Since then, other landmark documents have increased our focus on basic or core values, such as "The Family: A Proclamation to the World" and "The Living Christ."

Delegation. As the church grew throughout the world, the First Presidency delegated an increasing load to the Quorum of the Twelve Apostles. The Twelve, in turn, delegated an increasing load to the Seventy and to stake presidents.

For example, there was a time when general authorities ordained every bishop, an apostle ordained every patriarch, and general authorities set apart every missionary. Now those ordinances are performed locally by stake presidents.

Decentralization. The church's governing bodies have been decentralized to meet the needs of a growing and global church. In 1965 there were twelve assistants to the Quorum of the Twelve and seven Seventies serving as general authorities. Regional representatives were first called in 1967. Now there are eight quorums of the Seventy. Most of the men who serve in these quorums reside in their own countries and in their own homes.

In 1997 President Hinckley, after announcing the formation of some of these quorums, said: "With these respective quorums in place, we have established a pattern under which the Church may grow to any size with an organization of area presidencies and area authority seventies, chosen and working across the world according to need. Now, the Lord is watching over His kingdom. He is inspiring its leadership to care for its ever-growing membership."[13]

These new quorums of the Seventy and the increasing responsibilities of area presidencies indicate a decentralization of authority necessitated by growth.

Strategy. In the 1980s and 1990s, according to Elder Hafen, members of the Twelve and the First Presidency focused more on their spiritual ministries and let the Seventies and stake presidents take charge of operational matters. In 2000 Elder Maxwell said members of the Quorum of the Twelve were "Apostles first and then we may have assignments, rather than having the assignments seem to dictate our role to us."[14]

The Twelve became "more strategic and less tactical," less specialized or tied to a program, auxiliary, or geographical area. Elder Bruce R. McConkie would say he wasn't "the Archbishop of South America" even though he oversaw church affairs there. In other words, his role was not to specialize in South America; rather, he was an apostle of the Lord first and foremost.[15]

APPLICATION TO THE CHURCH HISTORY DEPARTMENT

So once again I ask, How should the Church History Department implement a worldwide program of acquiring, preserving, and making available church history records that will bless the lives of Latter-day Saints?

I believe that by following these four principles—a focus on core values, delegation, decentralization, and strategy—we will be able to support area presidencies with Church History Department programs, thereby ensuring that the history of the church is relevant to all Latter-day Saints. We are already well underway in applying some of these principles.

A focus on core values. Under the direction of Steven L. Olsen, Church History Department staff focused on defining the department's core values. Steve insisted that these definitions be simple and easy to understand—no easy task for those of us who sometimes revel in the complexities of history and historiography and their theological underpinnings. But we sought to follow this direction in describing the department's efforts to *preserve* and *share* the history of the Lord's work on the earth with the purpose of blessing Latter-day Saints worldwide.

The process of defining the department's core values helped us better communicate to church leaders and members what we do and why we do it. It also helped department staff stay focused on the larger vision.

Delegation. Delegation began back in the 1960s with the professionalization of the History Department. The department no longer consists of a church historian surrounded by clerks and research assistants; rather, it is staffed by a core of professional curators, librarians, and archivists. Instead of Elder Marlin K. Jensen, our current church historian, giving all the presentations, writing all the books, recording all the oral histories, and determining what to acquire, now the professional staff shoulders those responsibilities. I believe Elder Jensen trusts the staff's expertise.

The staff has also taken a major step forward in delegating some of our work to church-service missionaries. Our next step is to delegate even further to missionaries in the field, who can help with the acquisition and processing of church history records and other Church History Department programs. This is already happening in Mexico and Ukraine. This naturally leads to the notion of decentralization.

Decentralization. Decentralization depends on our ability and willingness to empower local Latter-day Saints, who already have the requisite language skills and cultural understanding, to represent the Church History Department and do the work of documentation in their own nations.

In 2008 we began a concerted effort, with area presidency approval, to implement two Church History Department programs, one in Mexico and the other in Ukraine.

Mexico. We had long set our sights on Mexico because:

- It has the second-largest Latter-day Saint population in the world (after the United States), with 212 stakes, 41 districts, 21 missions, and 13 temples.[16]
- The church has a lengthy history in Mexico, going back to 1874.
- Several themes in Mexican church history have become significant themes in the globalization of the church.

In analyzing our collections, we discovered that most manuscript records in the Church Archives relating to Mexico are either from the Mormon colonies in northern Mexico or from Anglo missionaries, mission presidents, or general authorities. We have a good collection of records relating to early efforts to establish the church in Mexico, but not much reflecting the growth of the church in the last half of the twentieth century. Virtually all native representation was either in the local records, such as minute books, or in the oral histories recorded by Gordon Irving in the 1970s and 1980s.

For the most part, there had been no concerted effort by our department to acquire records relating to the church throughout Mexico. Private collecting efforts in the country had preserved many records that would not have survived otherwise.

Given the incomplete state of the Church History Department collection, and with the encouragement of the Mexico Area Presidency, we put together an experimental program headed by a Mexican couple called to serve as Church History Department missionaries. Santiago and Rosa Mejia of Puebla were called as area church history advisers by the area presidency. The Mejias have launched programs in two areas, Puebla and Tecalco, where they are focusing on three acquisition projects: (1) they are recording interviews with some of the released Seventies from Mexico; (2) they are locating elders' and sisters' missionary journals in the possession of stake and ward leaders in the Puebla area; and (3) they are recording oral histories with ten Puebla women to be sure that female perspectives are captured.

Not long ago the Mejias held "cultural and historical nights" in five stakes. Local church members were encouraged to bring personal records, photographs, artifacts, and artwork to these events. More than four hundred people attended and learned more about the purposes of the Church History Department.

Within a year's time, one hundred significant new collections about Mexican church history were acquired for the Church History Department, including twenty oral histories, eighteen of which were recorded and processed by the Mejias.

For example, the Mejias had the wonderful opportunity to record an interview with ninety-five-year-old Dario Perez. Brother Perez, a second-generation Latter-day Saint, was born and raised in the town of Tepecoculco, where he still lives. In his November 2008 interview, Brother Perez shared many fascinating details about his life. He described how he reluctantly agreed to be president of the town at a young age, believing the Lord wanted him to serve in this manner. He was able to accomplish much in this position, but certain corrupt individuals sought to take his life.

On one occasion he was walking home at night when a force pushed him to the ground. This happened three times. Finally he remained on the ground until he heard the sounds of a group of men who had been lying in wait for him. They eventually left, and Brother Perez was able to return home safely.

As Brother Perez shared this and other experiences with the Mejias, Church History Department staff and local members made scans of his personal documents and photographs. The materials are now preserved in Mexico as well as in the Church History Library, enabling future generations to learn about this stalwart pioneer.[17]

We hope to use this model to build a permanent program for documenting Mexican church history. It may also serve as a template for preserving history in other areas of the world.

Ukraine. The Lord often opens doors when we are ready to walk through them—or when we are *almost* ready. The program we are establishing in Ukraine is a testament to this principle.

In May 2008 Marc and Cherylee Hall were called to serve as church history missionaries in Kiev. Like the Mejias in Mexico, the Halls were an inspired gift to the Church History Department. They had already served five missions, including one in which they presided over the Russia Yekaterinburg Mission, as well as two other missions in Russia.

Europe East Area president Paul B. Pieper charged the Halls to prepare a book that would capture the first twenty years of the church's history in Ukraine and would be part of the celebration for the Kiev temple dedication. The Halls traveled throughout Ukraine gathering photographs and personal records, as well as recording interviews. These records will be used for the book and will also be sent to the Church History Library to build the Ukraine collection.

Now, I realize there is one minor problem with the Ukraine program: Elder and Sister Hall are Americans from Sacramento, California. But at this point, some places in Ukraine lack experienced local members to run Church History Department programs, and so expatriates will have to do. One of the Halls' responsibilities is to try to find local church members who can replace them when their mission is completed.

The Mejias and the Halls represent a huge step forward in the Church History Department's attempts to delegate and decentralize. Their missions were made possible by the vision and endorsement of the Mexico and Europe East area presidencies.

This brings me to the final way in which the Church History Department can mirror the evolution of the church's global governance model.

Strategy. Just a few years ago the History Department staff had a model for documenting the global church, which we developed to near perfection. We called it the "Team-of-One-and-a-Budget" approach. A staff member would select a country, gather records from former missionaries or immigrants up and down the Wasatch Front, and then travel to the country, where he or she would spend a week or two recording interviews with the locals.

It was great while it lasted, but it was also fraught with problems. As I have illustrated, there were severe language barriers. There were also health and safety issues. In November 2005, Clint Christensen and I almost wound up in a Nigerian jail in Port Harcourt. It took a seventy-five-cent bribe to get us and our two Nigerian friends away from the crooked cops and back on the way to the airport.

Also, each of us who traveled throughout the global church came home with the nagging frustration that we had only scratched the surface. We realized that as church archivists, we could not do everything that needed to be done.

Now our task is to become global program managers. The Church History Department, with inspired direction from the church historian and recorder and also with crucial input from the area presidencies, will soon offer a variety of programs to the worldwide church. The area presidencies may select those programs that fit the area's needs and circumstances or develop their own projects, which the Church History Department will support. This is how we will move into the future.

In some respects I am sorry to say, "Gone are the days of being a team of one with a budget." Being a latter-day Andrew Jenson was fun. But I know our new direction is necessary and inspired. Church History Department staff now work to support local initiatives that meet area presidency objectives. In return, we will reap the benefits of extending our reach through local church members. In doing so we also hope to raise up a new generation of Latter-day Saint record keepers.

This may be what former church historian Leonard Arrington envisioned many years ago when he said: "As the Church becomes more international, it will become increasingly important to write the history of Latter-day Saints in their homelands. By reconstructing these people's lives, we give their heirs a sense of their LDS heritage as well as provide real models for their own lives, models with whom they can identify." He said further, "When history comes from the grassroots, from where the people live and worship, the individual can identify personally with the general Church experience."[18]

In conclusion, I have taken some liberty with a verse of scripture that I believe sums up our need to make church history more accessible and therefore more relevant to Latter-day Saints worldwide: "For it shall come to pass in that day, that every man shall hear the fulness of the gospel [including church history] in his own tongue, and in his own language, through those who are ordained unto this power, by the administration of the Comforter, shed forth upon them for the revelation of Jesus Christ" (D&C 90:11).

NOTES

1. Dennis B. Neuenschwander, "Reflections on Establishing the Gospel in Eastern Europe," *Liahona*, October 1998, 38.

2. Conversation with Rosemary Chibota, Statistical Records, Finance and Records Department, The Church of Jesus Christ of Latter-day Saints, January 5, 2009.

3. Gordon B. Hinckley, "I Was an Hungred, and Ye Gave Me Meat," *Ensign*, May 2004, 58.

4. Jay M. Todd, "President Gordon B. Hinckley: Fifteenth President of the Church," *Ensign*, April 1995, 6.

5. Andrew Jenson, *Latter-day Saint Biographical Encyclopedia*, vol. 1 (Salt Lake City: Andrew Jenson History Company, 1901), 262–63.

6. Russell M. Nelson, "Drama on the European Stage," *Ensign*, December 1991, 9.

7. Johannes Henry Burkhardt Oral History, interviewed by Matthew K. Heiss, 1991, typescript, The James Moyle Oral History Program, Church History Library, The Church of Jesus Christ of Latter-day Saints, Salt Lake City.

8. Alexei Vasilevich Akimov Oral History, interviewed by Matthew K. Heiss, 1995, typescript, Moyle Oral History Program.

9. Thomas L. Friedman, *The World Is Flat: A Brief History of the Twenty-first Century* (New York: Farrar, Straus and Giroux, 2006).

10. Bruce C. Hafen, *A Disciple's Life: The Biography of Neal A. Maxwell* (Salt Lake City: Deseret Book, 2002), 449–53.

11. Hafen, *A Disciple's Life*, 453.

12. Spencer W. Kimball, "A Report of My Stewardship," *Ensign*, May 1981, 5.

13. Gordon B. Hinckley, "May We Be Faithful and True," *Ensign*, May 1997, 6.

14. Hafen, *A Disciple's Life*, 453.

15. Hafen, *A Disciple's Life*, 453.

16. Telephone conversation with Rosemary Chibota, February 18, 2009.

17. Clint Christensen, "'Go Ye into All the World': An International Church," in *Behold, There Shall Be a Record Kept among You: Collections of the Church History Library of The Church of Jesus Christ of Latter-day Saints*, ed. Richard E. Turley Jr. (Salt Lake City: Church History Library, 2009), 58–60.

18. Leonard J. Arrington, "On Writing Latter-day Saint History," in *Voyages of Faith: Explorations in Mormon Pacific History*, ed. Grant Underwood (Provo, UT: Brigham Young University Press, 2000), 1, 4.

Church members in countries such as Peru, Chile, Argentina, and others in South America are building a rich heritage of faith and devotion to the gospel of Jesus Christ. The preservation of their vibrant history is vital to understanding the Church as a whole. (Courtesy of Corbis.com.)

Mark L. Grover

11

DOCUMENTING THE HISTORY OF THE CHURCH IN SOUTH AMERICA: RECOVERING THE PAST

W HEN I was studying history in graduate school, my professors said I would likely spend most of my research time in
archives looking at historic documents and reading dusty, antique
books. After thirty years of working on the history of the church
in South America, I have modified my graduate school expecta-
tions of the research process. Though I have passed many hours in
archives, I have spent significantly more time traveling on buses
from city to city, staying in two-star hotels, sitting at kitchen
tables looking at photographs and documents, and occasionally
shedding tears while listening to members' reminiscences about
the early years of the church in South America. From cafe bars or
park food carts, I have purchased many late-night meals—often

---

*Mark L. Grover is a senior librarian at the Harold B. Lee Library at
Brigham Young University.*

Argentine empanadas or Brazilian pastéis, with soft drinks being Quatro Pomelo or Guaraná Antarctica.

My experience as a historian is less like the description of my college professors and closer to the adventures of early church historian Andrew Jenson, who spent considerable time in the field interviewing and collecting documents. I have no complaints about this difference and consider my work to be one of the great spiritual blessings of my life.

Researching the history of the twentieth-century global church is no easy task. Although the Church History Library in Salt Lake City continues to collect important administrative records and has an active oral history program, access to interviews and records may be restricted by time or by content.[1] A second challenge is that the church's impressive document-collecting program has only recently been extended significantly outside the United States.[2]

Consequently, while the Church History Library contains many personal records relating to nineteenth-century Mormonism, few comparable records are available for the twentieth-century global church. This is also due to the fact that international members are not migrating to the United States as they did in the past. Without local church archives to collect personal records, the documents often remain in local ward or stake clerks' offices or in the possession of members. In almost every place I visit, I hear stories of bishops and stake presidents running out of space or moving to a new building and therefore discarding historical documents. Luckily, some members have saved those records, often retrieving them from garbage cans and keeping them in their possession.

Most local leaders appreciate the story of the church in their areas, but often they do not know what documents to collect and preserve. They also may feel overburdened with administrative tasks and may believe they do not have time to focus on history. As a result, unofficial approaches to collecting and disseminating global church history have evolved.

Latin America provides an interesting case study. There the work of preserving history has been influenced by personalities, geographical considerations, mixed support from local church leaders, and different levels of training. Local, often amateur, historians have great passion for the story of the church in their countries and are providing valuable service.

This paper will review and evaluate three approaches to collecting Latter-day Saint historical documents in Latin America and will conclude with general observations on the challenges involved in preserving the global history of The Church of Jesus Christ of Latter-day Saints.

SEMINARY AND INSTITUTE INSTRUCTORS

The Seminaries and Institutes of Religion program has played an important role in the development of local historical preservation programs. The curriculum of institutes worldwide includes a class on the history of the church; the approved manual for the class focuses on the church in the United States, with some information on global expansion. Teachers may also discuss local history in these classes. In most cases no published local history of the church in Latin America is available, so teachers often collect information and develop lessons on their own. These lessons may result in a printed document that is distributed to students and occasionally sold to members. Most of the initial volumes of church history for individual countries have come from this type of activity.[3] These lessons have in some cases resulted in the creation of regional historical volumes.

Néstor Curbelo is one of the most prominent examples of an individual involved in this type of history collecting and publication.[4] Néstor was born in San José, Uruguay, and joined the church as a teenager. After serving in the Argentina North Mission and marrying Rosalina Goitiño Ramirez, he moved to Buenos Aires to work as a photographer and planned to study at a university. After his daughter was born, he had to work long hours and abandon his goal. Unable to support his family as a photographer, he was employed as a custodian at the Belgrano Institute building in Buenos Aires. He began teaching classes there, and his teaching abilities were soon recognized. He moved into a full-time position as a teacher and later became director of the institute in Buenos Aires.[5]

Because he needed information on the history of the church in Argentina for his institute classes, Néstor began interviewing early members. He developed a passion for the history of the church in South America. The South American South Area Presidency eventually called him as the area historian, gave him an office, and provided some funding to collect documents and do interviews.

Néstor also served for ten years as a stake president, after which he was called as director of public affairs for the South America South Area. He was able to combine his history interests with public affairs responsibilities, and he traveled and interviewed church members all over southern South America. Eventually he expanded his institute lessons into a book on the history of the church in Argentina; the book is for sale at cost in the Church Distribution Center in Buenos Aires. It was translated into English and published in the United States in 2009.[6]

Néstor's collection of documents is housed in the area office in Buenos Aires. He recorded his initial interviews with audiotape but soon moved to video recording. His interviews are the most important component of what he has done, and his collection includes more than two hundred videos of early members and significant events such as temple dedications. He regularly donates copies of his interviews to Brigham Young University's Harold B. Lee Library and to the Church History Department in Salt Lake City.

Néstor has collected more than one hundred thousand pages of documents and several significant church artifacts, and he also has a valuable collection of more than one hundred thousand historical photographs. He has been careful to do everything under the direction of the area presidency and has cultivated positive relationships with each area president. Most of what he acquired is owned by the church.

After retiring from the Seminaries and Institutes in 2007, Néstor began work as a private historian and filmmaker. He received a grant from a private donor to write, in Spanish, a set of small one-volume histories of the church throughout Latin America. He is also producing documentaries on the church in Latin America for BYU Television International. He admits that he is not a professionally trained historian, and he does not try to write using the historical method. His books are not traditional histories but combine chronology, stories of local pioneers, and numerous photographs. They serve wonderfully for the members but lack the depth and analysis typical of rigorous academic works.

What Néstor has done for the church is remarkable. He is single-handedly responsible for the collection, preservation, and dissemination of much of what we know about the history of the church in Argentina, Uruguay, and Paraguay. He has unselfishly made all of his work available to the Church History Library and BYU. With financial help from the BYU Religious Studies Center, BYU has digitized most of the documents he has collected, and they are available to researchers at the Harold B. Lee Library.

PRIVATE HISTORIANS AND COLLECTORS

Private historians and collectors also contribute to the preservation of local church history. Fernando R. Gómez Páez from Mexico is one such example. Fernando was born in Monterrey, Mexico; his grandmother Genoveva González Gómez was baptized in Pachuca, Hidalgo, Mexico, in April 1925. After serving a mission in his home country and graduating from BYU in 1967, Fernando worked in Mexico but eventually moved to the Philippines, where he bought an electronic components assembly company. Seven years later he sold the company, returned to the Americas, and established residencies in both Mexico and the United States. He has served the church in a variety of capacities, including regional representative; mission president in Merida, Mexico; president of the Missionary Training Center in Santiago, Chile; and president of the Merida Mexico Temple.[7]

Fernando's interest in family history evolved into a hobby of collecting documents relating to the early church in Mexico. He has been aggressive in locating, copying, and collecting historical resources principally by visiting with early members throughout the country. Not only does he own unpublished documents and photographs, but he also has collected early church publications.

Because he lacked the space to adequately house what he owned, Fernando purchased a building across the street from the Mexico City temple and opened the Museo de Historia del Mormonismo en México (Museum of Mormon History in Mexico). He hired a codirector, Sergio Pagaza Castillo, who cares for the materials and conducts tours. The museum maintains a permanent display as well as rotating exhibits that focus on different aspects of the church in Mexico.

Fernando recently purchased an additional building in Provo, Utah, where he plans to create similar exhibits. He conducts historical conferences and develops portable displays directed to church members in Mexico and Hispanic members in the United States. He regularly presents at Mormon History Association meetings and has published four volumes, including an important book on the first Latter-day Saint in Mexico and a book that includes his analysis of the Third Convention movement in Mexico. In 2009 he examined contacts between the church and the Mexican government before the establishment of the missions in the late 1800s.[8]

Fernando has a passion for the history of the church in Mexico. He has spent time and capital to preserve and defend the church throughout the country. He has been cordial and open to students and professionals, and he has been particularly receptive to non-Mormon academics. Though not formally trained, he has learned the historian's trade. Fernando has provided an invaluable service to the church through his collection, preservation, and dissemination of church history to members and historians in Mexico and in the United States. Our knowledge of the early history of the church in Mexico is significantly enhanced by his activities.

MISSIONARY HISTORIANS

Brazil, like Mexico, is home to more than a million Latter-day Saints. Many years ago area authority seventies recognized the need to make a record of the church's history in the country. Their solution was to call local members as missionary historians. The missionaries had a variety of qualifications, though the most important requirements were a willingness to serve and an availability of time.

Flavia Erbolato, an early member from Campinas, was significant in the preservation of foundational records of the church in Brazil. Shortly after her marriage in the late 1940s, she went to

BYU with her husband, Oscar, and then returned to Brazil. She worked several years as a translator and eventually became director of the Church Translation Department in São Paulo. When historical documents were scheduled to be discarded, she saved thousands of pages and kept them in the Translation Department's library. Under her careful supervision, researchers, including myself, were allowed to use the documents.

In 1987 Oscar Erbolato was called as the first history missionary in Brazil and began to organize available records. He was able to collect additional documents as well as conduct a few interviews with early members of the church. Since then, seven missionaries have worked in this position: Elder Paulo Machado, Elder and Sister Demetrio Teixeira Fel and Marilucy Borges, Elder and Sister Roberto and Lucia Viveiros, and presently Elder and Sister Norberto and Rosângela Lopes. Under the direction of these various area historians, calls went out to church members in Brazil and the United States for documents and stories.

Elder and Sister Borges provided a monumental service by collecting and organizing the records geographically. Elder Borges wrote a chronological history of the church based on records collected from the members; the history has not been made available to the public.

Michael Landon of the Church History Department and I spent several years collecting and digitizing church documents in Brazil. In 2004 we went to the states of Santa Catarina and Paraná with two BYU students, and in 2006 I went to the state of São Paulo with three students. We conducted a total of 198 interviews and digitized 32,603 pages. BYU gave us an additional grant in 2008 for a similar project in the state of Rio Grande do Sul and central Brazil, principally Rio de Janeiro. Copies of all the materials we collected and the interviews we conducted are deposited at BYU, the Church History Library, and the Brazil Area Office. A website at the Harold B. Lee Library was established where many of the documents are available online.

OBSERVATIONS

These three different examples are important indicators of the need for some type of systematic approach to collecting the history of the church worldwide. We owe a great debt to faithful members throughout the world who have recognized the importance of local history and have worked to preserve valuable records. The lack of assistance and control by professional archivists and historians has resulted in mistakes but not serious errors. My concern is for the areas that do not have a Néstor Curbelo or Fernando Gómez.

I offer the following observations concerning the collection of historical materials worldwide:

1. In the past, church members were encouraged to send historical materials to Salt Lake City for preservation. As a result, the materials were not accessible to most members and researchers. Today the Church History Department is making efforts to keep records in local areas—an important and needed development.

2. The ability to digitize enables historians to collect documents that would not be available otherwise. Most members are willing to allow their documents to be digitized but are not ready to give them to an archive. I have had numerous experiences in which I was allowed to digitize documents as long as they never left the owner's home. The issue of obtaining proper permission to use the information is important, and a release agreement has to be signed.

3. Digitizing also allows for parts of documents to be copied that are important to the history of the church, when the rest of the document contains personal and private information that should not be released. This is particularly true with missionary diaries. Many former missionaries do not want their personal expressions of weakness or immaturity to be exposed, while sections that describe the opening of a city or a special baptism can be copied.

4. The changing nature of official record keeping in the church is affecting how we will research the story of the church worldwide. For a time, official historical records of branches, districts, wards, and stakes that often contained rich descriptions of events and people were replaced by brief, often lifeless chronological histories of limited value, or by no record at all. More recent records have begun to include better histories. The practice of publishing letters, descriptions, and reports about regions of the church in church magazines does not occur much anymore. Consequently, the primary sources for the history of these areas will have to come from oral histories and missionary diaries.

5. Members outside the United States do keep personal documents related to the church. Almost without exception, when I go into the home of an early member, he or she brings out a box with documents, written histories, diaries, letters, photographs, handouts, notes taken at important meetings, manuals, old scriptures, blessings, and so on. President Spencer W. Kimball's advice many years ago to keep a journal was heeded by many. These personal histories are often as much a history of the local church as they are the story of a family. Descriptions of

spiritual experiences are prominent in members' writings. And native local missionaries keep diaries just as their American companions do.

6. Serious scholars of recent global church history do not have the option of doing all their research in an archive. Going into the field, finding the early members, and copying documents are integral elements of the life of the global church historian.

7. The value of oral histories of both missionaries and early members is significant. Interviewing leaders is not enough. Local members need to be recorded. Though many of these interviews provide limited data on specific events, they often include descriptive stories, particularly of spiritual events. These oral histories have secondary but important functions beyond that of recording historical information. Often older members and missionaries feel they have been forgotten or left behind. The act of recording their history can be a validating experience for them, highlighting the sacrifice and work involved in accepting the gospel in trying times. The interviews may be emotional for them as well as for the interviewer. If the interviewer follows up by sending a transcript to the person interviewed, that document may become a meaningful treasure for the member and his or her family.

8. Returned missionaries may have valuable historical records that need to be collected. Missionaries keep diaries, take photographs, and collect documents such as flyers, lessons, and histories. These documents are important to the local members because in some cases they are the only documentation that exists. Copies of these materials need to somehow get back to the areas for use by the local members.

CONCLUSION

What I have described is probably not significantly different from what has historically occurred in the church, regardless of time or place. Private collectors, church administrators, and missionaries have always been involved in the development of church collections. I also understand that history may be a low priority on the list of church challenges, goals, and responsibilities. But as I have spent the past thirty years eating empanadas and drinking Guaraná, I have learned that members all over the world have great interest in the history of the church.

Most of us want our story to be remembered, particularly when it relates to such important events in our lives as accepting the gospel. The stories of modern pioneers in Mexico, Brazil, or Croatia are as important to the church as the stories of nineteenth-century pioneers in Utah. As a historian, I am eternally grateful for Latter-day Saints such as Néstor Curbelo, Fernando R. Gómez Páez, and Flavia Erbolato who have a passion for local history and who understand the value of a written story, letter, or interview.

NOTES

1. Due to privacy issues, oral history interviews may be accessed a minimum of ten years after the date of the original interview. Access to some interviews and records may also be restricted due to sacred or otherwise confidential content.

2. The Church History Department has collected internationally for many years. However, recently it began decentralizing its operations and is now training local people to identify and collect important records.

3. The following are examples of these publications: Carlos Pedraja, *Historia de la Iglesia en Bolivia* (Cochabamba, Bolivia: Sistema Educativo de la Iglesia, 2001); *Historia de la Iglesia en Colombia: Suplemento para el Curso de Historia de la Iglesia* (Bogotá: Sistema Educativo de la Iglesia de Jesucristo de los Santos de los Ultimos Días, 1986); *Un Bosquejo de la Historia de la Iglesia en Venezuela, 1966 a 1986* (Caracas: Sistema Educativo de la Iglesia, La Iglesia

de Jesucristo de los Santos de los Ultimos Días, 1986); Néstor Curbelo, *50 Años de la Iglesia en Argentina* (Buenos Aires: Sistema Educativo de la Iglesia de Jesucristo de los Santos de los Ultimos Días, 1986); Néstor Curbelo, *50 Años de la Iglesia en Argentina: Cronología para el Estudiante de Seminario* (Buenos Aires: Sistema Educativo de la Iglesia de Jesucristo de los Santos de los Ultimos Dias, 1986).

4. Though I will not focus on Chile, an important though somewhat different model occurred in Chile under the direction of Rodolfo Antonio Acevedo. His thesis at the Pontificia Universidad Católica de Chile was published as *Los Mormones en Chile* (Santiago: Impresos y Publicaciones Cumora, 1990). He has finished two other unpublished histories on the Santiago Chile Temple and the Missionary Training Center in Chile.

5. Biographical information comes from an interview with Néstor Curbelo by Mark L. Grover, July 2001, Montevideo, Uruguay.

6. Néstor Curbelo, *Historia de los Mormones en Argentina: Relatos de Pioneros* (Buenos Aires: Néstor Curbelo, 2000); *The History of the Mormons in Argentina* (Salt Lake City: Greg Kofford, 2009).

7. Biographical information on Fernando R. Gómez Páez can be found in Brittany Karford Rogers, "A Historic Collection," *BYU Magazine*, Fall 2007, 62.

8. Raymundo Gómez González and Sergio Pagaza Castillo, *"El Aguila Mormón o el Anarquista Cristiano": Plotino Constantino Rhodakanaty, el Primer Mormón en México* (Mexico City: Museo de Historia del Mormonismo en México, 1997); Fernando Rogelio Gómez Páez, *Sixta Martínez: A Living Testimony* (Mexico City: Museo de Historia del Mormonismo en México, 2002); Fernando Rogelio Gómez Páez, *The Church of Jesus Christ of Latter-day Saints and the Lamanite Conventions: From Darkness to Light* (Mexico City: Museo de Historia del Mormonismo en México, 2004); Fernando Rogelio Gómez Páez and Sergio Pagaza Castillo, *Benito Juarez and the Mormon Connection of the 19th Century* (Mexico City: Museo de Historia del Mormonismo en México, 2007). The Third Convention was a group that broke away from the church in 1937 over issues of leadership. The group included about a third of the membership in Mexico. They functioned outside the church until 1946, when most returned.

INDEX

Index

professional era, 233–34
provenance, 194

Quorum of the Anointed, 101–2
Quorum of the Twelve Apostles,
126–30, 243–44
Quorums of the Seventy, 243

Ramirez, Rosalina Goitiño, 256
Rays of Living Light (Penrose), 24
record keeping: advances in,
225–28; alphabetic arrangements in early, 142–47; Andrew
Jenson and, 180–83; Church of
Jesus Christ of Latter-day Saints
and, vii–viii; classification of
Old Testament terms in early,
147–54; commandment on, 4;
conclusions on early, 154–55;
godly perspective through, 7–9;
Joseph Smith and, 4–6; ledger
volumes in early, 137–39; notations in early, 139–42; oral histories and, 239–41; practices in
early, 136–37, 225–28; Wilford
Woodruff on, 122–23; William
Clayton and, 90–91
Reinwand, Louis, 176, 178, 184
Reorganized Church of Jesus Christ
of Latter Day Saints, 30, 65–70
restricted records, 226–27
Revelation Book 1, 147
Revelation Book 2, 145
Rich, Charles C., 128, 169
Richards, Franklin D., 21–22, 23,
26, 169–71, 179–81
Richards, Willard: as church

historian, 115–16, 187, 233;
Franklin D. Richards and, 21;
John Whitmer and, 56–57;
Joseph Smith history and, 145;
legacy of, 188–89; William
Clayton and, 87, 99, 103, 107
Rigdon, Sidney, 50, 54
Roberts, B. H., 21, 27, 28–29,
116–17, 233
Robinson, Ebenezer, 146
Rockwell, Porter, 104, 124
Romig, Ron, 72, 73
Russia, 240–41

School of the Prophets, 90
Schweich, George W., 61–62,
65–69, 80n42, 81n47
Schweich, Julia Ann Whitmer, 65
Searle, Howard, 130
seminary, 255–57
Sessions, Gene, 215
Smith, Emma, 14–15, 104, 110,
125
Smith, F. A., 69
Smith, Frederick M., 30, 69, 71
Smith, George A.: *History of the
Church* and, 95; Joseph Smith
history and, 123–24, 126, 189;
Wilford Woodruff and, 20, 120,
130
Smith, Heman C., 66–67, 70–71
Smith, Hyrum, 32, 103, 104
Smith, Joseph: Bible revision and,
151–52; birthplace of, 32;
"Book of the Law of the Lord"
and, 103–5; on church clerks,